To Fiona

Spread Liberty!

3/29/03

LISTEN AFRICANS:

FREEDOM IS UNDER
FIRE!

Emma S. Etuk, Ph.D.

Emida International Publishers
Washington, D.C. - Uyo, Nigeria

Publisher's Cataloging-in-Publication
(Provided by Quality Books, Inc.)

Etuk, Emma S., 1948-
    Listen Africans: freedom is under fire! / by Emma S.
Etuk. -- 1st ed.
    p. cm.
    Includes bibliographical references and index.
    ISBN: 1-881293-04-1

    1. Africa--Politics and government--1960- 2. Human
rights--Africa. 3. Nationalism--Africa. 4. International
relations--Philosophy. I. Title.

DT30.5.E88 2002   960.3'2
                                   QBI33-267

LISTEN AFRICANS: FREEDOM IS UNDER FIRE!

By

Emma S. Etuk, Ph.D.

Text copyright © 2002 by Emma S. Etuk

Cover design by George Foster

Emida International Publishers
P. O. Box 50317
Washington, D.C. 20091

For additional copies, contact the above address.
E-mail: emida1@yahoo.com

Emida International Publishers is a division of
Emida International Services, Inc.

ISBN: 1881293-04-1

Printed in the United States of America.

ADVANCE PRAISE FOR THE BOOK

"A book on an important subject. Africa needs freedom in all its dimensions. By researching the writings of some of the leading African political figures of the 20th century, this prolific African writer has assembled in one volume ideas about freedom in Africa that deserves serious attention. His book will serve as one of the sources of information about African opinions on and attitudes towards freedom. I strongly recommend it to libraries and to students of African politics."

Professor Sulayman S. Nyang, Department of African Studies,
Howard University, Washington, D.C.

"An excellent study of freedom in Africa. The book represents a significant addition to our knowledge of post-colonial Africa and deserves the widest possible distribution."

Alusine Jalloh, Ph.D., Founding Director, The Africa Program,
The University of Texas at Arlington

"Etuk has so excellently put forward a factual comment on African leaders and their leadership philosophy. ... I recommend this work to be read by anybody who cares about Africa and its destiny."

Dr. Njue Moses Gachoki, Consulting Clinical Pathologist,
Central Province, Kenya

"Excellent research."

E. F. Ekpo, Ph.D., Professor, Bethune-Cookman College,
Daytona Beach, Florida

"Readers of this carefully documented history and contemporary analysis of the concept of freedom in Africa may find Dr. Etuk's descriptions to be painful, shocking and revealing, but its message must not be ignored. The sad history of foreign domination is viewed as a precursor of abject denial of freedom by contemporary African leaders. This present book may be Etuk's most significant one because of its cosmic grasp of salient issues of the dimensions of freedom in Africa today."

Alvin L. Anderson, Ph.D., Professor Emeritus,
Malone College; Author and Fulbright Professor,
University of Calabar, 1977-79

DEDICATION

Dedicated to ALL those, blacks and whites,
who fought for the freedoms and human rights
of Africans. May we never live and act
as if their sacrifices were in vain.

ACKNOWLEDGMENTS

The original manuscript of this book began during Nigeria's President Ibrahim B. Babangida's administration and was completed in May 1994. When the manuscript was submitted to St. Martin's Press in New York, the editor, Micheal Flamini, suggested that it be revised to reflect more of a continental scope. Therefore, I wish to thank him very much for that suggestion which has enhanced the original manuscript.

I wish to thank my ardent financial supporters, particularly those in the Church of the Living God in Hyattsville, Maryland, who have constantly encouraged and prayed for me. Without their prayers, I would be unable to complete these self-imposed assignments. I must especially thank the senior pastor, Reverend Stephen Gyermeh, for his magnanimity.

Special mention must be made of some supporters: Dr. E. F. Ekpo, Jennifer Ferranti, Ben and Valeria Forjoe, Iniobong Ebong, Michelle Abu, George and Veronica Abu, Eze and Kelly Nwoji, Cynthia and Isaac Larbi, Eidu and Margaret Barnes, Dr. Chim and Edna Ogbonna, my former roommate Steve Onu, Mrs. Zelma Wilson, Dr. Mfon Umoren, Dr. Matthew Sadiku, Ameze Edobor and Ben Dadson. May God richly bless you all.

Few books can be successful in today's market without the help of some good reviewers, promoters, publicists, editors, and typesetters. I thank Kathy Scriven for her editorial assistance and George Foster for the beautiful covers to all my ii

books. I recommend Kathy and George to all who need their services.

I also wish to thank the staff of the National Interest newspaper based in Lagos, Nigeria: Emmanuel O. Obinyan, George Elijah-Otumu and Sam Egburonu for their interest in my books and for already reviewing this book for the African market. They have really made my days by their kindness.

I thank Professor Sulayman S. Nyang, Dr. Alusine Jalloh, Dr. E. F. Ekpo, Dr. Njue M. Gachoki and my precious friend, Dr. Alvin L. Anderson (and his wife Lucy) for their advance recommendation of this book. I really appreciate their kindness.

I cannot forget my comrade-in-publishing, Arit Ita, for all her constant encouragement. More than anyone else, she makes me feel that she understands how difficult, exacting, and frustrating the task of writing and publishing books can be. Thank you Arit.

Finally, I thank my family for bearing with me throughout the years of writing this book. I thank God whose wonderful grace is sufficient for all who trust in Him. May the reading of this book lead us to the joy of discovering the true meaning of human freedom and liberty.

PREFACE

If you have picked up this book, it is likely that you have some interest in the subject of freedom and liberty, perhaps, specifically for Africa. "In the evolution of mankind and civilization," wrote Professor William Ebenstein of the University of California at Santa Barbara, "no concept has played a more important role than liberty."[1]

Throughout history, men and women have fought long-lasting wars in the name of freedom and liberty. In the 19th century, the United States of America fought a brutal civil war to abolish slavery. It was a war for the preservation of freedom and liberty. Yet, in considering the history of freedom in Africa, little or nothing has been written on it.

Recent writings on Africa are more or less about the woes of political and economic failures on the continent. Such writings have revealed the betrayal of the vast majority of the African peoples. But not much thought has been given to analyzing the role of freedom and liberty in the course of the development of Africa.

Some analyses seem to suggest that all that Africa needs is democracy. But one must first be free in order to belong to a truly democratic society. Democracy and human rights, or even civil liberties, presuppose that the citizens in the particular country are free to choose their forms of government. They must be truly free before they can enjoy the benefits of democracy and human rights.

After 40 years of political independence from European

colonization, it is time that Africans start to give serious thought and reflection to this matter of freedom. They ought to do so especially because of certain recent experiences, like the killings in Rwanda and Burundi and the incidents of religious terrorism in Nigeria. The past 40 years have not brought to Africans the much longed-for El-Dorado. Why?

I believe it is because those who fought for independence in the different parts of the continent did not carefully and thoroughly consider the kinds of freedom that they were fighting for. It is evident now that independence from foreign rule was assumed to be tantamount to human freedom.

What emerged after independence was neo-colonialism bolstered by the new task masters in dark skins. Tyranny, despotism, dictatorship, oppression, state-sponsored terrorism and barbarism have become part and parcel of the post-colonial experience. The Africans have been terribly betrayed.

In this ground-breaking work, I have sought to provide a new perspective, a refreshing new approach to analyzing Africa's problems by considering the vital and fundamental value which we all cherish, that is, freedom. I argue that while Africans have a penchant, a natural love for human freedom, their military and political elites who succeeded the colonial masters slowly but surely opened the way for the evils that have plagued contemporary Africa.

Indeed, much of these evils and problems are man-made. They arise out of the poverty of thought on the part of African leaders regarding the preservation of what is really important to man. If Africa ever had an era of enlightenment, or an era of the renaissance, it must have been a very long time ago.

If there was ever an "African Reformation," it was a long, long time ago. America had her eras of "Great Awakenings." Africa today badly needs such an awakening. But the road to it lies in the pursuit of freedom, of choice among several alternatives, not censorship, intolerance and dictatorship. Africa must change!

Therefore, I insist that the place to begin the work needed for a better Africa is at the schoolhouse of freedom. Africans must begin to think and think very hard about the survival and preservation of freedom because freedom and liberty have eternal rewards. Freedom and liberty are crucial for the sustenance of a healthy civilization. The price of liberty is eternal vigilance.

Africans should no longer take for granted that the State will be the guarantor of their freedoms since the State today is the prime **abuser** of African freedoms! Africans must be prepared to defend their freedoms and liberty passionately. Like Patrick Henry, one of the American founding fathers, they must be ready to say to the tyrants: "Give Me Liberty or Give Me Death!"

This book has been written toward that objective. This book is not primarily a history text on the progress or development of freedom in Africa, although it is linked to that general subject. In fact, I believe that such a book badly needs to be written immediately in order to educate Africans on this issue. My book, however, is a thought-provoking advocacy for freedom in contemporary Africa.

This book analyzes the meaning of freedom by examining the Western and African conceptions of the idea. In trying to explore what most Africans mean by freedom, I have drawn insights from the writings, speeches and actions of some of the most prominent African nationalists such as Kwame Nkrumah of Ghana, Tom Mboya and Jomo Kenyatta of Kenya, Kenneth Kaunda of Zambia, and Julius Nyerere of Tanzania.

Other nationalists that I have analyzed in this book are Obafemi Awolowo and Nnamdi Azikiwe of Nigeria, Leopold Senghor of Senegal and Nelson Rolihlahla Mandela of the

Republic of South Africa. Also, I have noted that a linguistic study of the African ethnicities would confirm that Africans have always had a notion of freedom. For instance, in East Africa, the *kiswahili* term for freedom is *uhuru*.

Up until this time, African nationalists may not have done much to define the African conception of human freedom, but nonetheless, from time immemorial, most Africans have had notions of freedom. Ironically, while the average African has a high esteem or regard for freedom, their so-called political leaders tend to choose the path of tyranny, oppression and corruption. As Chinua Achebe, the celebrated Nigerian novelist once put it, the problem of Africa is squarely the problem of leadership.

In this book, ten chapters deal with the meaning of freedom. Then two chapters deal with the eight moral imperatives for, and the ten challenges to African freedom. The concluding chapter provides a challenge that if Africans desire a better continent, they themselves must become people who care about fundamental values like freedom and not people whose preoccupation is with crass materialism. Finally, there is a rich bibliography and an index.

Africans must be people who take the time to work on seeing that the principles of freedom are incorporated into day-to-day living in Africa. Africans must choose freedom now or they must choose slavery. There is no middle road. For a world that may increasingly be concerned with religious and global terrorism, freedom is the only road ahead. And, Africa is intricately tied to such a world which is marching toward freedom.

TABLE OF CONTENTS

Advance Praise for the Book
Dedication
Acknowledgments   i
Preface   iii
CHAPTERS
  1. Before 1960   1
  2. African Freedom – Forty Years Later   17
  3. Africans Betrayed   35
  4. "What Is Freedom?" - The Western View   53
  5. "What Is Freedom?" - An African View   63
  6. African Freedom: Nkrumah, Mboya and Kenyatta   69
  7. African Freedom: Julius Nyerere and Ujamaa   87
  8. African Freedom: The Humanist Kaunda   103
  9. African Freedom: Awolowo and Azikiwe   121
 10. African Freedom: Senghor and Negritude   141
 11. African Freedom: Nelson Rolihlahla Mandela   159
 12. The Eight Moral Imperatives for Freedom   181
 13. Ten Challenges to African Freedom   211
 14. Freedom or Slavery – We Must Choose NOW!   239

Notes   245
Selected Bibliography   275
Index   301
About the Author   307

CHAPTER ONE

BEFORE 1960

The cause of Freedom is the cause of God.

—- Hon. Edmund Burke, 1791

I remember now the day as clearly as if it was yesterday: October 1, 1960. I was in my last year of elementary school education. In those colonial days in Nigeria, it took eight years to graduate. For nearly a year before that day, the students at my school had been in much anticipation of the advent of the great day of independence from Great Britain.

At my school, Ipu Central School, in Imo River, in the former Asa County Council in Eastern Nigeria, in preparation for this day, all of the students had been practicing the march-past and the salute, and we sang and rehearsed a hymn of political freedom. We sang the song in the local Igbo language. When translated, the words of the song ran something like this:

Azikiwe and Mbadiwe.
Be strong so that we
May enter into the year 1960.
The whites will leave Nigeria.
Mazi Zik, be strong.
We'll govern ourselves.

It has been forty years since I sang this song. But I still fondly remember the words of that childhood hymn of political freedom, sang when I was only twelve years old.

All over Africa (and, especially in Nigeria), 1960 was "the year of Africa," the year of African emancipation or liberation from foreign rule, political domination, social discrimination, segregation, and economic exploitation. There are fifty-three countries in Africa today. In 1960, at least seventeen African countries gained political independence from European colonial powers.[1]

Ghana had set the ball rolling in 1957. Other African states soon followed the example of Ghana and Nigeria.[2] But, before 1960, except for Ethiopia and Liberia, nearly all of the fifty-one countries in Africa, the world's second largest continent, were controlled by the Europeans. Even before the Europeans, there were the Arabs who, around the seventh century, had conquered North Africa and a greater part of West and Central Africa.

The Arabs had conquered the indigenous peoples. They were, perhaps, Africa's first foreign conquerors. They brought literature and commerce from the countries of the Middle East. They also brought a foreign religion, Islam, which they imposed upon the conquered indigenous peoples.

In Islam, a person is not converted by persuasion. Thus, Africans were forced to accept a religion which was to have dire consequences in its future. The current socio-political crises in Africa in the struggle for supremacy between Islam and Christianity goes back to the manner in which Islam introduced itself into Africa.

From the seventh century to the fifteenth century when the Europeans arrived in Africa, the Arabs were the new masters. The socio-cultural and political domination which they maintained was through Islam. For 800 years, Islam dominated the African mind, establishing such intellectual centers as the University of Timbuktu, Jenne, Gao, and Walata. There was also a University at Sankore.

There was no other competent challenger to Islam as this new religion destroyed whatever was left of the Christian Church in North Africa. During those 800 years, the political states we now know of – Ghana, Mali, Songhai, Gao, Kanem-Bornu – emerged, largely, of course, as Islamic states. Still, one must ask, what have been the lasting legacies and benefits of those Islamic states which have now become extinct?

In 1415, the Europeans began their forays and intrusion into Africa. Beginning with their successful conquest of the Mediterranean port of Ceuta which belonged to Morocco, and led by Portugal, Europeans slowly but surely seized nearly all of Africa and became the second wave of new masters whom the indigenous Africans had to contend with.

Like their Arab forebears, the Europeans dominated all forms of economic, political, and social life in Africa. They also influenced the religious life of the Africans to their advantage. At first, they came as traders seeking a sea-route to India. But, before long, they settled down to engage in the most barbaric "trade" that our modern civilization has known — the infamous slave trade which included some African elite class collaborators.

Thus, Europeans were actively involved in the human sale of the Africans for 450 years, from 1415 to 1865, when slavery and slave trading finally ceased in North America! One should also bear in mind that the Arabs had been buying and selling African slaves during the 800 years of their political domination of Africans.

Chancellor Williams, in his book, *The Destruction of Black Civilization* (1987) wrote:

> And as Arabization spread among the Blacks so did slavery and slave raiding. The Arabs' insatiable and perpetual demands for slaves had long since changed slavery from an institution that signaled a military victory by the number of captured prisoners to an institution that provoked warfare expressly for the enslavement of men, women and children for sale and resale. Human beings had now openly become very profitable articles of trade and the slave dealers had found shorter routes to quicker riches.[3]

There is no record, at least known to me at this time, that the Trans-Saharan slave trade or the Trans-Pacific slave trade were ever banned by the Arabs during their occupation of Africa. The indigenous Africans bore the brunt of the pain and suffering which this kind of "trade" brought to them. It was a serious violation of their personal sense of freedom.

To be sure, there was domestic slavery in Africa before the arrival of the Arabs and the Europeans.[4] But, as some scholars have argued, African domestic slavery was similar to slavery practiced in other parts of the world of antiquity. What we now know of this slavery is that domestic slavery in Africa was not chattel slavery. It was not racialized though it may have been ethnicized. The slave could, however, rise above his or her social condition or status.

African domestic slavery was probably not as brutalizing and psychologically damaging as the kind of slavery which the

Arabs and the Europeans engaged in. One main reason was that once a slave was shipped to either Saudi Arabia or to Brazil, that slave lost contact with Africa forever. Herein lay the psychological and enormous mental disorientation. The pain of alienation was obviously great.

What I have stated in the preceding two paragraphs is not an apology for domestic slavery. For, to me, slavery is slavery whether it is domestic or foreign. In either case, liberty or freedom is denied and individual freedom and rights are violated. During the 800 years of Arab domination of Africa and the 470 years (1415-1885) of European intrusion into African life, we do not read of any great Arab abolitionists or defenders of the freedoms and rights of indigenous Africans.

Nor do we read of any great European defenders of African rights and freedoms until Granville Sharp, William Wilberforce, John Wesley, William Lloyd Garrison and Frederick Douglass emerged in Europe and in North America.[5] By then, slave dealers like Francis Drake and Jim Hawkins had already made huge profits from the sale of Africans.

Three phases of this trampling upon the freedoms and individual rights of Africans become discernible: the Islamic era running for 800 years, the 470 (1415-1885) years of European incursion into Africa, and the 75 (1885-1960) years of European physical occupation and colonization. Thus, for more than half a millennium, the Europeans were in Africa, not to promote any kind of freedom and human rights, but primarily for their own economic self-interest.

A modern-day apologist of colonialism may point to the "good" work done by Christian missionaries in the course of African development. But we must seriously question whether any such foreign missionary would have offered his or her life in the defense of African freedoms and human rights in the heyday of European colonialism. Such a benefit of freedom for an African was unthinkable given the racist ideology of many foreign missionaries at the time.

Besides, the promotion of African freedoms and human rights were probably considered the necessary by-products of the missionary enterprise. As for Moslems, freedom, as we shall discuss later, was out of the question since a true Moslem was bound to a theology of absolute submission to the will of God as defined by the Imam, a leader of a local mosque.

The pursuit and promotion of African freedom was not the primary or even a secondary motivation for doing missionary work on the continent. As many Westerners have put it, they were in Africa to civilize the pagans in order to Christianize them. In those times, social and racial equality did not dominate the minds of the missionaries such as to cause them to see human freedom as an important benefit for the indigenous Africans.

As African people have often said regarding the nineteenth century missionary effort, the foreigners were in Africa teaching them to look up to the skies and mind heavenly things while those same foreigners picked up the gold, silver, and other mineral wealth that belonged to the Africans.

Moreover, the missionary agencies collaborated with the colonizers when their mutual interests coincided with one another. At times, the missionaries relied upon the military might of a colonizing agency in order to punish a recalcitrant and unrepentant African potentate.[6] Such was the case when the British gunboat, *H. M. S. Pioneer*, bombarded the towns of Onitsha, Aboh, Yamaha, and Idah in Nigeria in 1879.

Since many Africans have come to view the Arab conquest of indigenous Africans as benevolent — vis-à-vis the reign of Islam in Africa – I shall not dwell too much upon the damage which that conquest did to the cause of indigenous African freedom and their quest for the attainment of fundamental human rights. I shall consider this matter later when I examine the connection of religious intolerance with freedom in the post-colonial era.

But, here, I would like to address what many Africans find unacceptable to them, that is, European colonialism and its devastating consequences. For one to fully understand why freedom has come under fire in much of Africa, it is important to know and to do two things: first, delineate the world which the European colonial masters created in Africa, and second, conceptualize the mindset and spirit of colonialism.

If colonialism was really about freedom and the betterment of the lot of Africans, then, it was a serious contradiction in terms, conceptualization, and practice. Colonialism was not about African freedom. Rather, its basic idea created for the Africans a world of coercion, brute and arbitrary force, commands, economic exploitation, political subjugation, wars, enslavement, banishments, loss of sovereignties, and, oftentimes, murder and death.

Colonialism promoted violence, not peace; arbitrary behavior, not mutual agreements; graft and not negotiation. There was rarely any persuasion. Colonial treaties were usually deceitful and dishonest. There was rarely any adherence to the principles of equality and justice, certainly not in an environment of white superiority and supremacy.

The colonizers' interests were paramount to that of the indigenous African. The colonizer could often use brute force to obtain whatever he wanted. Cheap labor was often obtained at the colonizers' command. The rights to the minerals and natural resources of Africa belonged to the colonizer.

Africans could not stop the robbery of their lands and countries because they knew they would be conquered if they resisted. And, when they did, they were conquered militarily.

Author Frederick Lugard, one of the arch-imperialists of England, best expressed the colonial logic in his book, *The Dual Mandate in British Tropical Africa* (1965). In it, he stated as follows:

> The partition of Africa was, ... due primarily to the economic necessity of increasing the supplies of raw materials and food to meet the needs of the industrialized nations of Europe ...
>
> These products lay wasted and ungarnered in Africa because the natives did not know their use and value. ... who can deny the right of the hungry people of Europe to utilize the wasted bounties of nature?

Then Lugard added:

> Let it be admitted at the outset that European brains, capital, and energy have not been, and never will be, expended in developing the resources of Africa from motives of pure philanthropy; that Europe is in Africa for the mutual benefit of their own industrial classes, and of the native races in their progress to a higher plane, that the benefit can be made reciprocal, and that it is the aim and desire of civilized administration to fulfill this dual mandate.[7]

Here, Lugard clearly told Africans that the Europeans were not in Africa for the interests of the Africans. They were there for the sake of meeting "the needs of the industrialized nations of Europe." The colonizers, he said, were in Africa for the sake of "the hungry people of Europe." They were in Africa for economic reasons, not for philanthropy or altruism.

Lugard clearly stated that "European brains, capital, and

energy have not been, and never will be, expended in developing the resources of Africa." Why should they? Lugard was bluntly honest about the European mission to Africa. Regrettably, 40 years after 1960, many African kleptocrats had not read these honest remarks by a colonizer. These kind of Africans keep stealing Africa's resources and hide them away in Europe! It is incredible.

European military mindset with respect to Africa goes back to the Berlin Conference of 1884-1885. After years and years of intelligence gathering and espionage, the Europeans came to the silly conclusion that the interests of the Africans were unimportant. They had fully and carefully assessed the military capabilities of the African kings and kingdoms and concluded that the conquest of those Africans was simply a matter of time.

The Europeans had the Maxim guns, gunboats, and artilleries while Africans had bows and arrows. The Europeans presumed that Africans would readily lay down their arms and capitulate in the face of superior weaponry. They did not seem to count on the determination and resolve of Africans to defend their sovereignty. So, in Ethiopia, for example, the Italians were soundly defeated at the battle of Adowa on March 1, 1896.

European colonialism sowed the seeds for the military barbarism which was to afflict Africans in the post-colonial era. African despots and tyrants learned very well from their European mentors. Belgium provides a classic example. Emile Banning was an archivist of the Belgian government who also supported and collaborated with King Leopold II of Belgium. Banning was a participant at the 1884-1885 Berlin Conference.

He wrote that the Conference signaled "the peaceful penetration of Africa" by the Europeans. What a lie! But,

Banning also wrote that,

> The visible entry of Africa into the empire of civilization, the distribution of its vast territories among the nations of Europe, the initiation, under European guidance, of millions of Negroes into superior conditions of existence truly seems to be one of the most considerable revolutions of our time, one of the richest in the economic and political consequences.[8]

We should note that, here, Banning was putting a pat upon his shoulder for the European robbery of African territories from Africans. He was right, though, about the economic motives for colonization. King Leopold II, Banning's boss, and a second cousin of Queen Victoria of England, declared at the same Conference, that:

> Since history teaches that colonies are useful, that they play a great part in that which makes up the power and prosperity of the states, let us strive to get one in turn. ... let us see where there are unoccupied lands ... where are to be found peoples to civilize, to lead to progress in every sense, meanwhile assuring [to] ourselves new revenues, to our middle classes the employment which they seek, to our army a little activity, and to Belgium as a whole the opportunity to prove to the world that it also is an imperial people capable of dominating and enlightening others.[9]

Yes, indeed! Belgium's army needed "a little activity" in Africa. Belgium needed to prove that it, too, was capable of "dominating" others. The first part of Leopold's declaration was the very antithesis of what really happened in the Congo.

The second part of his statement revealed the true aim of the Belgians in Africa – to dominate and exploit.

The Conference awarded Leopold the African territory of the Congo as his personal real estate under the pretext that he (Leopold) would eradicate a so-called Arab slave trade in that part of Africa. We now know what the Belgian enterprise did in Africa. It exacted the maximum degree of forced labor in the collection of wild rubber, ivory, and such other resources as would benefit Belgium. The eradication of Arab slave trade was soon forgotten.

Only one thing mattered to King Leopold: the assurance of cash flow into his pockets. He did make a huge profit from the backs of the Congolese whom he enslaved. Between 1888 and 1897 (a nine-year period), ivory brought about 38 million Belgian francs into Leopold's pocket. In 1900 alone, the value of ivory from the Congo was 5.3 million Belgian francs. Between 1887 and 1909, Leopold netted 478,324,558 Belgian francs from rubber used in the manufacture of motor tires, hoses, and other industrial products.

These economic benefits were derived at a terrible human cost to the Africans, a cost which the Western world has pretended not to notice. There were unspeakable atrocities – genocide, pogroms, and bodily mutilations – committed against the Africans. In a word, King Leopold and Belgium murdered **ten million** Africans between 1886 and 1908. A terrible holocaust far exceeding that of the Jews during World War II occurred and the world paid no attention because Africans were the victims!

The evidence for these atrocities were well documented by Kwame Nkrumah, former Prime Minister of Ghana, Ritchie Calder, Edmund Denille Morel, Mark Twain, Arthur Conan Doyle, and Judge Pierre Etienne Dostert of the 23rd Judicial Circuit Court of West Virginia in the United States of

America. The twenty-three years of Leopold's "little activity" in Africa cost Africa five to ten million lives.[10] The Congolese paid dearly for the European colonial "enlightenment."

In the light of this historical experience, does anyone wonder how the Belgian political experiment in the Congo produced a Mobutu Seso Seko and his collaborators who murdered Patrice Lumumba, the first nationally elected Prime Minister of independent Congo? In the light of the Belgian relations with Africa, what good examples of freedom-loving and respect for human rights did Belgium set for the Africans? And, Belgium was a part of "Christian" Europe!

In 1974, the Nigerian historian, G. N. Uzoigwe wrote that the "Berlin West African Conference [was] a landmark in world history." He added that:

> The Berlin Conference [was] the culmination of Europe's desire ... to impose by force, ... its collective will over those of the non-European world, to exploit the resources of the world. Africa happened to provide the best classic example of this ambition.[11]

As one might now fully realize, the early Portuguese adventurers to the Gold Coast (note the name!) of West Africa did not go there for the exotic African beaches and naked lusty women. They went there for gold. Author Brian Lapping, in his book, *End of Empire* (1985) observed that,

> In the fifteenth and sixteenth centuries the Gold Coast exported a tenth of the world's supply of gold. In the seventeenth and eighteenth centuries the country remained one of the three or four largest sources of a major element in world trade but gold sales were overtaken as the principal export by slaves. By the late nineteenth century ... the gold was almost exhausted.[12]

I have introduced the element of gold export out of Africa to show that Africans have always had something useful to offer to the rest of the world. Even the human labor exacted through slavery was a benefit to the rest of the world. Yet, the rest of the world, with their African political and military collaborators, have often mistreated Africa and grossly violated her rights and freedom. We must put a stop to this perennial problem, now.

By Lapping's own admission, the Gold Coast (now Ghana) supplied Europe with gold and slaves for nearly 450 years. No one quarrels with these Europeans for their materialism expressed in their lust for African gold, if only Africans received a fair price for their products. But did the Africans have to pay so dearly with their lives so that Europeans would have a better life and higher living standards?

Did Africans have to perish because they opposed foreign economic exploitation? And how much did the economics of slave trade and of slavery help in advancing the cause of African freedom, human rights, and development? Africans who today collaborate with foreigners to ruin Africa must think about (and answer) these questions. Once the oil resources are exhausted in a country like Nigeria, the world will have no need of her.

In his book, *Imperialism in the Twentieth Century* (1977), A. P. Thornton analyzed the colonial terms of reference, assumptions, framework, and assertions. He concluded that a basic imperialist assumption was the right of expansion no matter what rules were broken and no matter what harm was done in the process of expansion. In the United States of America, this mindset was termed "manifest destiny" and mission.

Thornton declared that "imperialism makes use of other people: coercion is its natural habit. The ultimatum waits at the far side of all imperial diplomacy."[13] He insisted that colonialism "bred irresponsibility and lack of self-confidence, since everything important was always controlled by unknown men who did what was not understood for reasons that were not stated."

Then Thornton added this keen insight:

> Colonialism most commonly produced not an eager pupil of superior wisdom but a personality type characterized by *anomie*, rage, compulsion, and withdrawal. It encouraged a state of mind that rejected everything and aspired to nothing, a state of mind basically pathological.[14]

If this psychological evaluation of colonialism's impact is true, then Africans should be given a handshake and praise for doing so well. For, by Thornton's standard, the African ought not to be doing anything useful after over 500 years of European domination over Africa. Yet, in spite of all her struggles, Africa is grossly lambasted again and again by the international press today. This is unfair.

In his own view, Charles Reynolds, author of *Modes of Imperialism* (1981), defined imperialism as:

> An idea that denotes a relationship of domination whether explicit, in the form of a political sovereignty asserted by force over subject peoples independent of their will or consent, or implicit, as a system of constraint and control exercised over peoples and territories, independent of their political organization, and directing their activities to the satisfaction of needs and interests themselves generated by the system.[15]

One must reflect carefully on these views expressed by

Thornton and Reynolds because they reveal quite clearly what was at the core of the colonial mindset and spirit. They tell us something about **the soul of colonialism**. These views also explain the consequences of colonialism as the very antithesis of democratic liberalism and libertarian objectives which the Europeans purported to cherish and practice within their countries.

When it came to Africa, the mindset and spirit of colonialism certainly were not that which evolved out of a Christian consciousness which would have promoted universal love, brotherhood, and a genuine respect for African freedoms and human rights. Instead, the opposite occurred because the impetus for colonialism was unchristian.

Therefore, I must reiterate my firm conviction that the colonial mindset was essentially that of economic exploitation, political subjugation, and spiritual demoralization. Africans should be convinced of these things and pass the message along to their children and grandchildren.

If colonialism was meant to promote African freedoms, then, it was a contradiction each time that the mortar and the canon exploded in the faces of innocent African men, women, and children whose only crime was their resistance to foreign rule and oppression. Africans must not and should never forget the harsh lessons of their colonial experiences.

In this respect, it is appropriate to recall the words of Kamau Wa Ngengi of Kenya who is known to many Africans and Westerners as Jomo Kenyatta. He was the man who bravely fought the British imperialists for many years in the so-called Mau Mau Rebellion. In 1938, Kenyatta wrote that:

> The African is conditioned, by the cultural and
> social institutions of centuries, to a freedom of
> which Europe has little conception, and it is not in

his nature to accept serfdom forever. He realizes that he must fight unceasingly for his own complete emancipation; for without this he is doomed to remain the prey of rival imperialisms.[16]

So, the African had to fight to secure his freedom or liberty. He had no other choice. On a single day, September 20, 1960, sixteen African countries took their seats at the United Nations as equal members of the world community. The march toward the realization of full equality and freedom had just begun. But would this dream be achieved or would freedom in Africa continue to be under fire?

CHAPTER TWO

AFRICAN FREEDOM – FORTY YEARS LATER

If a nation values anything more than freedom, it will lose its freedom.

— William S. Maugham

If anyone should love, appreciate and practice freedom – and fight for it – it should be persons who have known of and suffered most from oppression and brutality. Persons of African descent who had experienced the cruelties and barbarism of slavery, slave trade and colonialism should be the very people who fight the hardest for freedom.

Surprisingly, in Africa, this has not seemed to be the case. New political leaders and the elites in post-colonial Africa have not shown a high regard for freedom. Freedom is still under fire. In many instances, living in Africa has been a nightmare to many of its citizens.

It is interesting to note that Elizabeth Isichei, a scholar of African history, makes the observation that "colonialism makes its victims its defenders."[1] Hence, African political leaders who ought to have known of, if not experienced, the harsh realities of colonialism have not shown a high degree of sensitivity to matters respecting personal freedom and the sanctity of human life.

Political opponents or enemies of the new leaders have often been treated as if they were not human beings worthy of some degree of respect. African leaders have not become the strident apostles and defenders of freedom. Rather, these leaders and the elites have tended to emulate and practice the same things which their erstwhile colonial mentors had done!

Thus, post-colonial Africa has produced cannibals like Idi Amin of Uganda and brutes like Francisco Nguema of Equatorial Guinea. It has fought many unnecessary wars that have no meaningful purpose. Such wars have occurred in Rwanda, Burundi, Liberia, and Sierra Leone. In countries like Angola, Namibia, Sudan, Somalia, Ethiopia, Eritrea, and Nigeria (where a 30-month civil war claimed nearly one million lives between 1967 and 1970), there has been no peace after the wars.

Military tyrants, despots and dictators, claiming to offer political sanity and rectitude, have turned out to be the worst scoundrels that Africa ever produced. When such tyrants are eventually pushed out of office, the particular country they ruled over becomes economically worse off because the tyrant had been a kleptocrat who had cleaned out the national treasury.

To add insult to injury, there is now a resurgence of slavery and slave trading engaged in by the Africans themselves. Currently, in North and East Africa, Arabic Africans are selling black Africans to the Middle East and to wherever the price is right. What a shame! It is as if the African leaders and their political historians have totally forgotten the past.

What is worse, there is no general or popular outcry by the

African masses against this new barbarism and heinous crime. A conspiracy of silence pervades throughout the air. The few courageous abolitionist voices are persecuted and hounded with threats and real acts of incarceration. In some quarters, the existence of this sordid evil, in spite of the overwhelming evidence, is even denied. Does it mean that modern Africans love slavery more than they love freedom? Today, in Africa, freedom is seriously under fire.

Between 1945 and 1960, Africans advocated for independence for themselves. Essentially, they sought for political independence from foreign rule. Personal or individual freedom was implicit in this quest. The whole struggle for decolonization was rooted in this quest for political freedom. Africans were inspired by a universal sense of human freedom inherent in themselves.

Also, one may say that the Africans of the decolonization era drew their inspiration from two other sources. One source was Woodrow Wilson's speech, "Fourteen Points," which embraced the notion of self-determination for colonized peoples everywhere. The other source was Franklin D. Roosevelt's idea of the "Four Freedoms" which included freedom of speech and expression, freedom of religion, freedom from want, and freedom from fear.

Africans who fought in World War II understood that the war was about freedom, and more particularly, about their own freedoms, including the freedom from colonial rule. Theo Ayoola, a Nigerian military recruit in the British colonial army stationed in India, said: "We have been told what we fought for, ... 'That is freedom.' We want freedom, nothing but freedom."[2]

Ayoola's statement was part of a letter he had sent to Herbert Macaulay, who was generally regarded as "the father of Nigerian nationalism."[3] There were other Africans, besides

Ayoola, who also harbored this kind of expectation. Although not a British military recruit, Dr. Nnamdi Azikiwe was one of the staunchest apostles of African freedom at the time.

Educated at various colleges and universities in the United States of America, Azikiwe (or Zik as he was popularly known) returned to Africa in 1934 to become a journalist, publisher, orator, politician, author of many books, and Africa's most popular leader at the time. He earned the title "Zik of Africa" and, in some quarters, was regarded as the African Gandhi.

According to James S. Coleman, an authority on Nigeria, "Nnamdi Azikiwe was undoubtedly the most important and celebrated nationalist leader on the West Coast of Africa, if not in all tropical Africa," during the 15-year-period beginning from 1934 to 1949. "To the outside world," Coleman said, " 'Zikism' and African nationalism appeared to be synonymous."[4]

Azikiwe became the first Governor-General of the newly independent state of Nigeria in 1960. When it became a Republic in 1963, Azikiwe was its first president. In a letter to Herbert Macaulay dated April 30, 1929, Azikiwe made public what was to form the cornerstone of his philosophy regarding Africa. Azikiwe intended to be "independent in all things and neutral in nothing affecting the welfare of Africa."[5]

Later on, in his book, *Renascent Africa*, which he published in 1937, Azikiwe expounded more on his "philosophy of the New Africa" as follows:

> I believe in the God of Africa. I believe in the black people of Africa. I believe that it is not the will of the God of Africa to sentence the black people of Africa to servitude in any form forever. I believe that there is a destiny for the black people of Africa and that such destiny can only be realized

successfully under the aegis of free and independent African nations.[6]

Moreover, Azikiwe wrote that "If there is any African who disbelieves his capacity to enjoy the fruits of liberty, mark him well, he is not sane, he is destined to be the footstool of his compeers, and his doom has been sealed."[7]

Azikiwe considered himself to be "a living spirit of an idea – the idea of a New Africa." He rejected the notion of a self-appointed messiah, but insisted that he was "a living spirit of an ideal – the ideal of man's humanity to man. I am a living spirit of an ideology – the ideology of the effacement of man's inhumanity to man."[8]

Thus, the concept of freedom was central to his political philosophy. Azikiwe was quite willing, he wrote, to die for the attainment of his new ideal of freedom for Africa. He also predicted a future global era when blacks would rule the world by A.D. 2944, a prediction which did not escape the notice of the international press. For some of his positions, some black Americans branded him a radical and despised him.

Mazi Mbonu Ojike, another contemporary of Azikiwe, who also studied in the United States of America in the 1930s and 1940s, stated in his book, *I Have Two Countries* (1947), that "It was the search for freedom that brought a little black man like me to America."[9] Ojike had come to America in search of that kind of liberal education which would help him develop himself to become a well-cultured citizen. To him, illiteracy and ignorance were forms of enslavement and he wanted to be truly free.

Nobody in his or her right mind today would say that Africans in times past would have preferred slavery and colonialism to self-rule and freedom. Indeed, many, many Africans before Ojike had maintained that the African loved, and still loves, freedom. Such Africans included King Prempeh I of Ghana; King Behanzin, the last emperor of Dahomey; Hendrik Wittboi, the Nama leader; and Wobogo, the Moro-Naba, king of the Mossi.

Others were Machemba, king of the Yao in Tanzania; King Kabarega of Bunyoro; King Menelik II of Ethiopia; Kabaka Mwanga of Buganda; and Mirambo-Ya-Banhu, the Nyamwezi warlord who, in some circles, was regarded as the Napoleon of East Africa. These African potentates all told the colonialists that they preferred death to servitude and slavery. In the colonial days, Africa had her Patrick Henry's. Where are they now?

In the geographical area which became Nigeria, King William Dappa Pepple of Bonny and King Jaja of Opobo were proud Africans who loved their freedom and fought to defend it. They were ready to defend their freedom with their last drop of blood. But the post-colonial African leaders, the inheritors of such sacrifices, sadly soon forgot these disquieting facts of their own history.

But how could one so easily and so soon forget the scramble and the bloody conquest of one's motherland by foreigners? They soon forgot it all because they were blinded by greed, selfishness, avarice and covetousness. All the criticisms against him notwithstanding, Jomo Kenyatta of Kenya believed in and fought for his freedom and pride rather than submit to the British invaders under a false guarantee of "protection."

Some writers on Africa have stated that "Africa developed for thousands of years *in harmony with nature and in equilibrium* with its environment."[10] Such a harmony, I would argue, was sustained in a state of relative freedom known to the Africans themselves. But European colonialism overturned that relative harmony, peace and freedom. The center of life in Africa could not hold any longer. Life would no longer be at ease.

So, after 1960, as Chinua Achebe, one of Africa's greatest novelists had lamented, things began to fall apart. Freedom was more and more under siege. In fact, personal safety, freedom of speech and expression, and freedom from fear came with a greater price. Even freedom of worship and of religion was at stake in many of the newly independent African states.

By 1977, Azikiwe was disillusioned and publicly decried the new trend toward tyranny and oppression. In an article he published in the *Drum* magazine in April of that year, he stated as follows:

> Look at Africa today, see how we have become wolf to our own people; see how man's inhumanity to man flourishes ... I used to say to myself: Did you fight to drive away the white man to enable us to exploit and oppress our people? Certainly not. But that is the trend.[11]

The above jeremiad was written seven years after Nigeria, Zik's own country, had lost nearly one million lives in a civil war that now seems to have been meaningless except that it was fought "to keep Nigeria one." Is Nigeria better united today than it was in 1967 when the war began?

Azikiwe's jeremiad was written in the same decade when an estimated 50,000 Africans were massacred by former President Francisco Marcias Nguema of Equatorial Guinea.[12] Also, the jeremiad was penned at a time when more than 800,000 Ugandans were brutally murdered by Idi Amin, Milton Obote, and Tito Okello, all former rulers of Uganda.[13]

Azikiwe's African lamentation was also written at a time when Mobutu Seso Seko, as the sole dictator in the state of former Zaire Republic, destroyed virtually every Zairean's fundamental human rights and freedoms. Other African leaders kept silent about these atrocities because they were not supposed to meddle in the internal affairs of a sister country.

Mobutu once said that "democracy is not for Africa."[14] He probably believed the same thing regarding freedom for the African, given his record on human rights. One wonders what Azikiwe may have thought of the crimes of bodily harm, tortures, imprisonments, and murders committed by military tyrants like Ibrahim Babangida and Sani Abacha of Nigeria on their own people.

How many innocent Africans were murdered by Haile Mariam Mengistu of Ethiopia between 1974 and 1991? More than 150,000 Ethiopians![15] In 1988, how many Africans did fellow Africans massacre in the Rwanda-Burundi debacle? Did the Tutsis have to kill an estimated 20,000 Hutus, to gain only God-knows-what?[16] It was, perhaps, in the light of these horrific atrocities that one foreign observer remarked that the gods must be crazy in Africa.

In 1987, the Reverend Bishop Desmond Tutu of South Africa said that "It is ... very sad to note that in many black African countries today, there is less freedom than there was during that much-maligned colonial period."[17] This admission was made at a gathering of Africa's religious leaders at Nairobi, Kenya, another African country still plagued by a long history of autocracy under a civilian Head of State. But was anybody listening to Tutu's confession?

Forty years after colonial rule had ceased in Nigeria, President Olusegun Obasanjo, who was jailed in 1995 by the Sani Abacha military regime, had this to say of the road less traveled with respect to Nigerian freedom:

> Not so long ago, many of us indulged in the intellectual luxury of seeing Nigeria as a free and Democratic nation with full freedom and human

rights guaranteed to every citizen. Instead, Nigeria was steadily pushed into a most brutal dictatorship which corrupted everything and almost everybody, not excluding our cherished traditional and religious institutions. Nigerians became so impotent to the extent that a brutal dictatorship could ride rough shod over the collective will, freedom and voice of the people, openly plundering every public treasury or account, arresting, detaining, torturing and even killing its perceived enemies, and to still have among our men and our women disgusting but rich sycophants loudly cheering it. No one would have thought that Nigeria would suffer such prolonged and brutal tyranny of a few people over the rest, and to be saved only by divine Providence.[18]

That pretty much sums it up. The above statement was part of the Independence Day Speech on October 1, 2000.

Earlier that year, following religious riots and killings in several parts of Northern Nigeria, Obasanjo told a shocked nation:

I had decided to make a personal visit there, because I was very concerned by the security and other reports I was getting from the officials on the ground. I could not believe that Nigerians were capable of such barbarism against one another. But what I saw there was perhaps more gruesome in detail.[19]

Yes, many Africans have forgotten what civility and freedom mean. A military dictatorship ruled and reigned for 30 years in the 40 years of post-colonialism in Nigeria, climaxing in a new political mood and climate best described as babangidamania which entrenched graft, deceit, religious intolerance and state-sponsored terrorism in a maradonic grand style.

Thirty years of despotism and tyranny! How could the new politicians of Nigeria's Fourth Republic so quickly forget the hardships and pain of those thirty years? Truly, oppression does perform its wonders. Thousands of Nigerians have been murdered by Islamic fundamentalists in the name of an imposed *sharia* upon fellow non-Moslem Nigerians. Is this freedom?

In Tanzania and Kenya, the story is the other way around. Moslems are persecuted by the authorities acting at the behest of some so-called Christians. In Chad Republic and in Ethiopia, Moslems were repeatedly mistreated. Is this what the ordinary person wanted from African leaders after the colonialists had gone? Can Africans not live in peace, harmony and freedom with one another? Why is the savagery so grotesque?

In his Independence Day Address in 2000, Obasanjo reminded his countrymen and women that "Nigerians are great believers in freedom," a view which Azikiwe had expressed in the 1930s regarding the Africans. "We are not colonialists," Obasanjo continued, "and have not been put there to replace the British colonialists."

He insisted that "We are supposed to be better than they were. That is the whole point of Independence. We certainly have no right to act even worse than the colonialists did. The nation owes us citizenship, liberty, justice and opportunity."[20] But, again, was anybody really listening to this voice of reason?

The demographers tell us that one out of every four Africans is a Nigerian. Therefore, in many ways, as Nigeria goes, so goes Africa. So, how has this giant of Africa fared in terms of the pursuit of human freedom? Not very much better than the rest of the other 52 countries on the continent. In 1992 alone, at least 8,000 Nigerians perished at the hands of their fellow citizens in civil riots. Was this freedom?

According to the *Washington Post* of October 20, 2000, more than 1,000 people have died in ethnic or religious clashes across Nigeria since (Obasanjo) took office in May of 1999. Is this the kind of freedom that Africans want? In my Nigeria, freedom has been under fire for over 30 years.

The most painful aspect of the tragedy of modern African civilization (if one may use this term at this instance) is the resurgence of slavery and slave trading. Imagine this – Africans selling fellow Africans at the dawn of the 21st century! It is shameful. It is disgraceful. It is very embarrassing to any sense of decency and to African pride. I wish that I had the radicalism of William Lloyd Garrison or the eloquence of Frederick Douglass so that I could denounce this slavery as best as I can.

Oh! Africans, how can this be? Have we Africans totally lost our minds and our senses of honor and dignity? How can we do this to ourselves? Does this new wave of slavery mean that we are lost to the destinies of darkness and barbarism? Why is there no outburst of universal denunciations against this heinous crime? Is modern Africa's slave trade not a crime against humanity anymore? Shall we blame the white man for this?

Since some, like people of the American Nation of Islam, have denied the existence of this evil, let me present some available information on this contemporary African slavery and slave trading. In fact, there is nothing new about Islam and slavery in the history of Africa.

As we saw in Chapter One, the Arabs had been engaging in slavery and slave trading since their arrival into Africa around

A.D. 642. Dr. Joseph E. Harris, a professor of history at Howard University in Washington, D.C., documented this part of history in his book, *The African Presence in Asia: Consequences of the East African Slave Trade* (1971).[21]

Dr. George B. N. Ayittey, also a professor of economics at the American University in Washington, D.C., cited Peter Wickins's book, *An Economic History of Africa* (1981), in which the barbarity of the Arab slave trade was described in the following horrific terms:

> Enslaving and slave trading in East Africa were peculiarly savage in a traffic notable for its barbarity. Villages were burned, the unfit villagers massacred. The enslaved were yoked together, several hundreds in a caravan (for) a journey to the coast which could be as long as 1280 kilometers.... It is estimated that only one in five of those captured in the interior reached Zanzibar. The slave trade seems to have been more catastrophic in East Africa than in West Africa.[22]

Later in his book, *Africa Betrayed* (1992), Ayittey also stated that,

> Arabs largely organized and controlled this trade. Africa also lost large, if not equal, numbers from the East African slave trade. Estimates of Africans exported range from a low of 3 million to a high of 20 million.... In the mid-nineteenth century between 40,000 and 45,000 African slaves were exported from Zanzibar alone.[23]

When slave trade was abolished in the 1840s, it left black Africans with the stigma of "inferior" status in the eyes of the Arabs. One would have thought that with the shared experiences of colonialism and occupation of a vast African territory, many Arab Africans would treat their black African neighbors as brothers. But this was unfortunately not so. Ayittey added:

> More shocking is the continued enslavement of black Africans in this day and age, not by Westerners but by Arabs in Sudan and Mauritania. The slavery of blacks was abolished in Mauritania only in 1980. In Sudan it was officially abolished in 1987, but was still continuing in 1990. Arab militias, formed and armed by the Islamic government of Lt. Gen. Omar Bashir, were trafficking in slaves from the southern Dinka tribe.[24]

Ayittey's writing suggests that while the rest of the world had ceased to trade slaves since the 1840s, Mauritanians and the Sudanese were still mistreating black Africans through the sale of human beings up until the 1980s and the 1990s! Think of this, dear reader. Should this be tolerated or not? Should any black-skinned person (much less any person of any race) anywhere feel apathetic when one of his kind is under this sort of existence? I say, no. Absolutely, no.

Some empty-headed attackers might denounce Ayittey's revelations as window dressing. But it is not only Ayittey who has made these revelations. Thank goodness he did, though. They have been fully authenticated by international investigators. We should not ignore the issue of modern African slavery, no matter at what level or scale it is being perpetrated.

Many African leaders and the elites simply chose to ignore the crime all along. But they can no longer do this because the former slaves are speaking out. Ayittey cited credible sources which showed that in Mauritania, "between 100,000 total slaves and 300,000 part slaves and former black slaves (were) in the service of Arab masters."[25] That was in 1990. By 1992, the stories of two former slaves appeared in the *Washington Times*.

As late as in 1988, Arab Moslems in the Sudan were selling black Africans for $90.00 per slave. There were so many slaves that in 1990, the price had fallen to $15.00 per slave child. And the child is often black. So said Dr. Charles Jacobs, the Executive Director of the American Anti-Slavery Group based in the state of Massachusetts and working to end slavery in the Sudan.

Dr. Jacobs, responding to a CBS-TV News broadcast that reported that over 1,000 slaves in the Sudan had been bought back into freedom, disclosed on March 10, 1999 that "tens of thousands of African slaves have been seized by government-armed militia units." He said that "slave raids have become a terror weapon of choice, employed by a government whose goal is to Arabize and Islamize Sudan's African south."

Jacobs continued to say that in the Sudan, black Africans today are still "bought and sold, branded and bred, and forcibly converted to Islam."[26] As in Mauritania, there are no penalties for the crime of slavery in the Sudan. "To an Arab, being a non-Muslim is a crime in itself,"[27] explained James Mayan Benjamin, a 60-year-old Sudanese teacher who was forced to flee from his home in the upper Nile and now presides over a camp of 2,700 refugee children in southern Sudan.

Dr. Jacobs stated that atrocities against the women and children include capture, torture, buying and selling, and branding. The names of the slaves are changed from African and Christian names to Islamic names. Those slaves who refuse to convert are crippled for life or murdered.

Those who deny the existence of slavery in the Arab nations of Africa must be living in a fool's paradise. Recently, my children came home from school to report that they had successfully collected money and bought back a Sudanese child from slavery. My daughter was only ten years old at the time. She asked me so many questions about this slavery, some of which made me cringe to be a black African. By engaging in this type of enslavement, the Arabs are guilty of debasing our people!

Anyone today who denies that slavery still exists, even after reading this analysis, must be totally devoid of all sensibilities. Even the Western press is slowly warming up to the fact of slave trading in today's Africa. I personally heard on WCIN 1480 Talk Radio in Cincinnati, Ohio, on September 25, 2000, a news report that some hundreds of slaves had been bought back into freedom in Africa.

Many human rights organizations like the *Amnesty International* and *Africa Watch* have reported that slavery still exists in parts of Africa. *Friends in the West*, a Christian organization based in Arlington, Washington, recently released a paper titled: "Special Report: A Country in Crisis – The Forgotten Children of Sudan."[28]

On page four of their report, there was a news item captioned "Slave Trade Flourishes in Sudan." This report stated that there was "an exploding slave trade that is being carried out in the name of Islam." The report added: "The most extensive raids take place in the Bahr El Ghazal region of southern Sudan, where women and children are kidnapped by the Popular Defense Force, an Arab militia that receives horses and guns from the government-controlled National Islamic Front."[29]

The report said that recently 19 boys, ages 14 to 20, were abducted from their village in Northern Uganda by the West Nile Bank Front, a rebel group backed by the Sudanese government. The boys were taken at gunpoint, their hands tied, and were tied together by their waists in groups of five to be sold at a place called Juba.

The United States Government is fully aware of and admits that there is slave trading in Mauritania and in the Sudan. According to the State Department's own 1997 Human Rights Report, the average price per slave child is "about $300 worth of cattle or $550 if the purchaser was a Westerner."[30]

Non-governmental agencies in the U.S. are also trying to stamp out the evil slave trade by working to bring pressure on the government to do something about it. For example, the Africa Fund, an agency based in New York, sent a letter in December 1999 to Secretary of State, Madeleine Albright, "demanding a stronger U.S. policy against slavery."[31]

Also, the Africa Fund is working with former slaves, by providing them with a platform to publicize their stories. One such former slave is the Mauritanian abolitionist leader Boubacar Messaoud, who has appealed to the African-American community in the U.S. to join in the fight against this modern African slavery. The American Friends Service Committee has also responded to this appeal.

Indeed, as recent as January 8, 1995, Tony Brown aired a television program on his "Tony Brown Journal" which discussed the subject of slavery in modern Africa. The *Newsweek* magazine also had an article in its March 1992 issue. Even inside Mauritania, there is a Committee For the Defense of Human Rights. Mohammed N. Athie is one individual very involved with this organization. It is my belief that this evil will one day see its end.

But today, where is the general outcry and vehement denunciations by the Africans which should be expected? Where are the student marches from country to country against this crime? Where is the official anger by the black African nations? Instead, one reads of the possibility of slavery also still existing in some remote region of Ghana.

According to a CBS "60 Minutes" broadcast on November 30, 1997, a kind of slavery goes on in Ghana. Author E. Ablorh-Odjidja admitted that "there is no deny[ing] the existence of this practice of bondage for young maidens in an isolated tribal sector in Ghana today."[32] Good heavens!

But, should any African woman be involuntarily sentenced to any kind of bondage or servitude at all today? What kind of society are we developing? Forty years after colonial rule, should we be talking about slavery and bondage and attempt to provide stupid defenses for their existence?

Should the African intellectuals be rationalizing whatever sort of servitude the powerful Africans are imposing upon other unfortunate, powerless Africans? Should we be celebrating the enslavement of our peoples or should we join in the glorious march for full liberty, forty years later?

CHAPTER THREE

AFRICANS BETRAYED

The condition upon which God has given liberty to man is eternal vigilance.

— John Philpot Curran

Several years ago, an African-American historian, Rayford W. Logan, authored a book titled *The Betrayal of the Negro* (1965) in which he analyzed how the African-Americans were mistreated in the years following the end of the Civil War.[1]

Instead of enjoying a new lease of freedom as citizens, Logan argued, African-Americans faced a new era of discrimination, prejudice, segregation, and lynching. The post-Reconstruction era climaxed into what Logan termed the "nadir." The African-American was betrayed.

There is a parallel or similarity of experiences between post-colonial Africans and post-Civil War African-Americans. Both were seriously mistreated and betrayed. The majority of the African people have been betrayed since the end of colonial rule.

Instead of enjoying a new lease of freedom and the fruits of national independence, the majority of African people have been exposed to a new kind of oppression, mistreatment, and savagery. This time the brutality is perpetrated by their own leaders, not foreign colonialists. The brutality includes bodily mutilations, starvation as an instrument of war, genocide, kleptocracy, and slavery.

Let us pause here and ask some guiding questions. What did the Africans want or need after the colonialists had left Africa? What were their expectations in a new era of independence? Were the Africans justified to hold such expectations? In what ways were the Africans betrayed? What, if any, are the implications of this betrayal?

As one whose first twelve years of life ran through the colonial era, I can categorically state what the people of my generation wanted and what we did not want or need. I completed elementary school education in 1960 at Ipu Central School, Imo River, in Eastern Nigeria. Thereafter, I looked forward to attending secondary school and the university.

Somehow, intuitively, I believed that education was very important as a tool for rapid upward social mobility. I was not alone in having this belief. I did not want to end up a wine-taper with a shroud of loin cloth wrapped around my waist, or a poor peasant farmer and a petty trader as my parents had been.

I wanted to do better in life than my parents had done. I did not want to relive the misery and hardship of eking out a living with a multiplicity of wives and children. Oh, no! I believe that, as a young boy of the post-colonial era, I wanted to complete my education with hopes of a good employment, a good family life, and have the opportunity to contribute to the national development of my country.

I simply wanted to succeed, to become a person who grew

up to be a responsible citizen. I did not want to grow up to become a street beggar, ruined by unnecessary wars and deprivations, emasculated and ashamed of my identity as an African within the community of nations.

I wanted to walk with my back erect, my head held high up as a man no longer in bondage or in the enslavement of Europeans but a free man from Africa. I believe that this simple description of my youthful dreams and hopes were similar to those held widely by other Africans around 1960.

If you continue to ask me what the common man or woman in Africa wanted or needed at the time of their national independence, I would reply that their needs included all of the above. What the Africans needed most was a suitable or favorable environment for the realization of their dreams, hopes for the future, and have, at the least, the minimum necessities of life, namely, food, clothing, and shelter.

The average ambitious African who was politically aware wanted the newly independent States to provide for security, some basic social amenities like transportation and communication, good water supply, electricity, a reasonably thriving economy, and a feeling of progress and prosperity. Africans wanted their burdens lightened by the alleviation of poverty.

I do not believe that the Africans wanted to return blindly to the dark ways of the past – to the cruel murder of twins, indulgence and fear of the witches, superstition, and nonsensical worship of trees, spirits, and to intertribal wars. I do not believe that all Africans wanted to become rich overnight.

They just wanted a little encouragement to move on with life. They had just emerged from the trauma of foreign domination and oppression. They needed a little inspiration from those who called themselves the new leaders of Africa.

The common man or woman needed hope that all will be well, that Africans were in control of their affairs, of their own destinies.

Perhaps, the common man or woman trusted their new leaders too much to steer them on to the promised land – to Canaan. There was nothing wrong with having that kind of trust except that the trust has now been betrayed. Today's Africans do not trust their government officials and leaders. Many political leaders really don't care about the common people.

In order to reach their levels of progress and prosperity, the Africans had to assume that there would be national peace and tranquility. Peace is vital to national progress and prosperity. There also would be a relative measure of freedom. It stood to reason that political chaos and disorder bred wars and wars retard the speed of progress in nearly every area of national life. Wars and instabilities lead to stagnation. These were common sense realities.

In fact, common sense also dictated that the affairs of the State be handled in ways which would produce the expected results, one such result being the general well-being of the citizenry. Where there had been serious cases of unemployment during the colonial administrations, the new leaders were expected to be concerned enough to create and provide jobs to as many as possible.

After all, the provision of new jobs was one of the things that the politicians had promised during their campaigns before they took their seats in their respective national assemblies and governments. But, the overriding element for the attainment of all these expectations was **FREEDOM**.

It was to be a freedom that guaranteed choice over several alternatives, a freedom that would pave the way for the unfettered use and application of personal and collective initiative, talent, skills, and God-given ingenuity which would translate into technology, technical-know-how, and, ultimately, lead to an industrial revolution for all of Africa.

Nobody wanted a perpetual existence in penury, a return to feudalism or to primitivity while the rest of the world marched steadfastly onward to modernity and technological breakthroughs. No African ever wanted to be left behind in the rat-race to conquer the land, air, and seas of our planet. Those who think otherwise must have totally missed the whole point of national independence.

For the sake of sheer argument, let us say that the African did not want or did not need to progress and prosper. Says who? Why would the African not want to prosper? Why would the African choose backwardness or prefer to be brutalized by a new political oppressor when he or she may have fared better under a colonial administrator? Africans are *not* that stupid!

It is my concrete belief that inherent in the expectation to be free from foreign rule was the desire and the earnest yearning by the African to do better than he or she did in the years of colonial rule. Most probably, the Africans felt that their new leaders, being one of their own kith and kin, would treat them better than the foreign imperialist did.

The expectations of the Africans were not totally unfounded. For one thing, the African had been taking care of himself or herself for centuries before the arrival of the first foreigner to the continent. God had provided the continent with a favorably warm and wonderful climate, a rich vegetation, abundant mineral wealth and human resources, and a healthy social philosophy which knew nearly nothing of the acute individualism prevalent in other countries.

Generally speaking, Africans tended to act "brotherly" when they met with each other. Also, Africans had some experience with survivalism over the centuries. They had not gone over to the frigid countries of Europe nor to the Asiatic East in order to escape from their continent. Ancient Africa was like the Garden of Eden teeming with abundant wild life.

Africans seemed to have been content with what nature had bestowed upon them. They did not voluntarily flood the shores of the Americas in search of a new paradise. When you seriously think about it, Africa seems to have endowed upon her sons and daughters sufficient blessings so that they did not need to abandon the motherland in search of greener pastures.

In the Biblical times, Africa was the bread-house for the wandering Hebrews. Africa offered a safe haven for mankind's coming messiah. Foreigners could come and were often welcome in Africa. Africans were people with a deep sense of hospitality. But they stayed close to home.

Africans of the post-colonial era did not expect that, after the imperialists had robbed and plundered the continent for nearly 500 years, the new political leaders would dare to continue this robbery by stealing from the people and depositing such ill-gotten wealth in the banks and treasuries of the very people who had robbed Africa! And to have the temerity to demand reparations from their erstwhile colonizers. Imagine such idiocy. Keep in mind that Africa's foreign debt in 1996 was $400 billion.

Let us move on to our next important question, which is, were Africans justified to expect a better life during the post-colonial era? Absolutely, yes. And why not? No society is truly static. And who would dare to insist that Africans were divinely destined to the yoke and banalities of her past, while that same Divine hand tolerated the other races of mankind to conquer many lands, overcome their maladies, and reach out to human victories and national glory?

Such a God did not even exist. God is a good God. At least, the Christian God claimed that He is a God of justice and love. So, the Africans of the post-colonial era were justified to expect the best from their new political leaders. As Dr. James Emman Kwegyir Aggrey (1875-1927) and Bishop Samuel Ajayi Crowther (1806-1891) had maintained years before, only the best was good enough for Africa.

Those who sought to pilot the national ship of State had the awesome responsibility to make good on their promises to their people. There were very few instances, if any at all, where an aspirant politician was forced to accept national responsibility. In general, the new leaders sought for the offices which they eventually occupied.

Those politicians who felt too much of the pressures of public life had the opportunity or option to resign or quit. Very few ever did. Therefore, Africans were justified in their expectations for a better life. However, those expectations and hopes were dashed or betrayed. The question we must now ask is: why were those hopes and dreams dashed?

I firmly believe that the hopes and dreams were dashed because of the gross misconception about the idea of freedom or liberty held by some African nationalists. Now, with hindsight, we may safely say that there were two levels of understanding of the idea of freedom or liberty by the nationalist leaders.

At one level, the greatest need of the time was the struggle to end colonial rule. There was much effort in securing political freedom or liberty from the imperialists. Scores of books were written to that effect. An example was *The Case For African Freedom* by Joyce Cary who was a British novelist and officer in the colonial administrative service around 1913. He had the far-sight that Africa needed independence from Europe.[2]

Dr. Nnamdi Azikiwe spoke and wrote profusely about the necessity for national independence from colonial rule. For example, on April 4, 1949, he stated in a speech: "I conceive the cult of imperialism anywhere it exists, as a crime against humanity." On his forty-second birthday, he predicted that "Nigeria shall become a sovereign state in our life-time, in spite of the might of the oppressor." His prediction came to pass fourteen years later because "the God of Africa ... so willed it."[3]

Kwame Nkrumah also spoke and worked hard for the independence of his country, Ghana, which became independent on March 6, 1957. Seven years before this date, he was arrested and thrown into a filthy jail for nine months for his political activism. He wrote several books in the defense of national independence. Two such books were *Towards Colonial Freedom* and *I Speak of Freedom: A Statement of African Ideology* (1961).

Creditably, the goal to secure national independence from the imperialists was finally achieved. As we saw in Chapter One, many African countries gained independence by 1960. But, at the second level, there was little or no serious thought given to an understanding of the kinds of other freedoms which the Africans were bound to enjoy after colonial rule.

Therefore, it is very doubtful if the nationalist leaders clearly thought through the other forms of freedoms, such as social freedoms, economic freedoms, freedom of speech and expression, and the freedom of religion. The latter one mentioned I believe is the most important, that is, the right to believe or not to believe and to choose what kind of God to worship.

Kwame Nkrumah, for example, did espouse the doctrine that one must seek first the political kingdom and then all other things would follow thereafter. This kind of political indoctrination had a serious error because politics alone was not and could not be the cure-all for Africa's problems.

It is doubtful if the African politicians who campaigned for political independence understood, at the same time, the serious ramifications of that independence in terms of what it meant to have an open, free, and pluralistic society with the rule of law prevailing. In fact, looking back now, one wonders if the nationalists ever publicly articulated the issue of human freedom except when it was tied in with political independence.

We should by now know that national independence from foreign rule does not completely mean the same thing as fundamental human liberty or freedom. The latter is larger in scope and deeper in meaning than the former. Africans have had independence quite alright, but have we enjoyed the fruits of full and true social liberty, economic liberty, and religious liberty?

In many African countries, have we been allowed the liberty to be who (not to talk of what) we really wanted to be? Think, for example, of the freedom to be what you really wanted to be. I, for one, really wanted to be a lawyer or a journalist when I was a teenager. But, around my religious circles at the time, it was believed that lawyers were chronic liars who would never go to heaven!

Nobody took the time to inform my young mind that St. Paul had a lawyer friend. Besides, the circumstances of my being a Nigerian from the former Calabar Province and not being a member of one of the three major tribes prevented me from realizing my dream. I had to meander through many academic tributaries before I reached the intellectual plateau of acquiring the Ph.D. in history, not in law or communications.

Many other Africans can testify to having had the same

experience. They can say the same thing about the liberty to choose one's career, but also the difficulties faced in attaining or achieving that goal. But let us stay with our main course of inquiry and ask the next important question. In what ways was the African betrayed?

Through years of observation and many experiences, I believe that most ordinary Africans feel that they have been betrayed by the mindless, official acts and **intolerable arrogance** of their political leaders. Second, Africans have been betrayed by the **lack of humility** on the part of those who see themselves as important agents of the State. Third, Africans have been betrayed by the presumption on the part of the leaders that **the ordinary people are fools**, weak in terms of power, and so, can be taken for a ride.

Fourth, Africans were and currently are being betrayed because of the lack of appropriate and adequate **institutions** which will hold State officials accountable for their actions. These four ways, I assert, are the means by which Africans have been betrayed. Let us consider each of them in some detail.

1. Intolerable Arrogance

The new political leaders began with the false start of arrogance toward the common people of Africa. What is arrogance? The Webster's *Dictionary* defines the term as "a feeling or an impression of superiority manifested in an overbearing manner or presumptuous claims." Thus, the arrogant person is one who exaggerates or is disposed to exaggerate one's own worth or importance in an over-bearing manner.

Many Africans believe that their public officials are terribly arrogant people. This arrogance was derived at first from the attainment of higher education and the acquisition of paper degrees whether at home or abroad. Having become the literate members of their societies, and seemingly accustomed to the ways of life of the Westerner, these elites assumed a new air of importance and were ready to flaunt it.

They seemed to have forgotten that their arrogance reflected a particular mode of character which was unhealthy for their own personal growth and national progress. But, not all Africans with degrees were guilty of this arrogance. One such exception was Dr. A. A. Nwafor Orizu of Nigeria.

Like many others before him, Orizu had studied in the United States of America and had returned to Nigeria in the 1940s. Between 1951 and 1953, he was a politician in the Federal Legislature. As he observed the new elite class, he had some harsh words for the arrogant African. In his book, *Without Bitterness: Western Nations in Post-War Africa* (1944), Orizu wrote:

> "The educated class became a privileged class – 'privileged' because they felt themselves above the Nigerian diet, above the Nigerian attire, above the Nigerian form of marriage, above the people's ceremonies, in fact above Nigeria. Later this privilege expanded into study abroad. ... This educated class now exploits the masses. It has no use for the poor and under-privileged millions of the country. All that its members care about is to have a beautiful mansion and many servants, and to be very respectful to their wives.[4]

If one were to substitute Nigerian with African, the meaning or sense of this keen social insight would not be changed. Forty years of experience and hindsight have shown that Orizu was right. Today's African elites have exemplified Orizu's 1944 general characterization.

The manner that the political leaders treat the ordinary people or speak to the common citizen by radio or television, the chronic or habitual attitude of lateness to meetings, their pomposity, all reflect the general characteristics which Orizu had highlighted. In fact, in some quarters, arrogance has been surpassed. Some African leaders are simply megalomaniacs.

To understand the import of this analysis, one should bear in mind that I believe that the quality of the character of the men and women who lead a people is very important. In Nwafor Orizu's early jeremiad, one notices the seeds of intolerance and despotism that would afflict a person who had both arrogance and power.

These seeds of intolerance and arrogance were rooted in the new set of values of the African elite class. We should note carefully what Orizu boldly stated. The educated, privileged class "felt themselves above " all that was dear to the ordinary African. That's sheer arrogance.

In their pride and arrogance, the political elites set out to "exploit the masses." Is this not what the Africans have suffered from their leaders? Mindless exploitation. Instead of becoming the true leaders and public servants of their countries, the post-colonial leaders have turned out to be oppressive rulers and arrogant scoundrels. Therefore, the ordinary Africans have been betrayed.

2. Lack of Humility

What is humility? It is "the quality or state of being humble." To be humble implies not being proud or arrogant. It is not being haughty. It is reflecting a spirit of deference or respect for others. It is considering others more important than yourself. It is one of the cardinal virtues in ethics or in any moral construction. Our people of Ibibioland in Nigeria say that "before honor is humility."

How can a society do well when most of its leaders are usually braggarts and arrogant? During the Shehu Shagari administration (1979-1983), one public official boasted that Nigerian leaders already had their fingers on the trigger of the nuclear bomb. Imagine this statement in the context of a country which does not enjoy a constant supply of electricity. Was the public declaration intended to frighten anyone in or out of the country?

Africans have been betrayed by the absence of humility in the character of her political leaders. How humble was Idi Amin? How humble was Mobutu Seso Seko? How humble was Murtala Mohammed? If pride goes before a fall, as the ancients had said, and as the Bible declares, then it goes without saying that the leaders who are proud and arrogant, leaders who do not know what sobriety means, cannot stand. They must fall and fail.

Africa has fallen because her leaders have fallen. They have fallen because they lack the virtue of humility necessary for the conduct of personal character both in private and in public. They lack the humility and wisdom to know that public service comes with an awesome responsibility. It comes with a sacred trust which must not be betrayed.

Nobody should presume to lead others if he or she has not dealt with intolerable pride and arrogance. For it is just a matter of time before people would resent this arrogance. Arrogance is not a requisite for good company. And, certainly it is not an asset at all anyone in a leadership position should possess.

I strongly believe that Africans have been betrayed because of the poor quality of the men and women that have led her the last 40 years and continue to lead her, that manage her affairs, and that claim to lead her armies. It is not an accident that Africans often have, therefore, been treated with contempt by the rest of the world.

3. The People are Fools

During the past 40 years, African leaders, by their utterances and actions, have seemed to presume that the ordinary citizens of the continent are fools. Normally, when a person has misbehaved or has committed an outrageous act, the person would manifest an attitude of shame or embarrassment.

In traditional African society, to show that one was ashamed of misbehavior was a good thing. For example, it would be considered a shameful thing to publicly disgrace or dishonor one's parents or the village chief. In some villages, it was sacrilegious to do such a thing since the chief was both a political leader and a priest-king. A thief held his or her head very low in shame once their crime was exposed. It is so in Japan.

Africa's new leaders have displayed a total lack of shame in their public conduct. They have lied to the people without shame. They have robbed their countries and their countrymen without shame. They have committed outrageous rapes on decency and democracy without shame. They have even committed adulteries without shame.

The very laws they made, they have violated without shame! They have murdered so many people without shame. In a word, they have acted as if the ordinary citizen was not worthy of any respect. But the people are no fools, as the latest violence in Ivory Coast has shown. There, the ordinary people rose up in protest of the political mistreatment by their leaders. African leaders have seemed to ignore the lessons of history and of modern civilizations.

I should also add that the African people have tolerated the foolishness of their leaders for far too long. In fact, this is one reason why the oppression of Africans has thrived for so long. It is about time that the African leaders of thought developed a countervailing power to enable the people to resist home-grown despots and tyrants. It is a terrible misconception for leaders to think that the people are fools.

4. Lack of Institutions

Africans have been betrayed and the betrayal has been effected because of the lack of adequate institutions which should hold the leaders accountable for their actions. As George Ayittey had shown in his book, *Indigenous African Institutions* (1991), there was a time when Africans ran their affairs harmoniously and in equilibrium with nature.[5]

It used to be that in Africa, the elders were respected, the traditions and customs were respected, parents were respected, and even in-laws were respected. In my village, it was believed that we should not go to war against a village where our daughters had been married to the people there. There was order and tranquility. Then the colonial intruder arrived in Africa and all hell broke loose upon the African.

Whatever institutions there were which held the societies together were denigrated, debased or even destroyed by the colonialist. He imposed a new "civilized" social order and a new set of values upon the Africans. Things have really fallen apart ever since he came. And, I am fully aware of the school of thought which blames the colonialist for *everything* that has gone wrong on the continent.

Granted that all our institutions were destroyed by the colonial intruders, but did we not retain any measure of personal ethics and morality which could have seen us through the turbulent years ahead? Does it mean that when the colonialist left, he also took away our senses of propriety, justice, goodness, decency, and love?

Did the European imperialist turn us into zombies who could no longer act in our own self-interest? If the African leaders for 40 years had been acting in the "self-interest" of Africa (they call this national interest in the West), would we not have been better off? Would it not have been in the "self-interest" of a national leader to have spent the money stolen from Africans in Africa rather than hide it away in a foreign bank?

Would we have been in the terrible mess that Africa is in today? No. I, for one, believe that we could have done far better. We have no excuses to have been so self-destructive as we have been. I am not exaggerating when I say that Africa today is in a very bad shape. This is why the motherland is bleeding.

Before we end this chapter, we have to ask one last important question, which is: what, if any, are the implications of the betrayal of Africans by their own political leaders? To begin with an obvious answer, the betrayal of the Africans implies that the pace of progress which we would have attained has been delayed or significantly postponed.

Africa has not kept pace with other geographical areas in the advance march of civilization. Even countries like those in Southeast Asia, which had similar circumstances as we had in 1960, have outpaced the Africans 40 years later. Malaysia is a clear example. Although colonized like many African countries were, Malaysia is a country which has made significant economic progress.

A second implication of the betrayal of Africans is that the people have been grossly demoralized. The poor performances of the African leaders have not offered any encouragement to the citizenry. Personal initiatives have been stifled by ubiquitous bureaucrats and administrators who have no vision nor goals for their countries.

If any corporation were run the way Africa has been run, it would have gone bankrupt long ago. Indeed, Africa is a bankrupt continent. Can she ever pay her debts unless, by the good graces of her creditors, her debts are written off? Think of it! It is said that nothing succeeds like success. Therefore, failures breed discouragements, despair, and hopelessness. Our African youths have been demoralized by constant betrayals.

The third implication is that Africans have to redouble their efforts and energies in order to keep their houses in order. They have to strategize and plan carefully. If this is not done, then Africa will get nowhere. Africans must find ways to curb the excesses of their so-called leaders.

African people must reconsider the role of standing armies and the military in national development. I used to be on the side of strengthening the armed forces of Africa in order to prepare for external attacks. But, since the African soldier is much more cruel and a threat to his fellow Africans, should we not find ways to deal with this domestic problem first before we worry about an external aggressor?

Dr. Ayittey has painstakingly shown how Africa was betrayed in three of his books. I do not intend to reinvent the wheel. So, I will not discuss this betrayal to the degree he has already covered it. He has done excellent research. His detractors have to offer us something better before condemning him. But, as I have stated in several of my speeches and writings, the problem of Africa is mainly the problem of the mind versus matter.[6]

The main need of Africans, as I see it, is the spiritual necessity of formulating a functional systematic theology for the African world. Whether we discover this formulation through an African renaissance, reformation, or some other "Great Awakening," we owe it to our future generations to provide a solid foundation upon which they may build. Otherwise, we present-day Africans are inevitably slouching toward our Armageddon!

CHAPTER FOUR

"WHAT IS FREEDOM?" - THE WESTERN VIEW

*That condition of men in which coercion of some by others
is reduced as much as is possible in society ... (is) a state of
liberty or freedom.*

— Friedrich A. Hayek

A popular American "Negro Spiritual" goes like this:

> Oh, freedom! Oh, freedom!
> Oh, freedom over me!
> And before I'd be a slave,
> I'll be buried in my grave,
> And go home to my Lord
> And be free.[1]

The anonymous author of the above poem expresses his or her preference for and value of freedom over slavery. This author would rather die than be a slave. His preference leads us to ask an important question: what is the type of freedom that a person may be willing to die for?

The former Israeli Prime Minister, Menachem Begin, said

in 1951 that "if you love freedom, you must hate slavery."[2] We seem to know what slavery is; but what did he really mean by freedom? Thomas Jefferson, one of the founding fathers of the American Republic, wrote in 1774 that "the God who gave us life, gave us liberty at the same time."

Years later, in a letter he sent to James Madison dated August 28, 1789, Jefferson argued that the "Almighty God hath created the mind free."[3] We are familiar with Patrick Henry's "Give me liberty or give me death" statement. But, what did Jefferson mean by "liberty" and "free," bearing in mind that this defender of liberty was himself a slaveowner?

What was so precious about freedom or liberty that Patrick Henry would prefer dying rather than being denied liberty? There seems to be some confusion about the exact meaning and nature of the term. Philosophers and historians have no consensus on the matter. As the historians Oscar and Mary Handlin rightly observed, "liberty ... is a complex, not a simple condition."[4]

It is very possible that one may experience a condition which we call freedom without possessing an ability to put a clear definition of the term into words. We may simply have to agree with Herbert J. Muller, author of *Issues of Freedom: Paradoxes and Promises* (1960), when he noted that "to the ordinary man, freedom means the feeling of being able to do as he likes, act at his own sweet pleasure."[5]

Several years ago, when my son was four years old, he expressed the above kind of meaning of liberty when he said to me that he did not like people telling him what to do. I promptly reminded him that he could have his liberty at any time if he got out of my house and owned a property where he would pay his rent since he felt that he needed his freedom!

But, is freedom merely a feeling? And, what about the fact that no one is ever truly free to do just whatever he feels like doing. I may feel like sleeping with a beautiful celebrity. But I have no right to stalk one and force myself upon her, do I? Would this kind of "feeling" of freedom not be license and lead to anarchy?

To be sure, we may never be able to deny that there is such a concrete thing which we call freedom or liberty. Some writers have even suggested that we are born with it or into it. For example, Jean Jacques Rousseau, in his book, *The Social Contract* (1762), stated that "man is born free."[6]

John Milton (1608-1674), the great English poet, insisted that "no man who knows aught can be so stupid to deny that all men naturally were born free."[7] And, in 1797, Johann von Schiller (1759-1805), stated that "man is created free, and is free."[8] "Really?" we may retort?

However, in spite of all the above affirmations, we know that throughout much of the history of mankind, the world has had slavery. So what did Schiller mean by "man ... is free?" Also, let us consider this statement by Herbert Spencer who, in 1851, said that "no one can be perfectly free till all are free."[9]

What did Spencer mean by "perfectly free?" Are some people "perfectly free" while others are imperfectly free? Is there no suggestion in Spencer's statement, howbeit, implicitly stated, that some segment of mankind is in slavery and not thus enjoying freedom? Fortunately, we are not going to grope forever in darkness.

We may begin to discover what freedom means by contrasting it with something that it is not. So, as we return to our "Negro Spiritual" quoted at the beginning of this chapter, we may notice that in the Western sense, freedom appears to be the opposite of slavery. The author of our poem preferred freedom to slavery. So did Menachem Begin, though he was not a Westerner.

Simplistically, this case seems to be closed at this stage if we assert that freedom is not slavery, or, that freedom is the opposite of slavery. Abraham Lincoln said on April 6, 1859: "Those who deny freedom to others deserve it not for themselves, and, under a just God, cannot long retain it."[10]

Given the context and the circumstances of the time he made that statement, Lincoln obviously had the slaveholders in mind. Therefore, freedom is not bondage nor slavery. It is not being in a state of servitude nor serfdom. It is not coercion. It is not acting under compulsion. A man or woman in slavery is not a free person.

Yet, our task is not finished nor made easier by these negative assertions – these contrasts between freedom and slavery. So, we must return to the opinion of some experts, to see what they have to say. What definition, if any, do they provide for freedom and what meaning thereof? We can draw from the fountains of their wisdom and knowledge.

If we are to make any progress in our plea that freedom or liberty is of supreme importance, then we have to fully understand positively what freedom really is. Let us begin with John Stuart Mill (1806-1873) who, in his book, *On Liberty* (1859), wrote that "the only freedom which deserves the name, is that of pursuing our own good in our own way, so long as we do not attempt to deprive others of theirs, or impede their efforts to obtain it."

Then, he added: "Over himself, over his own body and mind, the individual is sovereign."[11] The Handlins, historians mentioned in the beginning of this chapter, quoted the French philosopher Claude-Adrien Helvetius (1715-1771) as saying that "the free man is a man who is not in irons, nor imprisoned in jail, nor terrorized like a slave by fear of punishment."[12]

Thomas Hobbes and David Hume, great philosophers, were also cited by the Handlins. Hobbes believed that "liberty, or freedom, signifieth, properly, the absence of opposition. ... *A FREEMAN is he, that in those things, which by his strength and wit he is able to do, is not hindered to do what he has a will to do.*"

Hobbes added that liberty "is the antithesis of the power of others; the one exists when the other is absent. Freedom ... is a condition at which the individual arrives by safeguarding himself against compulsion or the threat of compulsion."[13] For Hume, liberty meant "*a power of acting or not acting ...*, that is if we choose to remain at rest, we may, if we choose to move, we also may."[14]

Frankly, these views, carefully analyzed, are about the absence of restraints or external coercions. Herbert J. Muller conceived his book, *Issues of Freedom*, as an introduction to a history of freedom. But he also viewed freedom in terms of its relation to culture and not merely to its relation to a political structure within any State.

Muller provided what he called a "neutral definition" of freedom by saying that it is "the condition of being able to choose and carry out purposes." He also pointed out that his definition included the "freedom of mind and spirit, which is hardest to specify but still distinguishes human freedom from the ability of other animals to carry out their instinctive purposes."[15]

Muller acknowledged that there were various "concrete" forms of freedom. Hence, one may speak of individual, political, and spiritual freedoms. But let us turn to Friedrich A. Hayek, another expert on freedom, for his insights. He is the author of the famous trilogy, *Law, Legislation and Liberty* (1973).

In 1960, Hayek had published his classic, *The Constitution of Liberty* in which he believed freedom meant "that condition of men in which coercion of some by others is reduced as much as is possible in society. That state we shall describe ... as a state of liberty or freedom."[16]

Hayek also stated that his definition was "the original meaning of the word." Like Muller, Hayek agreed that there was more than one kind of freedom. For instance, there was what he called the "inner" or "metaphysical" or "subjective" kind of freedom. He insisted that coercion was central in any understanding of the meaning of freedom or liberty. His definition belongs to the classical or orthodox view of freedom.

In contrast to Hayek, we have the view of Isaiah Berlin, who was a former professor of social and political theory at Oxford University. Berlin believed that there were actually only two notions of freedom or liberty. One was negative, that is, the freedom to do what we like.

The other notion was positive, that is, the liberty or freedom that is circumscribed by restraints, such as parental, legal, governmental or even societal prohibitions. Here, one asks the question: to what degree is my freedom or liberty limited? Berlin called one notion the "freedom from" and the other notion, the "freedom to."[17]

There are other scholars who seem to agree with Berlin and have amplified his notions of freedom. Two of these scholars are Randy E. Barnett, author of *The Structure of Liberty: Justice and the Rule of Law* (1998) and David C. Cochran, author of *The Color of Freedom: Race and Contemporary American Liberalism* (1999).

Barnett defines liberty as "those freedoms which people ought to have" and license as "those freedoms which people ought not to have and thus those freedoms which are properly constrained."[18] He argues that liberty has a structure which embraces both true freedom and the constraint of actions.

Cochran writes that "positive liberty is mastering oneself in accordance with truth or reason." This kind of liberty, he says, relies upon "internal self-realization or rational self-direction."[19] He warns that positive liberty may lead to autocracy, authoritarian or totalitarian regimes since people have to "be forced to be free."[20]

Negative liberty, Cochran contends, insists upon non-interference by others. Negative liberty always insists that the individual ought to be free from external coercion or obstruction from the hands of others. It counts upon the ability of the individual to act properly in the absence of external restraints.

In 1958, Mortimer J. Adler authored a 689-page book entitled, *The Idea of Freedom: A Dialectical Examination of the Conceptions of Freedom*. Adler and his research team analyzed 2,500 years of thought on the idea of freedom. Based on their research, they concluded that there were basically three **modes** of freedom, as follows:

1. the circumstantial freedom of self-realization

2. the acquired freedom of self-perfection, and, the

3. natural freedom of self-determination.

The first mode was defined as "the ability of a person under favorable circumstances to act as he wishes for his own good as he sees it."[21] This was similar to the view held by John Stuart Mill. The second mode was defined as "the ability of a person through acquired virtue or wisdom to will or live as he ought in conformity to the moral law or an ideal befitting human nature."[22] This mode was close to the beliefs or philosophy held by St. Augustine or Thomas Aquinas.

The third mode was defined as "the ability of a person to change his own character creatively by deciding for himself what he shall do or become."[23] This was the pragmatists' position. Adler also identified two other modes of freedom which, he noted, "[did] not add any new principles" to his classifications.[24]

Those two modes were political liberty, which is a variant of circumstantial self-realization, and collective freedom, which is a variant of acquired self-perfection. In his conclusion, Adler stated what he thought freedom meant. "A man," he wrote, "is free who has in himself the ability or power whereby he can make what he does his own action and what he achieves his own property."[25]

This tripartite conception of freedom by Adler leads us to yet one more expert opinion, that is, the view held by Orlando Patterson, who seems to share the same three-dimensional conception of freedom as Adler's. A Harvard University professor of Sociology and the author of two volumes on freedom, Patterson's tripartite conception of freedom comprises of personal, sovereignal, and civic freedoms.

According to Patterson, personal freedom "gives a person the sense that one ... is not being coerced or restrained by another person in doing something desired and ... the conviction that one can do as one pleases within the limits of that other person's desire to do the same."[26] This concept embraces both the negative and the positive notions of liberty.

Sovereignal freedom is "the power to act as one pleases, regardless of the wishes of others."[27] Patterson adds that "the sovereignally free person has the power to restrict the freedom of others or to empower others with the capacity to do as they please with others beneath them."[28] This sounds like the freedom which is often exercised by despots, dictators, and tyrants. A rabble-rouser may also exercise this kind of freedom unless he is stopped.

Patterson's third concept of freedom is civic freedom which he defines as "the capacity of adult members of a community to participate in its life and governance."[29] This notion is similar to Isaiah Berlin's definition of political liberty in the ancient Greek world. Patterson concludes that "these, then, are the three constitutive elements of the uniquely Western chord of freedom."[30]

It is instructive to note that Patterson admits that his three conceptions of freedom are the Western, not the African, notions of freedom. Western scholars who write on freedom generally give the impression that the rest of the world laid in bondage or slavery until the arrival of the ancient Athenians who then discovered freedom.[31] What a misconception! They should have listened to the words by Jomo Kenyatta which were quoted in Chapter One.

Even a modern-day historian like Donald W. Treadgold, whose book, *Freedom: A History*, appeared in 1990, dismissed the idea of an African conception of freedom in only eight lines of sentences buried within two short paragraphs in Chapter Four. Apologetically, he admits that "Africa deserves more space than it can be given here."[32]

This is all that one gets from a Western scholar whose book is 462 pages in length! Therefore, I felt obligated to search for and find some materials on the African view of freedom. What I have done in this chapter is really to examine the Western historiography on liberty. I hope that my investigation has shed some light on the Western view of freedom. But, this light leaves us in a penumbra if the African conception of freedom is lacking. To that, I now turn my attention.

CHAPTER FIVE

"WHAT IS FREEDOM?" - AN AFRICAN VIEW

I believe in the God of Africa. I believe in the black people of Africa. I believe that it is not the will of the God of Africa to sentence the black people of Africa to servitude in any form for ever.

— Nnamdi Azikiwe

Few books are available on the subject of the African conception of human freedom. Perhaps, one reason this is so is because Africans have spent so much time trying to free themselves from the shackles of centuries-old slavery and colonialism.

It should not be forgotten that, for a country like Nigeria, foreign domination of the peoples in that part of Africa lasted for 475 years, that is, from 1485 to 1960. That meant nearly 500 years of foreign control, exploitation and domination.

For Africans, the history of the loss of their freedoms and sovereignties dated back to 1415, the year that Portugal militarily captured the Moroccan city of Ceuta and established a foothold on the African soil. Ever since that year, the Africans have been struggling to free themselves from

European control and domination.

Until the second half of the 20th century, Africans, exept in a few states like Ethiopia, had lost their political freedom. Hence, they had little or no time to think of or engage in writing exhaustive books on the meaning and structure of freedom. Their preoccupation was with the actual regaining of political freedom from the European powers rather than with the rationalization of or the intellectual expositions on freedom.

Consequently, there are few or no works for the researcher to consult on the matter of the African conception of human freedom. This being the case, my analysis here is only an attempt to explore the subject. I will leave an exhaustive treatment to others and for another time.

My methodology is to draw from some of the more than 2,000 languages and words used by Africans themselves to describe or define freedom. I draw also from some writings, addresses and speeches by African leaders, to examine what ideas some political leaders of Africa had about human freedom.

I am particularly interested in knowing what the Africans who struggled to win independence for their peoples thought, said, and did regarding human freedom in the past and currently. I contend that the African nationalists since the 1440s would not have fought for political freedom from foreign domination if they had no conceptions of human freedom. This is one of my basic assumptions.

Also, I assume that human freedom is the bedrock for all the other kinds of freedoms: political, social, economic, intellectual, individual and spiritual freedoms. I insist that African peoples did and still do value true human freedom. They knew of and enjoyed some relative forms of freedoms during the precolonial years.

All of Africa did not go through what may be called the "age of the despots." We know from history that some parts of Africa had no polities which would be described as autocratic regimes since they had no kings nor military autocrats. An example is the Igbo people of eastern Nigeria. There was no "*eze-gburugburu ndigbo*," meaning the King of all the Igbos, as Chinua Achebe had shown in his novel, *Things Fall Apart*.

In his book, *Indigenous African Institutions* (1991), Dr. George B. N. Ayittey strongly argued that precolonial Africans enjoyed *some* kinds of freedoms and that such freedoms included the freedom of choice, association, speech and expression, movement, worship, economic activity and for the press.[1]

Ayittey's argument suggested that no one was brutalized because he or she chose to worship the sun or the moon or even the crocodile or the python. If you ask any African, young or old, he would confirm that Africans loved and enjoyed some relative forms of freedoms which may not be concretely defined in or made to fit into Western terminologies. One such cherished freedom was the freedom to sit under their trees to tell some moonlight stories to their children.

Indeed, contrary to Western misconceptions, Africans have many words and phrases that *correspond* to the English term which we know as freedom. In East Africa, the international language spoken there is *kiswahili*. The word for freedom there is *uhuru*. The late President Julius K. Nyerere, the first president of the Republic of Tanzania, wrote three books on *uhuru* as it related to socialism, development, and national unity.[2]

Nyerere is quoted as saying that "a man betrayed his birthright if he were not prepared to fight and even die for the cardinal principles of individual and national liberty."[3] Here, one should note that Nyerere was not only concerned with political freedom, but was also certainly interested in individual liberty as well.

In West Africa, there are many words and phrases for freedom. The Igbos of Nigeria have a phrase, not a single term, which corresponds to the English word freedom. They speak of "*madu nwere onyeya*,"[4] meaning the person who owns himself. In sharp contrast is another Igbo word, "*oru*," which means a slave, or a person who does not own himself or herself.

Dr. Nnamdi Azikiwe, the first president of Nigeria, was an Igbo man and a great African nationalist who fought hard for Nigerian independence from British colonialism. I believe that he understood what human freedom was and so stood up against any kind of enslavement and tyranny during his political career.

Azikiwe fought the British colonialists with the might of his pen, his chain of newspapers, books and speeches. The theme of freedom spanned his anti-colonial career. Like the Igbos, the Efik/Ibibios of southeastern Nigeria also have some phrases and words that denote the terms we know as freedom and free.

The Ibibios say: "*sio ke ufin, sana yak*" and "*nam ayak*." These phrases correspond to the English words "to set free" or freedom. The words "*unyene idem ikpon*" or "*enyene idem ikpon*" correspond to the Igbo phrase that means a person who owns himself or herself. Also, in the Ibibio language, a free person may be refered to simply as "*eyenison*," literally meaning a "son of the soil," or a free-born.

The freedom of one's will is expressed in Ibibio as "*ukeme ediduak nte amade*." The condition of freedom or the state of freedom is rendered as "*itie eyenison*" or "*editie ke idem esie*."[5] In my judgement, it seems proper to me that the single term, "*uboho*," would be the most appropriate term in the Ibibio language for the English word freedom. But, I do realize that this word, "*uboho*" refers more to deliverance than to freedom.

In contrast to the above notions of freedom are some Ibibio words for the slave and slavery. The word "*ofun*" stands for slave and "*ufun*" means slavery. The phrase "*unyene ofun*" means to own a slave and "*utom ufun*" means slave labor, work of slavery, or servitude. The Westerner who is ignorant of and unable to understand or even speak these African languages simply presumes that the African had no notion of freedom!

The Westerner's insistence that his presumption is right is sheer arrogance or downright stupidity. Imagine an African who is ignorant of American popular culture, who had never seen nor heard of Santa Claus, insisting that Santa Claus is actually a ghost who resides at the North Pole. Would he not be deemed ludicrous?

Let us move even further to the country of Ghana. There, the Ashantis have the word "*faahodi*"[6] for freedom. They also have other word variations for freedom, like *fahodzi* for the Fante and *fahodi* for the Twi. East of the country of Ghana, the Ewes in the Republic of Togo have the word "*ablodee*"[7] for freedom.

To the west of Ghana, in the country of the Gambia, there are three words which stand for freedom. The Mandinka-speaking people use the word "*foroyaa*" for freedom. The Wolof prefer the word "*gorrya*" while the Fulbe use the word "*woddakeh*."[8]

According to Rhoi Wangila, the founder and president of the Ark Foundation of Africa, Inc., an NGO (non-governmental organization) based in Washington, D.C., the word for freedom among the Muganda ethnic group in the country of Uganda is "*dembe*."[9] The Mugandas speak the Luganda language.

The above examples suffice for an argument that Africans

have notions of or conceptions of freedom. Throughout the continent, there are thousands of languages and dialects spoken. Among these languages and dialects, there are many phrases and words which portray the African notions of freedom.

Even if Africans had no words for freedom, one could still have argued that, as human beings, Africans are born with the experience of freedom. We shall now move on, in the next six chapters, to consider the writings, speeches and actions of some African nationalists, in order to further understand their conception of human freedom.

CHAPTER SIX

AFRICAN FREEDOM: NKRUMAH, MBOYA AND KENYATTA

The African is conditioned, by the cultural and social institutions of centuries, to a freedom of which Europe has little conception, and it is not in his nature to accept serfdom for ever.

— Jomo Kenyatta

Africa's political leaders, particularly those who led the struggle for independence, provide the best examples for any analysis of the African conception of freedom.

Many of those leaders included people like Kwame Nkrumah of Ghana, Nnamdi Azikiwe and Obafemi Awolowo of Nigeria, Tom Mboya and Jomo Kenyatta of Kenya, Julius K. Nyerere of Tanzania.

Others were Kenneth Kaunda of Zambia, Leopold Senghor of Senegal, and Nelson Mandela of South Africa. There were also women like Margaret Udo Ekpo of Nigeria, Deodolinda Rodrigues, the Angolan resistance leader, and Ruth First and Charlotte Maxeke, both of South Africa. Certainly, there were many others that space would prevent us from including them here.

The important thing to remember is that those leaders knew what freedom was in order to want political freedom from the colonial masters. Also, they were considered heroes and heroines of the African liberation movements which, in turn, brought about national independence.

Those leaders championed African nationalism. Some of them came to be regarded as the fathers and mothers of their respective countries. It is my firm belief that those leaders knew what human freedom meant. Europeans did not have to educate them on the subject. The idea of freedom was inherent in the Africans.

I believe that human freedom is the bedrock for the exercise of all other kinds of freedoms and rights. The belief in the value of human freedom was, therefore, the basis for the aspiration by Africans to be free and control their affairs. So, it is important to inquire into the thoughts, expressions, and writings of those leaders, with the aim of discovering what they understood about human freedom.

Since Ghana looms large in the history of decolonization in Africa, let us begin with Kwame Nkrumah. What did he think, say, write or do regarding freedom? In my book, *Destiny Is Not A Matter of Chance* (1989), I had analyzed the political career of Nkrumah in terms of his conception of the destiny of the African people.[1] Here, we are concerned with his conception of freedom.

Nkrumah (1909-1972) led Ghana to national independence in 1957. Like the other nationalists of his day, Nkrumah honestly and sincerely concerned himself with the task of obtaining independence for his people. In the book, *African Nationalism in the Twentieth Century* (1965), the authors say this of Nkrumah:

> As he was leaving the United States in 1945 after ten years of study and hardship, and his ship passed

the Statue of Liberty, Kwame Nkrumah through misty eyes vowed: "I shall never rest until I have carried your message to Africa." A dozen years later, as Prime Minister of the first African colony to gain freedom, Nkrumah, reflecting on the long and difficult road to self-government, again determined that "African nationalism was not (to be) confined to the Gold Coast – the new Ghana."[2]

From the above statement, it is obvious that Nkrumah was earnest about political independence from Britain. On November 14, 1947, he left Britain to return to Ghana (then called the Gold Coast) to accept the position of Secretary-General of the United Gold Coast Convention (UGCC), a nationalist movement formed on December 29, 1947, with the goal of obtaining self-government for Ghana "within the shortest time possible."[3]

While in the United States and in Britain, Nkrumah had developed his skills and talents for leadership. He had become an eloquent and effective spokesman for Africa. He did not share the conservative idea of gradualism about self-government which was held by people like Dr. Joseph B. Danquah, one of the founders of the UGCC. For Nkrumah, the attainment of self-government was to be immediate.

On February 20, 1948, when he delivered what he called his "Maiden Speech in Accra," Nkrumah realized that Ghanaians were ready to "strike out for their freedom and independence."[4] From that day onward, he emerged as the most strident advocate for Ghana's self-government and national independence.

Nkrumah was sent to jail twice because of this role. The first time he received a six-week term in solitary confinement. The second time he received a three-year term, for which he served only nine months. In 1951, he rose from prison to power, forming a government led by his own political party, the Convention Peoples' Party (CPP).

Now, whether Nkrumah was clear in his mind about the difference between the attainment of national independence from Britain and the exercise of the principles of true human freedom is a matter that no one knows for sure. But, as we shall discover, Nkrumah, like many of the nationalists of his time, did not provide us with any thorough synthesis or elucidation of the subject.

However, the utterances and writings of Nkrumah from 1948 to 1957, and even beyond that year, reveal a man who was passionate about political emancipation from Britain for Ghana. The desire for Ghana to be free and "to breathe the air of freedom"[5] was part of his passion, though he cared about the total liberation of all Africa from colonial rule.

As a practical step, Nkrumah established over a dozen educational institutions, including the Ghana National College, in order "to liberate the minds of our youth so that they should be ready to tackle the many problems of our time."[6] Also, in order to mobilize and inform the masses, Nkrumah founded three newspapers: the *Accra Evening News*, the Sekondi *Morning Telegraph*, and the Cape Coast *Daily Mail*.

Through these newspapers, Nkrumah successfully led a propaganda of "Self-Government Now" as opposed to the UGCC's philosophy of "Self-Government within the shortest possible time." In 1948, he formed the Committee on Youth Organization (CYO) which was transformed into the CPP the following year. Nkrumah's addresses to the CYO in December 1948, and subsequently to the CPP, were about political independence from British rule.

For example, at one CYO meeting, Nkrumah spoke for

nearly two hours on "The Liberty of the Colonial Subject." At the Kumasi Youth Conference held from December 23 to 26, 1948, he assisted in the drawing up of the Ghana Youth Manifesto that was published under the title "Towards Self-Government."[7]

On Sunday, June 12, 1949, the CPP was born and Nkrumah was poised "to fight relentlessly by all constitutional means for the achievement of full 'Self-Government Now'."[8] On that single day, Nkrumah mobilized a crowd of about 60,000 people who demanded immediate self-government for Ghana from the British. Two days later, he resigned from the UGCC over differences of policy.

Clearly, Nkrumah was inspired by the ideal of freedom and the British tolerance of the press. He believed that "freedom had never been handed over to any colonial country on a silver platter; it had been won only after bitter and vigorous struggles."[9] Driven by this mindset, he applied the Gandhian principle of "Positive Action" to the Ghanaian struggle for self-government.

Nkrumah defined "Positive Action" as "the adoption of all legitimate and constitutional means by which we could attack the forces of imperialism in the country."[10] He was convinced that Ghana "wanted self-government and we had a legitimate right to decide for ourselves the sort of government we desired."[11]

He insisted that "the people of (Ghana) needed political power to manage their own affairs."[12] When he visited Liberia in 1953 at that country's official invitation, Nkrumah declared publicly that "A people without a government of their own is 'silly and absurd'."[13] He argued that Britain gained a foothold into Ghana through "the Bond of 1844." But, he also stated that the Fanti Confederation of 1868 was, in part, "an effort to oppose British imperialism."[14]

Nkrumah delivered the most important address of his life on July 10, 1953. He titled this speech to the Legislative Assembly "The Motion of Destiny." By it, he demanded a definite date for the granting of self-government to Ghana. This address showed Nkrumah's tact, knowledge of history, and brilliance. A great part of this address dealt with the reasons for independence.

Among other things, Nkrumah said:

> Throughout a century of alien rule our people have, with ever increasing tendency, looked forward to that bright and glorious day when they shall regain their ancient heritage, and once more take their place rightly as free men in the world.[15]

The reader should note the word "regain" used by Nkrumah above. As we shall find, the African nationalists assumed their possession of freedom and believed that imperialism and colonialism had robbed Africans of their freedom. They did not concede to the Europeans the right to decide whether Africans ought to be free or not.

Nkrumah held that the people of Ghana were ready to "regain" their political autonomy which they once had in order to run their own affairs. So, he said:

> The freedom we demand is for our country as a whole, this freedom we are claiming is for our children, for the generations yet unborn, that they may see the light as men and women with the right to work out the destiny of their own country.[16]

Nkrumah reminded the Assembly that the people of Ghana had governed themselves in pre-colonial times.[17] The Ashantis were warriors while the Fantis were constitution-makers. Between 1865 and 1871, the Fanti Constitution, believed by some to be "one of the most important documents produced in Africa in the nineteenth century,"[18] was drawn up.

This document also served as a petition to the British for independence for the Gold Coast. Nkrumah drew much from the past history of Ghana. He believed that his cause was just and said that the "demand for self-government is a just demand." He declared: "It is a demand admitting of no compromise. The right of a people to govern themselves is a fundamental principle, and to compromise on this principle is to betray it."[19]

Thus, Nkrumah placed this right to self-government at the same level as any of the other best known fundamental human rights such as the right to life, worship and expression. Therefore, Nkrumah argued as follows:

> The right of a people to decide their own destiny, to make their way in freedom, is not to be measured by the yardstick of colour or degree of social development. It is an inalienable right of peoples which they are powerless to exercise when forces, stronger than they themselves, by whatever means, for whatever reasons, take this right away from them. If there is to be a criterion of a people's preparedness for self-government, then I say it is their readiness to assume the responsibility of ruling themselves.[20]

Also, Nkrumah added that the people of Ghana had displayed such readiness and preparedness to govern themselves between 1951 and 1953. He demolished the European myth and logic that Africans were not ripe nor ready to govern themselves. Nkrumah called upon the members of the Assembly to realize that they held the destiny of their country in their own hands.

"A colonial people in Africa," he said, "has put forward the first definite claim for independence. An African colonial people proclaim that they are ready to assume the stature of free men and to prove to the world that they are worthy of the trust."[21] Nkrumah continued: "The vast continent of Africa and the New World are looking to you with desperate hope, as an inspiration to continue their grim fight against cruelties which we in this corner of Africa have never known."[22]

He concluded this speech with this affirmation: "We are ripe for freedom, and our people will not be denied. ... They claim it as their own and none can keep it from them."[23] The motto of one of his newspapers, the *Accra Evening News*, best summed up Nkrumah's stance on this political freedom. It said: "We prefer self-government with danger to servitude in tranquility."[24]

After this address, Nkrumah settled down to the task of preparing the CPP for the general elections of 1954. The day for that election was June 15. Ghanaians went out to the polls peacefully and orderly. The next day, the results revealed that the CPP had won. Nkrumah was again asked to form a government.

The entire country was electrified by this march toward colonial freedom. Wherever he went, Nkrumah received the "freedom salute." This was true when he visited the Ashanti region. It was true also when he made a stop-over at Lagos, Nigeria, on his way to Douala in the Cameroon.[25] He was at the time Ghana's Prime Minister. But the much coveted full independence had not yet been granted.

The British insisted upon another general election. Nkrumah wanted a fixed date for independence before any other election was scheduled. But the British were reluctant to do so. Therefore, Nkrumah sent an emissary, Kojo Botsio, to London, to impress upon the British that a fixed date for independence was absolutely necessary.

The general election of 1956 gave the CPP another political victory. The CPP won 71 out of the 104 seats in the Legislative Assembly. Thereupon, Nkrumah quickly introduced a motion for the independence of Ghana and it passed. On Monday, September 17, 1956, at 3 o'clock, he received the best news of his political career from the colonial governor: Ghana would become a free and independent country on March 6, 1957. And the British kept their word!

The next year, in August 1958, Nkrumah traveled to the United States of America. He delivered a foreign policy speech before the Senate and said: "I know that you will always find us aligned with the forces fighting for freedom and peace."[26] Also, he added that Ghana was dedicated to the ideals of liberty and justice.

Through this brief political biography, I have attempted to highlight what Nkrumah said, wrote or thought about freedom. It seems clear that he considered national freedom from colonial rule to be an integral part of human freedom. At the time, political freedom was his preoccupation.

In all of his writings, which covered more than fifteen books, Nkrumah nowhere offered any exhaustive treatment of the concept of freedom as we had seen in Chapter Four. After Ghana's independence was won, Nkrumah's actions betrayed any serious respect or regard for the freedoms and rights of other Ghanaians. The lust for power may have been responsible for this change of attitude.

In fact, as some scholars have pointed out, he actually practiced the politics of detention, repression against freedom of expression, and political dictatorship. He jailed some of his own colleagues who had suffered with him in prison at the hands of the British colonialists. One such victim of Nkrumah was Dr. Joseph B. Danquah. It was ironic, to say the least.

But, let us travel to East Africa, to Kenya, and examine the conception of freedom by another African nationalist. In Chapter Five, I had stated that, in the *kiswahili* language of East Africa, *uhuru* is the term for freedom. Dr. Tom Mboya (1930-1969) best articulated what *uhuru* meant when he published his well-known and most widely read book, *Freedom and After* in 1963.

Before his publication, Mboya was a world-renown trade unionist and pan-Africanist from Kenya. He had studied industrial management in London between 1955 and 1956. In 1958, he was the Secretary/Treasurer of the Pan-African Freedom Movement for East and Central Africa (PAFMECA) and worked with notable African leaders like Nyerere and Kaunda.

Mboya was committed to the African struggle for political freedom. Together with Nyerere and twenty-one others, the idea of PAFMECA was born in the quiet town of Mwanza near Lake Victoria. In three days of deliberations, in September 1958, the constitution and Freedom Charter for PAFMECA were written. In part, this Charter stated that,

> Freedom is our birthright; self-government our heritage, as sons and daughters of the free men and women who inherited Africa for the Africans. It is therefore not only just but imperative that we restore our birthright for ourselves and our children and our children's children. ... We declare that democracy must prevail throughout Africa, from Senegal to Zanzibar and from Cape to Cairo; that colonialism, the so-called trusteeship, and so-called partnership, apartheid, multiracialism and white settlerism are enemies of freedom, and can be eradicated only by African nationalism, virile and

unrelenting; that the right of self-determination is
God-given and no man or nation is chosen by God
to determine the destiny of others; that poverty,
ignorance, ill-health and other human miseries
cannot be satisfactorily eradicated under imperialism, but only under self-government and
international cooperation on the basis of equality
and mutual benefaction.[27]

Here, one must note the above-mentioned affirmations
by the authors of the PAFMECA Freedom Charter: the
insistence that freedom is a birthright, is God-given, and their
refutation of Rudyard Kipling's notion of "the white man's
burden," or of "manifest destiny and mission."

With Nkrumah, African freedom was to be regained; with
Mboya and his collaborators, it was to be restored. Clearly,
Africans assumed that they had always been free until their
contact with Europeans. Africans believed that they did not
need white "settlerism" nor civilization.

The Freedom Charter was not a racialist document. It
emphasized "the precepts and practice of democracy" and
denounced any kind of "discrimination, victimization, or any
form of segregation based purely on race or color or religion."

Also, the Charter provided that,

> The safeguards and protection of citizen's rights and
> human liberties will be buttressed by uncom-
> promising adherence to the Rule of Law; the
> maintenance of the absolute independence of the
> Judiciary; the exercise of the right to vote or stand
> for any office; the constant observance of the
> declaration of the Universal Human Rights and the
> United Nations Charter.[28]

In 1958 when Mboya, Nyerere, and other Africans expressed these lofty sentiments, white colonialists were adamant not to grant these basic rights and freedoms to Africans in their homeland.

Like Nkrumah, Mboya was seriously interested in the educational advancement of Kenyan youths. So, he negotiated for the air-lifting of many Kenyan students from East Africa into the U.S. between 1956 and 1963. According to Mboya, by 1963 there were 1,011 students in the United States and another 100 in Canada.

The air-lifting also included 132 Kenyan women who were to study in the U.S. These efforts were part of the preparations for provision of needed manpower when independence from Britain would be won. Mboya teamed up with Nyerere, Kaunda, and Joshua Nkomo of Zimbabwe, working under the auspices of the American Committee on Africa.[29]

For these abilities and his other contributions, Mboya was conferred with an honorary degree of Doctor of Laws in 1959 by Howard University in Washington, D.C. Mboya's brief life had greatly affected the politics and history of Kenya and of Africa. Sadly, on July 5, 1969, he was murdered while shopping in Nairobi.[30] Jomo Kenyatta and the officials of his government were suspected to have been involved in Mboya's death.

Mboya's views on freedom are to be gleaned from his autobiography, *Freedom and After*, mentioned already. In it, he states what *uhuru* was to Kenyans and to the East Africans. He states that *uhuru* meant different things to different people. For Kenyans, in particular, *uhuru* was a clarion call for political freedom from the British colonial masters.[31]

Like Nkrumah, Mboya believed that political freedom was to be granted immediately. Therefore, the Kenyans demanded *"uhuru sasa"* (Freedom Now).[32] Mboya declared: "So *uhuru sasa* was our declaration in simple words that we had always possessed the right to be free, and freedom had nothing to do with riches or schooling, or civilization."[33]

Some Kenyan independence politicians established their own newspapers and called it the *Uhuru*. It was owned by the Peoples' Convention Party (PCP).[34] Others formed a political party called the *Uhuru* Party (or the Freedom Party).[35] We should not ignore the significance of tying these Kenyan political developments to the idea of *uhuru*.

Like Nkrumah, Mboya believed that African freedom included the total liberation of all Africa from European imperialism and colonialism. Freedom meant "independence for all Africa."[36] Freedom or *uhuru* was the rallying cry that united the people in a common cause.

And, we should not ignore Mboya's insistence that Africans "had always possessed the right to be free." This assertion ran contrary to the imperialist worldview. Nevertheless, this view by Mboya was widely held throughout Africa by the Africans themselves. Now, we must examine the conceptions of freedom by another nationalist.

Although Tom Mboya did not become the president of the Republic of Kenya, the man whose cause he defended emerged to be the father of Kenyan nationalism. That man was Jomo Kenyatta (1891-1978) whom some Kenyans affectionately called the *Mzee*. When Mboya was on a visit to New York, he gave a speech on African Freedom Day on April 17, 1961, by which he revealed his respect for the *Mzee*. Among other things, Mboya said:

> Let me speak for a while about the father of my own country Kenya, the man who perhaps more than any other represents the African personality: Jomo

Kenyatta. He has been imprisoned for the past nine years, most of that time not only deprived of his liberty, but deliberately made to suffer ... Jomo Kenyatta is still imprisoned in this year of 1961, despite that wind of change we have heard so much about.[37]

Then Mboya added:

Denial of freedom to Jomo Kenyatta and the other detained people of Kenya is a mockery of justice. It is a sheer injustice and a contravention of the United Nation's Declaration of Human Rights to restrict anyone without a trial or after he has completed a prison sentence.[38]

Like Mboya, Jomo Kenyatta had studied in London and lived there for about fifteen years. In those years, he had visited Moscow and some other European cities. He studied anthropology under the famous professor B. Malinowski who encouraged Kenyatta to publish his first book, *Facing Mount Kenya: The Tribal Life of the Gikuyu* in 1938.

This book was an analysis of his own ethnic group, the Gikuyu. In it, Kenyatta stated that "the Gikuyu system of government prior to the advent of the Europeans was based on true democratic principles."[39] Also, Kenyatta argued that "the African can only advance to a higher level if he is free to express himself, to organize economically, politically, and socially, and to take part in the government of his own country."

Kenyatta insisted that,

The most elementary human rights of self-expression, freedom of speech, the right to form social organizations to improve their condition, and above all, the right to move freely in their own

country ... [were] the rights which the Gikuyu
people had enjoyed from time immemorial until the
arrival of the [British].[40]

Kenyatta ended the book with the assertion that "the
African is conditioned, by the cultural and social institutions of
centuries, to a freedom of which Europe has little conception,
and it is not in his nature to accept serfdom for ever."[41]
Although on the face of it, this was a book on anthropology, it
was also a political indictment of the colonial system and of
British imperialism in Africa.

In 1946, Kenyatta returned to Kenya. In London, he had
met with many other Africans clamoring for independence for
their countries. He had participated in the Fifth Pan-African
Congress the year before. He was encouraged by the
independence of India and Pakistan in 1947, to press on for
Kenya's freedom.

By this time, a radical secret movement, known as the so-
called Mau Mau, had been formed. Its sole aim was to drive
away the European settlers out of Kenya. There is no evidence that Kenyatta was a member of this Mau Mau. But the
British colonial authorities suspected that he was the brains
behind the movement.

When the British clamped down on the Mau Mau and
its sympathizers, a terrible guerrilla warfare erupted in
1952. By 1956, the British had killed 10,527 Mau Mau
fighters, excluding an additional 534 other Africans killed.
63 Europeans were also killed and 102 wounded.[42]

Kenyatta was apprehended and on April 8, 1953, at the age
of 62, sentenced to seven years of hard labor. He spent eight
years in jail and was not released from this imprisonment until
1961 when he was elected to lead the Kenya African National
Union (KANU).

KANU won the general elections held on May 28, 1963, and Kenyatta was invited to form a new government. On December 12, 1963, Kenya became a free and independent country with Jomo Kenyatta as its first Prime Minister. The Kenyan Independence Day was celebrated as the *Uhuru* Day.

On that first *Uhuru* Day, Kenyatta declared that "freedom ... means that we are now a member of the international community" and he added: "Freedom is a right, and without it the dignity of man is violated. But freedom by itself is not enough."[43] So, he asked all the Kenyans to embrace *Uhuru na kazi* (Freedom and Work).

Furthermore, Kenyatta believed that freedom meant deliverance "from the afflictions of poverty, ignorance and disease, otherwise freedom for many of our people will be neither complete nor meaningful."[44] Here, we find that freedom was reduced to the merely material and external levels. Qualitatively, this kind of freedom is superficial. Men and women may wallow in abundance and yet can be imprisoned or enslaved by their passions and maladies.

On May 25, 1964, the Organization For African Unity (OAU) Day, Kenyatta promised to "enhance personal liberty and freedom of expression"[45] in his country. About three months later, on August 13th, he delivered a speech by which he advocated a one-party system. The road to dictatorship was opened then.

On this occasion, Kenyatta reminded Kenyans that freedom was intended to promote an "Africanism" which he defined as the combination of "the best from the past, present and future: the Africanism which seeks to fulfill what our people want to be, to do and to have."[46] On October 20th that year, celebrated as the Kenyatta Day, he declared that "our struggle for *Uhuru* (had) ended."

Thus, in less than eleven months after the first *Uhuru* Day was celebrated, the man who had been imprisoned, reviled, banished into compulsory confinement for two years at Lodwar, appeared to have forgotten that true freedom involved a life-long struggle against man's inhumanity to man.

There is nothing in the speeches and actions of Kenyatta which showed a deeper level of understanding and appreciation for the principles which he had articulated before he became Kenya's Prime Minister and president. Although he once said that *uhuru* was "for all people of Kenya to enjoy and breathe the air of freedom, after so many years under the yoke of imperialism and colonialism,"[47] by January 25, 1964, the *Mzee* was already very worried about his state security.

For one thing, some of his soldiers had mutinied on this day. In his lifetime, Kenyans were made to celebrate "Kenyatta Day," an honor best reserved for the great ones who had passed away. This was a sign of the cult of personal rule and of worse things to come. Some of Kenyatta's former associates dissented with him and with the direction that the new country was heading. One such dissenter was his Vice-President, Oginga Odinga.

Instead of a steady march toward *uhuru*, Kenyatta practiced the politics of "retribalization,"[48] repression of political opponents, and of personal rule. In March of 1966, Odinga, with some other radicals, broke ranks with KANU and with Kenyatta. They formed their own political party, the Kenya Peoples' Union (KPU).

Kenyatta did everything possible to destroy this rival organization. Some prominent Kenyans were harassed, detained or banished. After Tom Mboya was murdered, Kenyatta cleverly banned the KPU and had Odinga detained indefinitely. Some Kenyans were no longer to enjoy *Uhuru* under the Kenyatta rule.

Even artists like James Ngugi (Ngugi wa Thiong'o), the famous author of *Weep Not Child* (1966), who protested against Kenyatta's dictatorship, were detained and not released until Kenyatta's death in 1978. Therefore, Odinga was right when he wrote that life in Kenya under Kenyatta was "not yet *uhuru*."[49]

Many other political opponents, like Ronald Ngala, the former president of the Kenya African Democratic Union (KADU), were either murdered or their deaths were attributed to alleged "car accidents," which reminds one of how many Ugandans under Idi Amin perished in similar so-called car accidents!

In the end, the man who had written that "in the eyes of the Gikuyu people, the submission to a despotic rule of any particular man or a group, white or black, is the greatest humiliation to mankind,"[50] himself became the despot who demanded political submission! Thus, in the eyes of the civilized world, Africans were humiliated and betrayed by one of their own leaders.

So, Jomo Kenyatta, Kenya's "Burning Spear," left no thorough elucidation or shining example on the burning subject of the African conception of true freedom. Unfortunately, he followed in the footsteps of his West African colleague, Kwame Nkrumah who also loved to be worshipped and called himself the *osagyefo*, Ghana's savior or messiah.

CHAPTER SEVEN

AFRICAN FREEDOM: JULIUS NYERERE AND UJAMAA

Africa is our own and only inheritance.... It is our main duty to recover its control from those who have grabbed it from us.

— Julius K. Nyerere

To the south of Kenya lies the country of Tanzania which was formerly known as Tanganyika. It was colonized by the Germans from 1884 to 1918. After World War I, the British took over the territory under the mandate guarantees of Article 22 of the League of Nations. The capital city of the country is Dar Es Salaam, meaning the City of Peace.

Tanzania is the home of Africa's highest mountain, the Kilimanjaro. According to anthropologist Dr. Louis S. Leakey, the Olduvai Gorge in Tanzania is probably the aboriginal home of all mankind. In the early years of the twentieth century, Dar Es Salaam and the Tanzanians had no peace.

The Germans, led by a man named Carl Peters, had arrived at Sadani in 1884 and aborted the peace there. In order to regain and restore their peace, the people of Tanganyika took to arms in what is now known as the Maji Maji Resistance of 1905 to 1907. The Germans ruthlessly crushed this resistance against foreign rule.

Author Judith Listowel, in her book, *The Making of Tanganyika* (1965), writes that "the price of Maji Maji was appalling. ...One hundred and twenty thousand men, women and children died either fighting, by execution or from famine."[1] She added that "the German military commanders had crops burnt and food confiscated so that the resisters could not be helped. Of course the main sufferers were the ordinary people, who died of starvation by the thousand."[2]

Julius Kambarage Nyerere, the future president of Tanzania, was born in March 1922 into this turbulent political history. He began his education at the age of twelve when he was sent from Butiama, where his family lived, to attend an elementary school at the Musoma Native Authority School. This school was twenty-six miles away from his father's home.

For secondary education, Nyerere went to a public school at Tabora from 1937 to 1943. On December 23, 1943, he was baptized at the age of 21 by Father Mathias Koenen. Thereafter, Nyerere remained a devout follower of Roman Catholicism.[3] Thus, his earliest intellectual and spiritual influences were of the Christian faith and scholarship.

After Tabora, Nyerere studied further at Makerere College (now known as Makerere University) in Uganda. He was there for the two-year diploma program in education. Upon graduation, he returned to teach biology and history at Tabora's St. Mary's School. But Nyerere was known for striving to improve himself. His life's dream was to be an excellent teacher.

Writings about him reveal that as early as 1946, he had wished to have an opportunity to study for a higher degree.

That opportunity came to him in April 1949 when he arrived in Scotland to study at Edinburgh University. He was there for three years and earned a Master's degree in education. He returned to his country in 1952 to continue with his teaching career. That same year, Nyerere also joined the Tanganyika African Association (TAA), a social organization formed by civil servants in 1929 for the Africans.

One year after joining the TAA, Nyerere was elected its president. It was from 1952 onward that the TAA was reorganized. It formulated a political platform and changed its name to the Tanganyika African National Union (TANU), with Nyerere still serving as its leader. TANU was formally launched on July 7, 1954. It was the first nationalist movement in the country.

Compared to the other nationalists like Nkrumah, Mboya and Kenyatta, Nyerere was a moderate. "He had seen freedom and democracy in Britain. He saw neither in Tanganyika."[4] But, he believed that "no colonial power, however benevolent, ha[d] the slightest right to impose its rule on another people against their will."[5] As he expressed this view publicly, Tanganyikans responded with the cry for "*Uhuru! Uhuru!*"

Nyerere had formulated his political and racial philosophy while in Britain. From parts of his Master's thesis titled, "The Race Problem In East Africa," one finds that he firmly believed in the right of the African to be the master of his own fate and destiny. He wrote:

> What we claim is the right to be masters of our own fate ... We resent the idea that the power to shape the destiny of our country should be exclusively vested in the hands of an alien and minority group which is sworn to use such power to maintain its own privileged position and to keep us for ever in a state of inferiority in our own country.

Nyerere added: "Africa is our own and only inheritance. ... It is our main duty to recover its control from those who have grabbed it from us."[6]

His future political platform and philosophy were rooted in the mindset expressed in the statement quoted hereunder:

> Africa is for the Africans, and the other races cannot be more than respected minorities.... Should it come to a bitter choice between being perpetually dominated by a white or an Indian minority and between driving that minority out of East Africa, no thinking African would hesitate to make the latter choice.[7]

In plain language, Nyerere believed that the African would fight for his or her freedom instead of remaining in perpetual slavery or servitude. So, bluntly, he stated that,

> For a small white minority to come to our country and to tell us that they are the people of the country and that we are not, is one of those many insults which I think we have swallowed for too long. The sooner we tell the Europeans that we will no longer tolerate such monstrous impudence the better for us all. ... The Africans' capacity for bearing insult is not limitless. The day may come when someone may want to incite them. How easy it is to inflame an insulted people! I shudder when I think of the terrible possibility, but it will not be a mere possibility if our White Neighbours insist on this vulgar doctrine of the Divine Right of Europeans and refuse to live like 'ordinary sort of fellows.' Such a doctrine may have to be uprooted with all the vulgarity of a bloody revolution. I say this in

perfect honesty. ... A day may come when the people will prefer death to insult and woe to the people who will see that day! Woe to them who will make that day inevitable![8]

Nyerere was about thirty years old when he made the above-quoted statements which were warnings that colonialism had to end. The British colonialists should have taken notice that a young African freedom advocate was in the making. Nyerere was a great organizer, with an affable personality, and some oratorical talent.

However, he was not a Macbeth. His heart's desire was still to become an accomplished teacher. But fate and destiny had other plans for the man whom Tanzanians would come to revere as their *Nwalimu* (teacher). So, on May 12, 1954, Nyerere was nominated by the colonial governor into the Legislative Council. It turned out to be only a temporary appointment.

In his first speech in the Council, Nyerere expressed his concerns regarding the material well-being of his people in terms of water supply and education. He sharply criticized the budgetary cuts by the governor while taxes were being raised. Consequently, Nyerere did not retain his nomination.

In March of 1955, Nyerere traveled against all odds to New York in order to speak on behalf of his people before the United Nations Trusteeship Council. There, he declared that the aim of TANU was "to prepare the people of Tanganyika for self-government and independence."[9]

Nyerere suggested, to the surprise of the Council, that independence should be granted within a 20-25 year period. Also, he persuasively argued that "although Tanganyika [was] multi-racial in population, its future government shall be primarily African." He asserted: "I have to emphasize the fact that we regard Tanganyika as being primarily African."[10]

In December of the following year, Nyerere appeared again before the UN Fourth Committee in New York to remind the world of his people's efforts to free themselves from colonial rule. He admitted that "the struggle against the Germans ha[d] proved to our people the futility of trying to drive out their masters by force."[11]

Therefore, Nyerere adopted the tactics of moderation, gradualism, nonviolence, multiracial accommodation, and political realism in approaching the British and the UN body. He pressed for a definite date for the granting of independence. This time, he suggested that Tanganyika "should be independent in about ten years' time."[12]

In June of 1957, for the third time, Nyerere went to the UN Trusteeship Council to report on the political developments in his country. He stated that TANU was opposed to "the idea of a restricted franchise even if we had not a single European in the country or a single Asian ... because it was discriminating against the vast majority of our people."[13]

When he returned home to Tanzania from this trip, Nyerere was banned from public speaking by the colonial authorities for some months, the ban being effective from December 14, 1957. However, the colonial governor re-nominated him into the Legislative Council. But in less than six months, Nyerere resigned, giving several reasons for his resignation.

One such reason was his complaint that he was personally opposed to the official policy of nominating Africans to the Council. He preferred them to be elected. He also complained about the lack of constitutional reforms. He said that his membership in the Council was "useless" since the government kept on rejecting his proposals.

Shortly afterward, Nyerere criticized two government officers in a published article and he was arrested, tried, and convicted for "criminal libel" in May 1958. At that point, Nyerere declared: "Colonialism is an intolerable humiliation to us. We shall wage a relentlessly determined battle against it until we are free. We shall use nonviolence. We shall stoop to no dishonest methods. ...We shall not submit to humiliation."[14]

He was ready to go into prison for his belief in press freedom. But the new governor, Richard Turnbull, advised Nyerere to pay the fine imposed instead. TANU called out a total boycott of all European drinks the next month. This was almost one hundred percent effective. Later, in the first general election ever held in Tanganyika in 1958, TANU won and Nyerere became the Leader of the Opposition in the Legislative Council.

The 1958 election was continued into the following year. In March 1959, Nyerere stated as follows:

> The right to govern ourselves being ours, ours by right, we are in this Africa which is becoming rapidly free. What are we, the people of Tanganyika, asking the British to do? We have stated it, stated it categorically. The right to govern ourselves is our right. We are in an Africa which is becoming rapidly free. What have we asked the British people to do in our case? We have not asked them for independence. No, Sir, we have not asked them for independence, which is our right. We have not even asked them for full responsible government. No, Sir, we have not. We have asked them for semi-responsible government, for a measure of responsibility which in concrete terms

would give to this House a majority of Elected Members and give to the executive a majority of Elected Ministers.[15]

Clearly, here Nyerere was applying his diplomatic skills to secure a democratic political change and victory, one that would be bloodless and peaceful. He believed that a democratic, constitutional process would turn the scales in the favor of his people. The essential elements for such a democratic process were open discussions of matters, equality, and freedom.[16]

Concerning such freedom, Nyerere had, in a 1958 publication, stated that,

> Man is nobody's property. He owns himself and cannot be someone else's possession. If, therefore, man possesses himself, it is clear that his health, his intellect, and his ability cannot be someone else's property. So, whenever he uses his intellect, his health and his ability to make anything, that thing becomes his property ... Land is a free gift from God to all His living things to be used now and in the future.[17]

During a PAFMECA Conference held in September 1959, Nyerere stressed the importance of human, not racial, rights. He did not believe that Africans who were clamoring for freedom and dignity would turn around to violate such rights against their own people. Although he admitted that he knew that man was depraved, however, he did not think that any African would sink so low to these levels of barbarism. In this respect, Nyerere was somewhat naïve.[18]

On October 22, 1959, in a speech he delivered titled, "A Candle On Kilimanjaro," Nyerere emphasized hope, love, light, and dignity as principles for human brotherhood. At another time, he publicly complained: "My friends talk as if it is perfectly all right to discriminate against Europeans, Arabs, and Indians, and only wrong when you discriminate against black men. The crime in the world today is the oppression of man by man."[19]

That year, his deputy in Parliament was a white politician by the name of Derek Bryceson and his membership signaled Nyerere's openness for a pluralistic society. He had preached racial tolerance and demonstrated this by the politics of racial inclusion. The new Tanzania would not be torn apart by racially-motivated conflicts.

In August 1960, TANU won seventy out of the seventy-one seats in Parliament. This time, Nyerere was asked to form a new government. His official title was that of Chief Minister. On May 1, 1961, he became the Prime Minister of Tanganyika. The country was granted independence on December 9, that same year.

On June 1, 1961, Nyerere had said in Parliament:

> We do care, passionately, about the development of justice, of well being, and peace throughout the world. We do care about the rights of man, about the independence and self-determination of nations or groups of nations. We do care about having peace both in Africa and in other parts of the world. On these great issues we cannot be neutral. But although our policy will not be one of passive neutrality, it will be independent.[20]

In Nyerere's view, national independence was "the attainment of *Uhuru*." On that day's speech made before a crowd of 75,000 at the new National Stadium, Nyerere said:

> All the time that TANU has been campaigning for *Uhuru* we have based our struggle on our belief in the equality and dignity of all mankind and on the Declaration of Human Rights. We have agreed that our nation shall be a nation of free and equal citizens, each person having an equal right and opportunity to develop himself, and contribute to the maximum of his capabilities to the development of our society. We have said that neither race nor tribe nor religion nor cleverness, nor anything else, could take away from a man his own rights as an equal member of society. This is what we have now to put into practice.[21]

The road into the future, he proclaimed, lay along the path of *uhuru na kazi.*

In yet another article which he wrote for a "Whites Only" school magazine in Natal, South Africa, Nyerere had "stated quite categorically that no part of Africa will ever become a duplicate copy of any part of Europe. An African in Africa will never become simply a black European."[22] That was written in June.

But now that independence had come at last, Nyerere flew to New York on December 14, 1961, to address the UN General Assembly. At the UN, he expressed Tanganyika's commitment "to honour the dignity of man," and added: "We believe, in fact, that the individual man and woman is the purpose of society."[23] Also, he said that he was opposed to colonialism anywhere in Africa and in the world.

Barely six weeks after independence, Nyerere resigned his prime ministership. He had made plans for this action long before that day. The reason for his action was to give Tanganyikans new confidence in themselves, to demonstrate to them that nobody was indispensable, and to act as a bridge between the people and the new government. Nyerere chose as his successor Rashidi M. Kawawa, a colleague who was equally dedicated to the service of his people. Nyerere chose not to be a member of the government. Rather, he wanted to serve as a member of Parliament and the leader of TANU. One year after independence, on December 9, 1962, he was solidly elected the new president of the country, with ninety-seven percent of the votes cast.[24] He served in this capacity until 1985 when he voluntarily relinquished power, only the third leader in all of Africa ever to do so.

As one can readily see, Nyerere's conception of freedom was reflected in his pronouncements, writings, and actions, in and out of government. Like the other nationalists of his day, Nyerere was deeply concerned about freedom from colonial rule. But he was far beyond many of his contemporaries in his concern for the elevation of the standard of life for the ordinary African.

Better than Kenyatta (who had no social philosophy) or Nkrumah (who experimented with a foreign brand of socialism), Nyerere understood the necessity of incorporating notions of personal and human freedoms into a social framework that would enhance national development. Nyerere termed this framework and philosophy *ujamaa*.

Nyerere seemed to have believed that the ideal of personal freedom was meaningless unless this freedom was translated into tangible material well-being for his people. Personal freedom was vital as a creative dynamic that propelled the twin engines of political stability and social progress. Tyranny would be counter-productive.

There is no doubt in my mind that Nyerere and TANU understood the importance of human freedom. In a paper which TANU officials distributed publicly on October 16, 1968, the question was raised: "For what do we mean when we talk of freedom?" Here was the answer:

> First, there is national freedom, that is, the ability of Tanzania[ns] to determine their own future, and to govern themselves without interference from non-Tanzanians. Second, there is freedom from hunger, disease, and poverty. And third, there is personal freedom for the individuals; that is, his right to live in dignity and equality with all others, his right to freedom of speech, freedom to participate in the making of all decisions which affect his life, and freedom from arbitrary arrest because he happens to annoy someone in authority – and so on. All these things are aspects of freedom, and the citizens of Tanzania cannot be said to be truly free until all of them are assured. Yet it is obvious that these things depend on economic and social development.[25]

Thus, given the circumstances into which Nyerere found himself, he was not so enthralled to possess the abstract forms of political freedom without its concrete social and economic benefits. This is why he always spoke of freedom with responsibility and of a government that was responsible to the people. Therefore, *uhuru na kazi* became the creed for his social engagement.

Nyerere chose a middle road between the harsh brand of Western capitalism, with its super-haves and have-nots, and the extreme brand of atheistic Eastern socialism (as was practiced in China, a country he had visited). He found this middle road in African familyhood and communal cooperation which he called *ujamaa*.

This *ujamaa* was his social philosophy, one in which the "leaders must not be masters" of the people and one in which "freedom must be maintained." This *ujamaa* was to be one with a "commitment to Tanzanian freedom and to the freedom and human equality of all citizens."²⁶ Here, all men were to be truly equal and the politicians upheld the supremacy of the people of Tanzania.²⁷

Some writers have said that the "ujamaa socialism is an attitude of mind needed to ensure that the people care for each other's welfare."²⁸ It is neither Marxist nor Leninist. It allows for the exercise of the freedom of expression which is a necessary ingredient in a democracy. It also allows freedom of worship, with no state-sanctioned religion.

Nyerere took a strong stand against any kind of state infringement of the rights of individuals. The Arusha Declaration of February 5, 1967, was intended to emphasize rural development along with a stand for freedom and human rights. A year before Arusha, Nyerere had complained that "Africa is in a mess."²⁹

But how was Nyerere going to succeed in promoting *ujamaa* and *uhuru*? By the sheer force of his example and character. And, "what manner of man [was] Nyerere?" This is the question which William R. Duggan and John R. Civille, co-authors of the book, *Tanzania and Nyerere: A Study of Ujamaa and Nationhood*, had asked in 1976. Here is their answer:

> Nyerere has a personality which can best be described as incandescent.... He lacks most of the vanities and conceits of the world's great. He is able to laugh at his own mistakes. He is never arrogant.³⁰

Another writer observed that,

> Nyerere was unique in Africa for his humble life-style; he shunned the fancy cars, elaborate villas, and foreign bank accounts so common among his counterparts. He practiced what he preached ... he urged those who enjoyed freedom to make a commitment to those who did not.[31]

"One of his most famous sermons," writes another admirer of Nyerere, "was a blistering letter to his colleagues asking their help in 'stamping out the disease of pomposity.'"[32] He did not like to live at the State House. He despised dictators like Idi Amin and actually sent in his troops in 1979 to rout the Ugandan tyrant out of office. Nyerere rejected the idea of being named president for life.

He was widely judged to be one of the best among the post-colonial leaders of Africa. Some other scholars have stated that,

> Nyerere offers the student of African rulers and regimes an example of a leader whose personal ideals will have made a significant difference not only to personal relations of power in the state, but also to social relations in the wider society ... Nyerere has been sub-Saharan Africa's most acclaimed political Prophet and perhaps the best example of the moral agent in political history.[33]

Nyerere's conception of power as it related to freedom was that power should be used "not for domination but for political construction and societal transformation ... His socialism reveal[ed] a blend of Christian ethics, particularly evident in his belief in the doctrine of 'needs' and in good works."[34] He lived simply, eschewed ostentation, and was in close and constant touch with his people. Nyerere was not sinless, however, so he had many critics.

One such critic is George Ayittey who faults Nyerere for mistaking "the peasant's emphasis on kinship and community as readiness for socialism – *Ujamaa*." Ayittey adds that "Nyerere ... focused on *intra-group* loyalty and cooperation and ignored *inter-group* rivalries." Then he charges that "Nyerere for 24 years stuck bullheadedly to a 'socialist' path even when things were going so obviously wrong."[35]

I may point out, though, that this blame is about the failures in the economic area, not about human freedom. Also, author and award-winning journalist Sanford J. Ungar, is even much more direct. He blamed Nyerere for the failure of the *ujamaa* villages and their relocation schemes. According to him, the entire exercise "proved to be undemocratic in practice, with a narrow elite controlling most of the decisions and resources."[36]

Ungar pointed to the widespread corruption in official quarters within the Nyerere administration. He stated that "Nyerere rejected the notion that he held any political prisoners, but his jails were full of people accused of 'economic crimes.'"[37] Many of the accused persons were often not entitled to due process.

I cannot totally exonerate Nyerere for the apparent contradiction whereby he insisted upon the preservation of the freedoms of Tanzanians, on the one hand, and, on the other hand, he ran a one-party political system where the opposition was not tolerated. In economics, the system was state-controlled. These two systems hardly work out harmoniously together. Nyerere succeeded in having Swahili as a national language.

When Nyerere died in London of leukemia in 1999, at the age of 77, the world lost a *Nwalimu* who had stridently urged his people to pull together peacefully, without having to slaughter each other. In the words of the American Secretary of State, Madeline K. Albright, who delivered a befitting eulogy on October 21, 1999, the world is immensely indebted to "President Nyerere who in our lifetime showed us how to be champions of peace and forces of liberty."[38]

We can safely state that Nyerere's conception of freedom was buttressed in his ideas of African socialism, unity, and development. Nyerere left no systematic synthesis. Nevertheless, he endeavored to show us the way to live in peace and in freedom.

CHAPTER EIGHT

AFRICAN FREEDOM:
THE HUMANIST KAUNDA

*Freedom is our birthright and we simply are determined
to achieve it.*

— Kenneth Kaunda

Further southwest of Tanzania lies the country of Zambia,
formerly known as northern Rhodesia. According to
historian Andrew Roberts, the British had colonized
this African territory since 1860. The first of the Europeans
to set foot into this part of Africa was David Livingston.
Later, Cecil Rhodes from South Africa expanded his
influence into the area in search of the rich copper minerals
of the territory.

Like Tanzania, Zambia is a multi-racial society. Between
1889 to 1914, a white minority administered the territory
through the British South Africa Company. Direct colonial
administration began in 1924 by the Indirect Rule system.[1]
Kenneth David Kaunda, author, musician, first Prime
Minister and later, president of the independent Republic of

Zambia, was born on April 28, 1924, at Lubwa, a village within the Chinsali province.

His father, David, who died when young Kenneth was only eight years old, was an ordained Church of Scotland missionary and teacher. He became the headmaster of the mission school at Lubwa. Kenneth's mother, Helen, had eight children, "three of whom died young."[2] The family was very poor.

Kenneth recalls that during his childhood "there was no free universal education at the time and every parent had to find half a crown a year"[3] to pay for their children's school fees. Neither poor Kenneth nor his mother had the money for his school fees. A kind neighbor came to their aid with a loan which had to be repaid. Thus, Kenneth was able to attend the local mission school.

During the holidays, he worked to earn his school fess. From this experience, he learned the value of hard work quite early in his life. He assisted his mother in doing the family chores. He also learned "the great value of self-help."[4] Later on, he would establish some self-help clubs for his people.

Though poor, Kenneth's family was a happy one. At nine, he had learned how to play music from one of his brothers. His father had taught him how to sing and pray. When he became a salaried teacher, Kenneth bought himself a guitar. With the guitar, he formed a singing and dancing group that helped out in the church choir and toured the province.

After elementary school, Kenneth attended the Lubwa Normal Training Course for two years. In 1941, he studied at the secondary school at Munali near Lusaka. The journey to this school took him about eight days by lorry. His subjects included Mathematics, South African history, and English Literature. He was about seventeen years old at the time.

At Munali, Kenneth came under the influence of Daniel Sonquishe, a teacher who had come from South Africa. He indoctrinated young Kenneth about the evils of the apartheid system. He urged Kenneth to follow a life that would change apartheid. With further encouragement from Sonquishe, Kenneth Kaunda perfected his dancing troupe, singing and playing his guitar during concert tours of the Copperbelt.

At the end of his second year at Munali, Kenneth Kaunda was recalled home and was appointed a boarding master at the Lubwa school. He taught there for four years. It was at this time that he met the woman who was later to be his wife. Her name was Betty, a hard working woman. She was a nursing aid as well as a teacher. She had been trained in cookery, dressmaking, and in other domestic science subjects.

Betty was introduced to Kenneth by his mother. In 1946, she married him. She gave birth to "six strong sons and at last a baby daughter, Musata, the joy of (their) hearts."[5] Betty became a strong supporter of Kaunda's political life. They have been married now for fifty-five years.

Like Nyerere, Kaunda was both a teacher and a Christian. Kaunda was greatly influenced by the gospel which his father had preached. Regarding this gospel, he would later write as follows:

> I was brought up in a Christian home and my Christian belief is part of me now. It is still my habit to turn to God in prayer asking for His guidance. I do not think I have ever seriously doubted the truth of the Gospel, but I seriously question sometimes whether God is really speaking to us in the voice of the organized churches as I see them in Northern Rhodesia.... I knew that the Christian religion had something important to say to us in our political

movement. We were always looking for Christians
to support us in our struggle.[6]

Kenneth Kaunda was also influenced by the biography of
Abraham Lincoln as well as by some other books which he
read. Two of his favorite books were *In Tune With the Infinite*
by Ralph Waldo Trine and *Talks To Boys* by Arthur Mee.
Equally important were the influences of his own family and
the Indian struggle for independence led by Mahatma Gandhi.

Kenneth Kaunda's ideas about freedom were derived,
first and foremost, from his home life and also from the
socio-political environment around him. His father had
been one of the founders of the Mwenzo Welfare Association
whose aim was "to bring African views to the attention of
the government."[7]

In 1937, the Northern Rhodesia African National Congress
(ANC) had been formed by a group of African teachers "to
protest against land alienation and discrimination against
African food production for the market."[8] The political
environment was downright racist and oppressive. It was not,
therefore, an accident that Kaunda joined the Chinsali African
Welfare Association, five miles away from Lubwa where
he taught.

Like the ANC, the members of the Association were local
teachers and clerks. This Association represented the interests
of the local community. Members made their complaints and
resolutions to the colonial District Commissioner (D.C.) or to
the missionaries. Kaunda was keenly interested in the
community's social issues.

Also, this Association reflected the elite interests of the
African society. In Kaunda's view, members of this Association
were "the mouthpieces of the inarticulate masses [that
expressed] their own feelings of frustration in a society

dominated by white settlers. ..."[9] The emergence of the Associations were foundational to the eventual establishment of Kaunda's own political party – the United National Independence Party (UNIP).

Kaunda once tried to escape from the dreary life at Lubwa. He traveled to Tanzania and Zimbabwe (known formerly as Southern Rhodesia) in a vain search for a better job. He had been invited to Tanzania by his teacher colleagues and Lubwa friends, Simon Kapwepwe and John Sokoni. These two were already in Tanzania, but Kaunda found no job there. He referred to this time as his "wandering days."

Back from "his wandering days," Kaunda had a temporary job at a mine in Nchanga. He was employed as a Welfare Assistant. But, soon, he was teaching again at Mufulira. He was once more a boarding master. His wife, Betty, also taught there. The family also engaged in petty trading for profit. Kaunda also continued to establish some self-help clubs and served as choir master at his church.

Life at Mufulira was not very different from that at Lubwa, his hometown. The shops were segregated and discriminated against the African population. Racial slurs were openly used against the Africans. Kaunda decided to do something about those "insult(s) to my race and my people."[10]

The white overlords called the Africans "black-skinned niggers." To these whites, Africans were simply "boys" no matter their age and education. Kaunda desired that his "people should be treated with reasonable courtesy."[11] Nothing changed in that direction. In 1948, Kaunda and his friends – Kapwepwe and Sokoni – decided to leave Mufulira.

But, before they did, the trio purchased bicycles to enable them to move about and attend meetings freely. Also, they bought watches in order that they might be on time at such meetings. They also bought sewing machines to mend used clothes meant for resale. However, Kapwepwe did not return with the team to Lubwa.

At Lubwa, Kaunda and Sokoni settled down to the task of founding and building the Chinsali Youngmen's Farming Association. In 1949, a year later, Kaunda opened a local branch of the ANC and served as its Secretary. That year, he was elected to the provincial council. The work of running the ANC presented "a tremendous challenge"[12] in that Kaunda had to travel a great deal on bicycle throughout the area.

Sometimes, he would bicycle for over 300 miles across the bridge over the Luapula River into the former Belgian Congo. This area had many man-eating lions. Indeed, during one of his travels, Kaunda came face to face with a lion standing right in front of him! Besides this danger, he also faced the risk of political imprisonment at the hands of the colonial authorities. It was risky to be a member of the ANC and be politically active.

The colonial authorities deemed any kind of political activity dangerous to and undermining of their interests. But the Africans saw things differently. Thus, Kaunda and his friends persisted and persevered in their efforts to organize and mobilize their people. They looked forward to the day when freedom from colonial rule would come.

Kaunda once asked: "What was the message that the Chinsali people were receiving at this time?" His reply was:

> We had to make our people conscious that they were human beings just as good or bad as any other... I was aware that most of our people who had gone to fight in defence of the British Empire had suffered for nothing; we were only employed as hewers of wood and drawers of water, and we could not eat from the same tables nor share the same beds in hotels.[13]

This statement clearly indicates Kaunda's anti-colonial stance. The local travels and meetings were part of this anti-colonialism. They constituted Kaunda's moral crusade against the injustices of a racist, colonial system. They were part of his search for freedom from foreign rule and the march toward national independence.

In 1951, the national president of the ANC was Harry Nkumbula. Kenneth Kaunda had first met him in 1944. In 1952, Kaunda met him again at an ANC meeting and the two men worked together as Kaunda became a member of the Supreme Action Council of the ANC. This Council was a sort of "War Cabinet" responsible for fighting against the Federation of northern Rhodesia with Southern Rhodesia and the rest of the region.

Africans in northern Rhodesia wanted "full adult franchise with no reserved seats or other special safeguards for minority groups."[14] These minority groups were, of course, the white settlers. By a memorandum which the Supreme Action Council sent to the British government, the Africans "strongly object(ed) to the necessity of becoming British subjects before they can become full citizens of their own country."[15]

The Africans regarded this policy to be "ridiculous." But the pleas of the Africans fell upon deaf ears. Also, the ANC opposed the demand for apartheid by the white European settlers. When a white member of the ANC was deported to London, Kaunda became very angry and sent "a terribly angry" letter to the missionaries at Lubwa.

At a Lusaka meeting of Chiefs and the people, Kaunda was appointed Organizing Secretary for the northern province of Zambia. His successes in political activism quickly moved him up the ranks within the ANC. In August of 1953, he was elected Secretary-General and moved to Lusaka, the capital of Zambia.

Early in April, Kaunda had sent a petition signed by 120 chiefs to the British Queen. This petition was a protest against Federation which was a move to unite three territories: northern and southern Rhodesia and Nyasaland. This move would have hindered Zambia's stride toward independence.

On October 13th, Kaunda issued a press release in which he stated, among other things, that,

> In Central Africa a major constitutional change has been imposed against the expressed wish of some six million Africans in favour of a handful of reactionary white settlers. This imposition has only been possible because the imperialists count on the strength of the British troops which they are ruthlessly using in crushing down the national aspirations of the colonial peoples. Nay, they have not solved the problem. They have only managed to shelve the inevitable racial strife in Central Africa. Serious trouble lies ahead.[16]

In this way, Kaunda revealed that Federation had been imposed upon the Zambians. As an ANC organizer, he "regarded himself honestly as a worker in the cause of freedom" and the ANC was simply "a means through which the frustrations of the people could express themselves."[17] However, the colonial masters saw Kaunda and his ANC differently.

It did not matter to those white masters that Africans had no representation in Parliament because "the mass of Africans were not voters." It did not matter to the colonialists "that Africans are people, not cattle to be herded together and driven here and there."[18] When in 1954 Kaunda and Nkumbula traveled to Southern Rhodesia to attend an important meeting, they were deported right at an airport, even though they were residents within the so-called Federation.

Even the ownership of a newspaper by the ANC was considered subversive and illegal by the authorities. So also was the mere possession of certain magazines. It did not matter that such magazines were printed and imported from Britain into Zambia. In fact, on January 6, 1955, Kaunda and Nkumbula were sentenced to two months' imprisonment, with hard labor, for this "crime"[19] of just possessing certain magazines.

Many other ANC officials in the provinces were similarly jailed. The University at Lusaka was segregated. There were no secondary schools that the African women could attend. A more militant response was the outcome and answer to these outrages. Thus, in 1956, the ANC resorted to mass sit-ins and boycotts of the white-owned businesses.

In May of that year, in the city of Mufulira, the ANC used legal action to redress some of the injustices over the pricing of commercial goods. They won. The goal of this litigation was to expose the unfair and unjust practices of the colonial government. But the primary objective was to pave the way toward freedom from colonial rule.

In 1957, Kaunda again vehemently protested against the racial mistreatment of the people at Kitwe. Here, the restaurants were segregated. Kaunda and Nkumbula would not be served a meal when they entered into one of the restaurants and asked to be served and were called "boys." Kaunda was then 33 years old!

When they persisted in their demand, a white police officer arrested Nkumbula, took him into a room, closed the door, and beat him up. Incidents such as this were rampant. Even in 1962, when Zambia was close to its independence, cases of police brutalities and racial malpractices were occurring in spite of laws against them. For instance, the Post Office at Lusaka was still segregated.[20]

Kaunda visited Britain for the first time in 1957. He went there at the invitation of the British Labor Party. On May 26, Kaunda and Nkumbula left Zambia to go to Britain in order to participate in a conference of delegates from twenty-six countries. In Britain, Kaunda spoke to some parliamentarians and won some sympathy for the situation in his home country. In his spare time, Kaunda also studied the British political party organization.

When he returned to Zambia, he recommended to the ANC that an African representative be permanently kept in Britain to counter the false colonial propaganda. Kaunda spent six months in Britain. While there, he received a scholarship grant to study at New Delhi University in India. But he was ordered back home by Nkumbula, his ANC boss, who had abruptly left Britain.

It is important to state here that Kaunda's method of resistance to colonial domination and search for freedom from that domination was by non-violence. In a letter which he sent to James Johnson, a British Labor Party member, and dated July 30, 1957, Kaunda said:

> I would be the last person to advocate violence because apart from the fact that it does not pay, we have only our people to get killed. What is the point in having the people one struggles for killed? Who is going to profit by those rights once they are achieved with half the population gone? ... We have no intention of running MAU MAU in our country but there are those dangers. I have pointed out those facts which I think it important for the British government to know.[21]

In another official ANC circular dated January 31, 1958, Kaunda stressed the use of "the powerful weapon" of non-violence as it had worked in India, pointing out that the Africans of Zambia would suffer most if violent resistance were resorted to. He insisted upon a new constitution based upon the principle of "one man, one vote." The colonial authorities spurned this proposal and imposed their own brand of constitution upon the Africans.

Between February and May of 1958, there were strains within the ANC because of the deepening frustrations of the African people as a result of colonial oppression. In May, Kaunda responded to an invitation from the Indian Council for Cultural Relations and traveled to India.

When Kaunda returned, he broke ranks with Nkumbula over the question of some constitutional proposals. There were also some squabbles regarding internal ANC policy implementation and style of leadership. Kaunda was unhappy with the manner that Nkumbula had abandoned his duties and abruptly left him in London in 1957.

Consequently, on October 24, 1958, the Zambian African National Congress (ZANC) was born, with Kaunda as its president. Membership included his long-time friend, Kapwepwe. Not long afterwards, the ZANC was banned by the colonial authorities. In the fall of that year, Kaunda made another trip abroad.

After ZANC was banned, Kaunda went to Ghana, to attend a conference at Accra which was chaired by Tom Mboya of Kenya. Kaunda used this opportunity to visit the Republic of Togo. He was in Togo for three days to see things for himself. He also attended a ten day "New Year School" of the Department of Extra-Mural Studies at the University College of Ghana.

In March 1959, in response to the false propaganda of the colonial authorities, Kaunda publicly wrote as follows:

I wish to state here categorically that we shall untiringly attack systems that for reasons of race alone deny about three million Africans the full enjoyment of democratic rights in this country. But I shall pray that no bitterness shall come into the picture and that we freedom fighters shall be for ever colour-blind. We make no apologies for being in the forefront in the struggle for national independence and self-determination. FREEDOM IS OUR BIRTHRIGHT and we simply are determined to achieve it.[22]

The colonial authorities were unimpressed. They were not only angry that Kaunda had gone to Ghana where he had consulted with "communist" Nkrumah. But they were also alarmed by Kaunda's growing boldness and popularity. On March 11 of that year, at 1:00 a.m., the colonial police broke into his home and he was arrested in his bedroom in the presence of his wife and children. He was handcuffed and marched off to prison.

The charge against Kaunda was that he had held an unauthorized ZANC meeting, even though the colonial government had been informed that such a meeting would be held. Other ZANC officials were also picked up, including Kapwepwe. They were all kept in detention, without trial, at Kabompo Boma. Furthermore, Kaunda was banned from addressing any public meetings for a period of three months.[23] He was 35 at the time.

Kaunda was re-arrested after a State of Emergency was imposed. There were rumors of a plot by ZANC to kill off all the Europeans. The UNIP was born at this time. Kaunda was sentenced to nine months and another three months prison terms, a total of twelve months but running concurrently.

Kaunda's crime was that he was becoming more and more of a threat to the colonial authorities. His popularity undermined their interests. To humiliate him, the authorities assigned him the prison duties which included cooking, cleaning of dishes and cleaning of the "primitive bucket lavatory" thoroughly. Again, he was banned from speaking to any fellow African prisoner.

In July, he was transferred from the Lusaka Central Prison to the Central Prison at Salisbury in Southern Rhodesia. All through this journey, he was handcuffed like a criminal. An officer of the colonial government jokingly told him that his crime was that of conspiracy "to blow up the British Empire." At Salisbury prison, Kaunda's duty was book-binding.

There were indignities here such as stripping the Africans naked and ordering them to jump on one leg. Kaunda was spared from this additional humiliation. But he was often locked up for fifteen hours in a stinking cell. Political prisoners were mixed with incorrigible criminals. According to his autobiography, there were cases of prison rapes, especially of the younger boys.

Kaunda noted that freedom fighters were at war with their political masters.[24] On December 18, 1959, he was returned to his Lusaka cell. He had served a little more than nine months and had been "shut off from all natural beauty" for five full months. On January 9, 1960, he was released from jail.

At once, Kaunda issued a press statement which said:

> Freedom! ... The Zambia African Congress was banned, but there is no power to ban our desire to be free, to shape our own destiny. In this struggle for freedom, we will tell the present rulers to realize that the colour of a man should not count; what should count is behaviour ... I am determined more

than ever before to achieve self-government for Africans in this country. Detentions, imprisonments and rural-area restrictions will only delay, but will not stop us from reaching that goal, which should be reached this year, 1960.[25]

On January 31, Kaunda was elected unopposed as the president of UNIP. More than ever before, he "was determined to combine Gandhi's policy of non-violence with Nkrumah's positive action." Around March of that year, he again called for a constitutional change. He submitted a case for immediate self-government to the British, basing his case upon a firm belief that "it is the God-given right of any people to rule themselves."[26]

He published his first book, *Black Government?* in 1960. This book dealt with his views on race, non-violence and politics. In August, he held a meeting of the UNIP delegates, preaching and emphasizing the necessity and importance of non-violence. When he addressed the crowds, there were shouts of "FREEDOM NOW." In colonial Zambia, such shouts could send an African to prison.

Kaunda encouraged his party leaders to organize and prepare themselves for independence from colonial rule. Often, he referred to Nkrumah's three "S's" – Service, Sacrifice and Suffering. He was quite optimistic. Iain MacLeod was the British colonial Secretary in 1961 and he had invited the UNIP to a Federal Review Conference in London. Reluctantly, Kaunda accepted this invitation.

The London conference was a failure. It did not meet the expectations of the African delegates. When Kaunda returned from London, he issued what the colonial authorities termed the "Mau Mau" statement. Actually, the statement was titled: "My People Are Tired," and was dated February 9, 1961.

In June, a disappointing new constitution was approved by the British. Africans were very angry. Even the Christian clergymen of Zambia denounced it. On July 9, an annual conference of UNIP, attended by over 3,000 people, met and denounced the new constitution. The British and its colonial government had dashed the hopes of the Africans. The time had come for the implementation of positive action.

The situation nearly got out of hand when schools and shops were burnt down by angry mobs. Eight Africans died during those civil unrests. Many were wounded by police brutalities. The following year, an entirely new constitution, acceptable to UNIP, came into effect. The dawn of a new day (or "Kwacha") was now in sight. Kaunda was elected to the Zambian Legislative Council in the October 1962 elections.

Initially, Kaunda was the Minister of Local Government and Social Welfare. He took his seat for the first time in the Legislature on January 15, 1963. The next year, on January 23, Kaunda was sworn in as Zambia's first Prime Minister.[27] On October 24, 1964, Zambia became an independent Republic, with Kenneth Kaunda at the helm of affairs as its President.

There is no doubt that Kaunda loved liberty and "has been the personification of the freedom struggle in Zambia."[28] He fought hard for four specific things: a color-blind society; freedom of speech and movement; "one man, one vote;" and an end to "Federation." He fought for human rights. He wanted political freedom for the African people of Zambia and he obtained it. He should receive credit for these things.

After independence was won, Kaunda championed the doctrine of African humanism, which, according to author Sanford J. Ungar, was "a blend of Christian precepts and African socialism."[29] His commitment to the total liberation of Africa was unquestionable. In his era, Kaunda's Zambia was one of the frontline states where freedom fighters from Zimbabwe, Mozambique and South Africa took refuge.

For this kind of support, Zambia was open to attacks from the Portuguese-held territory of Mozambique, from rebel Ian Smith's Southern Rhodesia, and from apartheid South Africa. But, Kaunda was not a blind apostle of pacifism. In his book, *The Riddle of Violence* (1980), he defended his support of armed resistance against Southern Rhodesia, apartheid South Africa, and any kind of militarism.[30]

Truly, Kaunda was a freedom fighter. In his book, *Letter To My Children* (1973), he admitted that Africa "is obsessed with the idea of freedom," and wrote that "personal liberty is the idol of the modern world."[31] But he provided no in-depth exposition on the meaning and concept of freedom and liberty. Like the other African leaders considered, he was too busy trying to free his people from foreign oppression.

Ironically, the man who broke ranks with Nkumbula, on the supposition that Nkumbula was becoming a dictator, turned around to be the very same thing he had reprehended – an almost life-time president who ruled Zambia for twenty-seven (1964-1991) years! Moreover, Kaunda ran a one-party system for almost twenty (1972-1991) years.

Unger wrote that during those twenty-seven years, "Kaunda became increasingly authoritarian" and "intolerant of opposition or criticism."[32] He failed to practice what he preached. Dr. George Ayittey pointed to other failures of the Kaunda era, such as the use of the State of Emergency laws for twenty years to suppress political opponents and their personal freedom.

Also, Kaunda mistreated many journalists and editors who dared to write or publish material that displeased his government. There was even an alleged case of personal enrichment and corruption.[33] Regrettably, the Africans in

Zambia were betrayed. The exercise of the right of true freedom became a mirage for many who were not members of UNIP.

Kaunda's humanism was no more or less one of the ideologies of liberation in Africa. In 1991, the people of Zambia threw out Kaunda from office in a multi-party election which many considered to be free and fair. He was 67. At the time of this writing, Kaunda is seventy-seven years old.

Perhaps, he is still dreaming of becoming the future president of Zambia someday. But now we move on to consider the concepts of freedom held by Obafemi Awolowo and Nnamdi Azikiwe, two prominent African nationalists from Nigeria.

CHAPTER NINE

AFRICAN FREEDOM: AWOLOWO AND AZIKIWE

If there is any African who disbelieves his capacity to enjoy the fruits of liberty, mark him well, he is not sane, he is destined to be the footsool of his compeers, and his doom has been sealed.

— Nnamdi Azikiwe

We return to West Africa, to Nigeria, to examine the conceptions of freedom by two of Africa's greatest political leaders and nationalists. We begin with Chief Obafemi Awolowo (or Awo, as he was popularly known). A self-made man, author of about a dozen books, and ex-Premier of the former Western Region of Nigeria, Awo was born to peasant-farmer parents on March 6, 1909, at Ikene, Ijebu Remo.

He first studied to be a teacher. Later on, he worked as a clerk, a trader, and a newspaper reporter. In his spare time, he organized trade unions. In 1944, he traveled to London to study law. While there, he formed a Yoruba cultural group known as the *Egbe Omo Oduduwa* ("Society of the Descendants of Oduduwa"), a cultural organization. In 1951, this group became the basis for the emergence of Awo's political party, the Action Group.[1]

Awo's ideas and thoughts about freedom first appeared in the title of his first published book, *Path To Nigerian Freedom*. This book was released in 1947 by Faber and Faber, a London based publishing company. In this 137-page publication, Awo provided his blueprint on the political economy of colonial Nigeria at that time.

He attacked continued British colonialism and wondered about "what [was] going to be Nigeria's ultimate goal – independence or self-government?"[2] Regrettably, the book was not an exposition on the concept of freedom. Rather, it was an advocacy for self-government which he championed for his region at the time.[3]

The same year that his book was published, Awo returned to Nigeria to practice law. Later that year, he gave a public lecture to the Assyrian Union of Teachers at Ibadan. Speaking on the topic, "What Is National Freedom?" he attempted to define the role of education in the attainment of such a freedom.

Among other things, Awo stated that "the passion for freedom is ineradicably ingrained in every human breast." He argued that "knowledge is necessary to the beneficial use of one's freedom, and courage and strength are essential to its preservation." "No one," he declared, "can claim to be truly free who is ignorant."[4]

The Reverend Dr. Francis Ishola Ogunmodede stated in 1986 that, "for Awolowo, there are three types of freedom: natural or absolute, individual and collective or political."[5] Awo believed that individual freedom must be subject to certain restraints of ethics, law, order, and convention and that freedom must be indivisible in order for it to be true and beneficial.

Given the context of his address to the teachers Union, Awo linked national political freedom with individual freedom when he argued that national freedom must be composed of those ingredients which constitute individual freedom. At this time, he did not precisely define what he meant by individual freedom.

Neither did he state exactly at what point individual freedom began and where national freedom ended. But, concerning Nigeria, he declared: "Our country is totally enslaved, and we as inhabitants therein are but only partially free."[6]

In a practical sense, Awo defined education to mean the fullest development of the body, brain and mind. He added: "In order to wrest our freedom from our British overlords, we need must develop our bodies and brains to the fullest. And in order to benefit by that freedom, ... we must also develop our minds to the fullest."[7] In accordance with this mindset, Awo championed the cause of a universal free primary education (UPE) in the Western Region when he was the Premier.

On April 28, 1951, Awo spoke again publicly. His topic was: "Freedom For All." Typically, this speech was not an elucidation of the concept of freedom. Rather, Awo outlined the aims and objectives of his new political party, the Action Group (AG). The motto of AG, he said, was "Life More Abundant, Freedom For All." He said that, in his region, Nigerians would be free if they were able to enjoy four basic freedoms.

These freedoms were:

1. freedom from British rule
2. freedom from ignorance
3. freedom from disease, and,
4. freedom from want.

More than a year later, on July 16, 1952, Awo addressed the Western Nigeria House of Assembly in Ibadan. His topic on that occasion was the "Charter of Freedom." He was about to make a motion for a Bill that would establish local government administrations. For him, the Bill was a "veritable charter of freedom, that is, freedom at the local government level."[8]

Perhaps, the most important statement which Awo made in the political history of Nigeria was on March 31, 1953, during a speech in the Federal House of Representatives in Lagos. Awo had become very unhappy with the northern Nigerian representatives at that meeting. He complained of their being in the custom "to threaten the rest of Nigeria with secession, if this is done or if that is not done."

Awo castigated them and stated that "political independence is the inalienable right of man." Then he added: "We were free before the British came and we ruled ourselves. It might be said that we did not rule ourselves well enough. But foreign rule however benevolent is not as good as self-rule."[9] Awo and his party then demanded for self-rule from the British. They were the first to do so in Nigeria.

In 1958, Awo and his party published a policy document titled *Freedom and Independence For Nigeria: A Statement of Policy*. In this publication, the AG outlined "the path the largest free nation in Africa should follow in both domestic and foreign affairs." Regarding freedom, this document also stated as follows:

> We must guarantee to all our people the fundamental freedoms, including freedom of assembly, freedom of religion and freedom of speech. We must not permit, in any region of our country, the slightest restrictions on the inalienable

rights of all free men and women. It is incumbent upon us to include in the new Constitution guarantees dealing with the rights of the citizens in a democracy, and preserving, from wanton violation, a parliamentary system of Government in such a manner as to make amendments subject to the popular will of the majority of our people.[10]

In essence, the document contained a major declaration on the type of political freedom which Awo envisaged for Nigerians. With hindsight, we may also say that the document was a warning to the northern leaders since Islam dominated the area. Therefore, Awo insisted upon the rights of Moslem women to vote in northern Nigeria. Hitherto, those women were disfranchised by tradition, custom and law.

In 1961, after Nigeria had gained her independence, Awo appeared to have placed national economic freedom above political freedom. Also, he warned fellow Nigerians of the danger posed by any attempt to islamize the rest of Nigeria. He observed that "the Sardauna of Sokoto, [Ahmadu Bello] with the express consent of [Tafawa] Balewa, is moving heaven and earth to drag Nigeria into a Commonwealth of Moslem States."[11]

By this warning, Awo seemed to have advocated for a separation of Church and State and a secular Nigeria. What Awo feared in 1961 has come to pass since Ibrahim Babangida assumed the reigns of power in 1985. From then until now, many Christians in Nigeria have systematically been purged in pogroms and arsons. Their churches are often razed to the ground, all because some Moslems want to dip the Koran into the Atlantic ocean.

On February 4, 1961, Awo gave a lecture at the former Nigerian College of Arts, Science and Technology, in Enugu, capital of the then eastern Region. He vehemently denounced a proposed Anglo-Nigerian Defense Pact. He argued that Nigeria was not only to be free but was to be seen as truly free. He did not want Nigeria entangled in European military pacts or alliances.[12]

In his autobiography, Awo credited the Nigerian "anti-imperialists [who] never went so far as to create a state of violent disturbances in our agitation for freedom." He added that the road to freedom "has been free from violence and bloodshed."[13] No wonder that the flag of independence was of the green, white, and green colors. No red!

Thus far, Awo may appear to be a symbol of a liberal democrat, an advocate of libertarian principles, a true lover of liberty. But a man is judged by not only what he says, but also actually by what he does. So, with hindsight, we can say that Awo may have sincerely believed in popular democratic ideals. His publicly stated preference for freedom was rooted in the English liberal tradition.

He had been to London, studied there, and read many of the books by British political theoreticians. He was also exposed to some American authors. However, like many of the other African leaders already analyzed, Awo failed to bequeath to future Nigerians a political climate where freedom was truly cherished. Nowhere did Awo provide a systematic synthesis of the concept of freedom or liberty which was clearly different from political independence from colonial rule.

In his days, barely six years after the British had left the country, Nigerians fought a brutal war whose origins went back to the political crises which afflicted the former Western Region of Nigeria. Awo is also credited with the statement that hunger and starvation were legitimate instruments of war. So, as the Federal Minister of Finance during the civil war,

Awo cared less if the children of "Biafra" and their parents starved to death in their millions! Nigeria lost about one million lives in that futile and senseless war.

Awo's worst critics perceived him to be "a rampant tribalist."[14] The editors of the popular *West Africa* magazine observed that "though a democrat, [Awo] was also an autocrat." They added that Awo was bound by the "three-cornered power trap of Hausa-Yoruba-Ibo which caused the Nigerian crisis."[15]

The editors pointed out that Awo learned ethnic politics from Azikiwe, "his alter ego, with whom he was locked in an epic struggle of love-hate, permanently foiling each other, dooming each other by their very divisions, two buds on the single stem of nationalism."[16] This political rivalry prevented the flourishing of a true national unity.

In the former Western Region itself, Awo's other arch-rival was S. L. Akintola, himself a Yoruba. Akintola described Awo as "the greatest enemy of democracy and freedom that I know in Nigeria."[17] Given the political rancour which existed between Akintola and Awo, which eventually led to the political crisis in the area, it is not hard to understand why Akintola reserved such harsh words for Awo.

What is really hard to understand is the contradiction which existed between avowed **principles** and the **practice** of freedom. This is what the editors of the *West Africa* magazine alluded to. How can it be that Awo was both a democrat and an autocrat? My answer is that Awo may have embraced the larger scope of the concept of human liberty, at least, in principle. But, he found the road between theory and practice too narrow to tread.

The hard realities of political greed, the acquisition of temporal political power, and the maintenance of that power for oneself were too tempting for Awo to ignore. It was one thing to possess an intellectual notion of freedom and quite another thing to defend the freedoms and rights of others, especially when doing so would stand in the way of personal gain and ambition.

Like the other African nationalists, it was difficult for Awo to defend the rights and freedoms of his political enemies who also had a right to enjoy the fruits which national independence from Britain had brought. This is the main problem which the African political leaders have had in the post-colonial era. Obafemi Awolowo died at his home-town, Ikene, on May 9, 1987. We move on to his political rival, Dr. Nnamdi Azikiwe.

In Chapter Two of this book, I had begun to examine Zik's perspective on the matter of freedom. So, we shall return to where we left him off, to analyze more of his views and actions as we have done with the rest of his comrades-in-nationhood. But, permit me here to make a quick digression.

On April 24, 1994, I was at Lincoln University in Pennsylvania, Zik's alma mater, to participate in a conference in honor of the *Owelle* of Onitsha, as Zik was then known. There, I met Zik personally for the first time. He was seven months short of being ninety years old, dignified, strong and impressive as ever, with a clear mind and a humble spirit. He sat on the same platform with all the presenters.

There, I presented a paper titled "Zikism and Some Troubling Issues in Nigerian Politics, Nationalism, and Democracy." In 1989, I had published my second book, *Destiny Is Not A Matter of Chance: Essays in Reflection and Contemplation on the Destiny of Blacks*. In it, I had examined Zik's views on the destiny of the African race. I surmise that I may have been invited to the Lincoln conference because of my book.

Like many of his contemporaries, Zik studied abroad in the United States of America in his 20s. He met Edem Ani-Okokon whom he later described as "this pioneer of freedom in Africa." Unfortunately, Edem died unexpectedly and Zik gave the eulogy at the Howard University Rankin Memorial Chapel on May 10, 1928.

As part of this eulogy, Zik vowed: "If God spares me to return home alive, I pledge that I will join crusaders for human freedom anywhere in the world and we shall intensify the struggle for democracy in Africa."[18] Zik returned to Africa in 1934 and kept his pledge. He teamed up with the other Nigerian anti-colonialists like Herbert Macaulay, Ernest Ikoli, and H. O. Davies.

Before he left the United States, Zik had obtained two masters degrees, but no doctorate. He had also published his first book, *Liberia In World Politics*, in 1934. He applied for a teaching job in Nigeria but the colonial government could not find a vacancy for him. He was denied the opportunity to return to work in his own native land!

After nine weary years abroad, Zik returned to Nigeria, but then, shortly afterwards, he moved to Accra, Ghana, to begin his career as a journalist. This was on January 1, 1935. According to Nyaknno Osso's book, *Who's Who in Nigeria* (1990), Zik was the editor-in-chief of the *Accra Morning Post* from 1934 to 1937. He was also the founder and editor-in-chief of the *West African Pilot* from 1937 to 1940. Then he was the Managing Director of his own company, Zik Enterprises Limited from 1937 to 1953.

At that time, he also established the African Continental Bank (ACB). He moved back to Nigeria in 1937, to settle permanently, and to work toward the political freedom of Nigeria from British rule. As a politician, Zik was a member of the Western House of Assembly from 1952 to 1953.

Between 1954 and 1959, he was a member of the Eastern House of Assembly and the Premier of that Region. As Nigeria moved toward independence, Zik was elected to the Federal House of Representatives in 1959. He was the president of the Senate in 1960. When Nigeria became independent that year on October 1, Zik was appointed by the British as the first and only indigenous Governor-General and Commander-in-Chief of the Armed Forces of Nigeria.

Three years later, when Nigeria became a Republic, Zik was the choice as Head of State and President of the new Republic. However, the executive power was conferred upon Balewa, who served as Prime Minister. Zik continued to be President until 1966 when the military overthrew Balewa's government.

After his first wife Flora died, he married another woman named Uche. He had many children and grandchildren. He spoke Ibo, Yoruba, and a "smattering" of Hausa. He wrote no less than 21 books and booklets. He died on May 11, 1996, at the age of 92.

Awolowo recalled that when he arrived in Nigeria in the fall of 1934, Zik gave three public lectures in Lagos. One of those lectures, delivered at the Methodist Boys' High School, was titled "There Is Joy In Scholarship." Awo conceded that "the fame of the brilliance of that lecture reached all corners of Lagos and the mainland in no time."[19]

At that lecture, Zik argued that scholarship was coterminous with social progress. In Zik's view, originality was the essence of true scholarship and creativity, the soul of the true scholar. Zik believed that it was "the scholar who makes or unmakes society." Therefore, he urged Nigerians to "consecrate themselves for scholarly research into all the aspects of world society in general and African society in particular."[20]

So, like Awo, Zik saw education as an instrument for political liberation as well as for social progress. Professor James Coleman, author of the book, *Nigeria: Background to Nationalism* (1971), pointed out that, even before 1925, when Zik had left Africa to the U.S., Zik had shown his interest in mass education by establishing branches of the Young Men's Literary Association.[21]

The other two lectures which Zik gave in 1934 were about his economic and political philosophies for a new Africa.[22] These philosophies were fully elaborated in his book, *Renascent Africa*, published in 1937. That year, Zik joined the Nigerian Youth Movement (NYM), an anti-colonial group whose members later included Awo, Akintola, and Oba Samuel Akisanya.

In his book, Coleman described the NYM as "the first Nigeria-wide multi-tribal nationalist organization in Nigerian history."[23] And Anthony Enahoro, one of those earliest Nigerian nationalists, wrote that, in 1937 "Dr. Azikiwe seemed to me to symbolize in some ways the new Nigeria," adding that Zik "was, if nothing else, a dedicated nationalist."[24] Zik continued in the NYM until 1941 and, in 1944, he formed his own political party, the National Council of Nigeria and the Cameroons (NCNC).

To understand Zik, one has to remember that he was the product of American democratic liberalism. He was exposed to the Jeffersonian political ideas about liberty. He read and was acquainted with the racial ideas and thoughts of Americans. He had studied at Storer College, a segregated Southern institution. He had been a student at two black institutions: Howard and Lincoln Universities.

He was exposed to the Who's Who in African and African-American intellectual tradition. These included people like William Leo Hansberry, Edward Blyden, W. E. B. DuBois,

Booker T. Washington, Claude McKay, Frederick Douglass, Richard Wright, and Cheikh Anta Diop. He was familiar with the works of L. S. B. Leakey and Melville Herskovits, noted anthropologists of the time.

Zik understood the history of African-American slavery and their quest for freedom. When he was at Howard University, he met with Alain Locke, the African-American professor of philosophy. Zik was influenced by Locke's generosity as well as by Marcus Garvey, Dr. J. E. Kwegyir Aggrey of Ghana, and by James A. Garfield, the twentieth president of the United States, whose biography he had read.

Zik's ideas about freedom were also rooted in his experiences as a child when he watched a young British colonial officer insult and humiliate his father. His ideas were fashioned through the American intellectual process. He became a prolific writer, a believer in the adage that "the pen is mightier than the sword." He gave many speeches and addresses. His *West African Pilot* newspaper is an important source for his views on freedom.

Without question, Zik shared the anti-colonial stance of the other Nigerian nationalists. On June 27, 1947, in New York, Zik publicly expressed his disgust for colonialism:

> I say without equivocation that such policy has been formulated in accordance with the logic of imperialism, buttressed by a false belief about the incapacity of the colonial peoples to develop initiative. To an extent, this policy was justified in the past, for historical reasons, but it can hardly stand the test of impartial analysis and criticism today.[25]

At the annual convention of the NCNC held on April 4, 1949, in Lagos, Zik said:

I conceive the cult of imperialism, anywhere it exists, as a crime against humanity, because it enables any section of the human race which is armed with the techniques of modern scientific knowledge without justification to dominate less fortunate sections of humanity, simply because the latter are unequal to the task of resisting the force which buttresses such domination. As I see the problem of imperialism in the world today, it is the only yardstick by which I can judge the good intentions of any nation or race. Continuance of such a philosophy cannot but be regarded by me as a chronic disease which must invite drastic remedy.[26]

Notwithstanding these inflaming sentiments, Zik was always careful not to advocate violence, as Elizabeth Isichei, the Nigerian historian has pointed out. Zik often argued that the colonial constitutions were "essentially autocratic." The "denial of elementary human rights such as freedom of speech and of the Press and freedom of association and assembly is rife."

Zik contended that social segregations and discriminations were rampant in colonial Nigeria and that education was merely a privilege. Economically, he said, the British used the colonies as the dumping ground for their unemployed ones. He complained that "the prisons [were] medieval" and that "the penal code [was] oppressive." Even religious freedom was "a pearl of great price."[27]

For all these injustices, Zik called upon all Africans and Nigerians, in particular, to resist the colonialists. I should add that, in spite of these anti-colonial agitations, Zik was not incarcerated nor tortured in jail, or even murdered, as many of the post-colonial African leaders have done to their other fellow Africans who spoke out for freedom.

At Trafalgar Square in London in 1949, when he was 40 years old, Zik addressed some West African students and said:

> The people of Nigeria cannot continue to accept as their destiny the denial of human rights. We, too, have a right to live, to enjoy freedom, and to pursue happiness like other human beings. Let us reinforce our rank and file in the fight for freedom, no longer suffering in silence and whining like a helpless dog, but striking back with all the force at our command when we are struck, preferring to suffer the consequences of pressing forward our claim to a legacy of freedom, than surrender our heritage to despoilers and usurpers. Be of good cheer, my compatriots.[28]

The above address was the closest that Zik came to what may be called an incitement to violence. But, it is doubtful if Zik was here recommending armed resistance. Perhaps, as an "African Gandhi," he may have had non-violence in his mind. Zik was no blood-thirsty revolutionary when he urged the African residents in London to strike back at the British. He was not such a fool to engage in that kind of suicide or futility.

What he recommended was action in self-defense. He did not advocate armed resistance but rather the use of the tactics of civil disobedience and non-violent positive action as Nkrumah was doing in Ghana. He used the power of his oratory, newspapers, and the Press to advocate labor unrest, strikes, propaganda, and mass education of the populace.

Zik was not afraid of martyrdom. He understood that risk with regard to leadership. On January 12, 1937, when he was residing at Accra, Ghana, he had written that "the New Africa is destined to become a reality." And he added:

> If because I am an instrument of destiny through which imperialism in West Africa is to be challenged and liquidated, and if in this mission I am compelled to pay the supreme penalty, then there is no need for me to quake or to quiver.[29]

Zik wrote profusely to educate and inform both the Western intelligentsia and Africans regarding the demands for political freedom. He was not interested in becoming a political messiah. And, lest anyone should think otherwise, he publicly declared: "I will publicly admit that I have never claimed to be a new Messiah."[30] He disclosed that "Fabianism became part of my life's strategy and tactics."[31]

Fabianism espoused the doctrine of slow rather than revolutionary change in government. It was a political philosophy associated with the English Fabian Society whose history went back to 1884. The English had borrowed the idea from the Roman General Quintus Fabius Maximus known for his defeat of Hannibal in the Second Punic War. Maximus' tactic was to avoid direct military contests. Zik embraced and applied this tactic in his politics.

In 1950, Zik revealed how committed he was to the cause of human freedom. At Enugu he said: "I am not a slave and I have no desire to commit my children to slavery; but if I were a slave, and preferred to have my children follow in my footsteps, then it were better that I had never been born."[32]

When twenty-one Nigerian coal miners were brutally massacred by the British on November 18, 1949, Zik called for restraint but offered this solemn warning:

> Let there be no mistake about our future; we are determined to be free, and history is on our side. It

is not whether Nigeria is right or Britain is right; it is what is right for Nigeria. In these days of struggle for national survival, let us not be bitter; let us bear no malice; let us be charitable and stand firm in the cause of justice and righteousness. God knows we hate none on account of race or colour, but we love our country, and we want our country to be free, and we shall be free.[33]

In 1957, when Ghana became independent, the Eastern Region of Nigeria became self-governing, but not yet independent. On his 54th birthday, November 16, 1958, Zik reflected on the stride toward Nigeria's political freedom in the following words:

In 1937, when I returned from Ghana, I joined forces with my compatriots in order to fight for freedom for Nigeria. We fought for political autonomy, economic security, social equality and religious toleration. Those were the days of the colonial regime, with its trappings of economic inequality, social discrimination and religious intolerance. It is gratifying to realize that today these specters of the past are being swept away by the forces of nationalism. Indeed, we have not fought in vain.[34]

Clearly, as the above quotations show, Zik knew what Nigerians wanted from their struggles with Britain. They wanted political, economic, social and religious freedoms. They admired Zik who, for twenty-six years (1934-1960), had become "a crusader in the cause of human freedom in Africa."[35] On October 1, 1960, all Nigerians joined with Zik in jubilation over the political freedom which was won at last.

They hoped that the other freedoms would follow fast upon the heels of this political freedom.

One important aspect stands out in the notion of freedom which Zik had. That is, Zik often conceived of freedom in universal terms. Like Nkrumah, he tied Nigerian freedom to his pan-Africanism. He believed that Nigerian political freedom from colonial rule would eventually lead to the emancipation of the entire African continent. This characteristic developed out of his racial consciousness formed during the years of study in the United States.[36]

There is also another difference between him and Awolowo or even Ahmadu Bello, the Premier of northern Nigeria. Zik did not see his political opponents as his perpetual enemies. If he did, he rarely expressed the opinion publicly. But, on several occasions, Awo called his opponents his enemies. Zik believed firmly in the unity of Nigeria, at least, up to the year of the Civil War in 1967. He once said that "the political union of Nigeria is destined to be perpetual and indestructible."[37]

I may safely say that Zik was much more of a believer in Nigerian unity and freedoms than any other nationalist leader that Nigeria had ever known. However, for the mistake of siding with Biafra for a brief moment, he has been very harshly criticized as one who cannot be relied upon. Even today, many of his own Ibo people are his worst critics![38] They seem to have totally forgotten his contribution to African education and enlightenment in the establishment of the University of Nigeria, Nsukka.

Zik's critics insist that he was a tribalist and no more different than Awo and Bello who used their geographical and ethnic platforms to bolster their political careers. But, *this is not the same thing as saying that Zik was a tyrant or dictator.* In the days of Zik's political campaigns, I do not recall the cases of the loss of innocent lives because Zik had to be kept in office at all cost.

But, I vividly remember the days of Dr. M. I. Okpara, Zik's successor-in-office, who caused terrible damage to property and the loss of many lives in Ibibioland. However, Zik was no political saint. And, very few people can be. Zik was once allegedly involved in some financial improprieties in the African Continental Bank.[39] Again, *this is not the same thing as saying that he was a megalomaniac.*

It is quite probable that Zik once used his ethnicity to his advantage in the overthrow of Professor Eyo Ita's government when the scales had turned against Zik in Awo's Western Region in 1953. Ita, an Ibibio, was the Parliamentary Leader and Minister of Natural Resources in the Eastern Regional government. He was also the Vice-President of the NCNC since 1948.

But, in less than a year, after Zik's political fortunes went downhill in the Western Region, Ita was replaced by Zik as Premier. Also, Ita was shamefully expelled from the NCNC by a letter which impugned the reputation and respect of the Efik/Ibibios. Ita was forced to found a new and rival political party – the National Independence Party (NIP), which later was renamed the United National Independence Party (UNIP).[40] There is no record that Zik, the doyen of freedom, defended Ita who belonged to a minority ethnic group.

Instead, Zik wrote disparagingly of Ita's nationalism, calling it "parochial" and "utopian."[41] It is probably true that the Ibo-dominated NCNC could not tolerate a man from a minority group as their leader. In this instance, Zik's conception of freedom was indented by the sharp sword of ethnicity.

One more case where Zik may have failed is provided by H. O. Davies, an eminent Nigerian. In his book, *Nigeria: The Prospects For Democracy* (1961), Davies recounted that in the

1940s, tensions between the Ibos and the Yorubas reached such heights that a war between them was imminent.

Davies stated that "The Ibos ... bought matchets by the thousands throughout the country in preparation for a civil war against the Yorubas."[42] The looming conflict was luckily averted by the massacre of the Enugu coal miners which galvanized the NCNC and the AG against a common enemy, the British. At the time, Zik was the national president of the NCNC. He is not known to have fought hard against the possibility of such a civil war.

These examples may give credence to the charge that Zik was a tribalist. But, as I have argued, there is no hard evidence that Zik was a dictator, a tyrant, or a megalomaniac during his political career. As Head of State and Commander-in-Chief of the Armed Forces of Nigeria in 1966, he could have broken the law and had the opportunity to assume absolute power, sacking the Prime Minister and holding on to the reigns of power.

One must not forget that the highest ranking military officer at this time, General Aguiyi Ironsi, was also an Ibo man. Zik could have collaborated with him to hold on to power, like others had done elsewhere in Africa. Nigeria would have had a different history had Zik done so. But, he did not. He believed that he had no constitutional authority to usurp power.

On the side of social freedom, Zik supported the abolition of the *Osu* or *Oru* or *Ohu* caste system in Iboland. An *Osu* was a person who had been dedicated to a shrine or deity and such a "person and his descendants [were] therefore regarded as social pariahs with no social rights which non-*Oru* [were] bound to respect."[43] An *Osu* may also have been a descendant of a slave family. In 1956, Zik publicly repudiated this caste system and had a law passed to abolish it.

After independence, Zik continued to speak out against the denial of freedoms to fellow Nigerians. Whatever one might say about Zik, he did attempt to be a true advocate for human freedoms and rights. I had cited his rueful lamentation of 1977 in Chapter Two, a lamentation regarding the new trend in politics toward despotism and tyranny.

And, there is nothing that Zik or Awolowo did that will ever compare with the harassments, imprisonments, tortures, and murders of innocent Nigerians during the corrupt and kleptocratic military administrations, particularly during the Ibrahim Babangida and Sani Abacha regimes.

But having said this, the early Nigerian nationalists in the person of Ahmadu Bello and Obafemi Awolowo, and to a lesser degree, Nnamdi Azikiwe failed to lay a solid foundation for the exercise and enjoyment of true human freedoms in a land that is so richly blessed by nature and nature's God. Imperialism and colonialism were partly to blame for the detour into tyranny. But the nationalists also deserve some of the blame. Africans in general and Nigerians, in particular, were betrayed.

H. O. Davies, already cited, best expressed the dynamic forces which worked for the betrayal of our freedoms. He observed that, "The Christian South was looking towards England and Western Europe. The Islamic North fixed its gaze on distant Mecca beyond the Sahara Desert."[44] In this religio-political contest, the pearl of freedom was trampled underfoot.

Nigerians and, indeed, many Africans living with the nightmare of the result of this contest, are still suffering from the dire consequences of the early nationalists' indiscretion, misdirection, and the poverty of their thought over the application of the principles of human freedom to national and international affairs.

CHAPTER TEN

AFRICAN FREEDOM: SENGHOR AND NEGRITUDE

I would like ... to assure the whites of our unshakable will to win our independence and that it would be stupid as well as dangerous for them to wish to make the clock march backwards.

— Leopold Sedar Senghor

To the west of Nigeria is the Republic of Senegal, Africa's westernmost state. Its capital, Dakar, was once the capital of the vast French West Africa, a territory which, in 1920, "comprised an area of some 4,600,000 sq. km., nine times the area of France."[1] French West Africa was made up of a group of eight separate colonies.

The eight colonies were: Mauritania, Mali, Burkina Faso, Senegal, Niger, Ivory Coast, Togo and Benin. By the coast of Senegal is the island of Goree, famed "as an entrepôt for successive European slave-trading companies from the latter fifteenth through early nineteenth centuries."[2] Today, Goree is an international tourist and historic site.

About 1542, the French had descended upon this part of West Africa. Colonization was not immediately possible due to rivalries from other Europeans like the Spaniards, Dutch, Portuguese, and the English. A first attempt by the French to colonize Senegal between 1817 and 1827 failed. The second attempt was effected between 1850 and 1920. "After the conquest, Senegal occupied a privileged place in France's colonial empire."[3]

According to historian Robert W. July, "the official French position regarding the colonies was rooted in the idea of a worldwide community of Frenchmen who shared the benefits of French language and culture."[4] This idea is known among scholars as the doctrine of assimilation.

This doctrine of assimilation "provided, to a large measure, the framework of French colonial administration." Its aim was to create black Frenchmen in Senegal and to make the colony an "extension of the mother country overseas."[5] The assimilation doctrine was a "more subtly racist doctrine."[6] Leopold Sedar Senghor was born into this kind of French colonial idealism.

A renowned poet, professor, politician and statesman, Senghor was born on October 9, 1906, in the small coastal town of Joal. The fifth of six children by his mother, Senghor came from the minority ethnic Serer group which occupied the most densely populated area of the peanut basin in Central Senegal.

Gnylane Bakhoum Senghor, Leopold's mother, was the youngest and last of the many wives of his father, Basile Diogoye Senghor. Basile was a well-to-do trader. He had become a success and owned many heads of cattle, fields and a large house on Joal's main thoroughfare.

Gnylane has been described as a woman who loved peace and her independence. She was quiet, reserved, and "of resolute character."[7] For she had refused to reside in her husband's house in Joal with the rest of the family. It was she who gave the name Sedar, meaning "impudent" or "he who is without shame," to her son. On or before May 24, 1913, Sedar was baptized into the Christian Church. This was when his other name, Leopold, was added to the Serer name, Sedar.

The Senghor family resided among the Wolof community, Senegal's most dominant ethnic group. The Wolofs are predominantly Muslims. Thus, Leopold came to be a Christian by religion as well as a minority by ethnicity, "on both counts."[8] However, he was not the product of one of the four coastal cities, or *communes*, created by the French.

Within the *communes*, Africans had French citizenship and some special privileges. But, being a Roman Catholic, Senghor was able to attend Catholic elementary and Secondary schools. At the age of seven, under the care of Father Leon Dubois, Senghor began his elementary school. It was Father Dubois who introduced him to France and to Normandy, the city of his second wife.

Dubois sent Senghor to a boarding mission school at Ngazobil, located six kilometers north of Joal. A year later, he was learning French, History, Geography and Mathematics. He also enjoyed music. This early educational training "did bind" this emergent Senegalese African elite to France.

At this time, Senghor decided to be a priest. He had excelled at Ngazobil and "won all the academic prizes."[9] In 1923, when he was seventeen, he enrolled at the Libermann Seminary in Dakar. There, he was influenced by the writings of Thomas Aquinas, the great Catholic philosopher.

Senghor also came into contact with Father Lalouse, a racist priest while at the seminary, who regarded Senghor a proud, pretentious boy who would never amount to anything. On the other hand, Senghor observed that Father Lalouse discriminated against the African seminarians and even called them "savages." Senghor's insistence that Africans had a civilization did not go well with Father Lalouse.[10]

A few days before graduation, Father Lalouse prevented Senghor from participation in the graduation, and so, effectively, barred Senghor from becoming a priest. But, putting this disappointment behind him, Senghor entered a secular school, the Lycee Van Vollenhoven, named after a young colonial governor.

While in Dakar, Senghor was exposed to the intellectual world of the *communes*. There, the Africans participated in the political debates of the time. Since an African within the *commune* was presumably a French citizen, he could participate in the political discourses of the colony. This was one privilege of the assimilation doctrine.

For Senghor, his mind was set upon higher education. With the help of a scholarship, he traveled to Paris in October 1928 to study at the Sorbonne. Later that December, he transferred to the Lycee Louis le-Grand. Among his classmates at this school was Georges Pompidou, who later became France's president. Those were the Depression years.

Senghor read whatever he could find about Africa. He was particularly attracted to African-American poetry. He met many Africans and Africans from the diaspora. He developed an intense intellectual interaction with them. He began to write his poems that exalted African culture. This brand of poetry eventually found expression in the much popularized philosophy known as negritude.

When Senghor completed his studies at the le-Grand, he was admitted into the Ecole Normale Superieure's School of Philosophy where he graduated as the first African to ever receive a diploma, an aggregation, the equivalent of an American Ph.D. In June 1933, he was naturalized as a French citizen.[11]

Senghor's teaching career began in 1935 when he was appointed a schoolteacher in Tours, described by biographer

Janet Vaillant as "a calm little town in the Loire Valley" southwest of Paris. He taught there for four years. Then he transferred to the Lycee Marcellin Berthelot in Paris where he taught literature. He began to emerge as the spokesman for his fellow Africans, expressing discontent with French cultural life.

The price for being a French citizen was military service. So, when World War II broke out in 1939, he was drafted. He was captured by the Germans and held prisoner for 18 months. But, in 1942, he was released. Promptly, he joined the French resistance movement. At the end of the war in 1945, he entered politics. General Charles de Gaulle appointed him to the Commission on Colonial Representation in the French Constituent Assembly.

The following year, in 1946, Senegal elected Senghor as a Deputy to the French National Assembly where he assisted in the drafting of the French Constitution as a member of the Socialist Party. Two years after this, Senghor founded his own political party, the Bloc Democratique Senegalais (BDS). During the next four years, he continued to teach African languages.

In 1952, the French Premier, Edgar Faure, appointed Senghor the Secretary of State in the French Cabinet. In 1960, Senghor became president of Senegal after an attempt by him to federate his country with Mali failed. Senegal was admitted a member of the United Nations (UNO) on September 28, 1960, with Senghor at the helm of things.[12] From the foregoing, it is clear that Senghor was not an outsider within the colonial system.

He served in various capacities in the French colonial empire. Thus, it is somewhat difficult to delineate his conception of African liberty or freedom. Unlike many of the other African leaders already analyzed, Senghor's concept of

African freedom is hard to pinpoint because, very early in his life, he was indoctrinated into the colonial philosophy of assimilation and he appears to have accepted it.

His views, writings and actions reveal a sophisticated Senghorian mind which, like that of W. E. B. DuBois, wrestled with the double consciousness of Africanity or "Africanhood," in the face of a strong and opposing foreign ideology. As I have indicated, it appears there were some attractions in France's assimilation ideology to him, and, perhaps, some benefits derivable and too tempting to refuse.

For, instance, in Senegal, there was no covert colonial policy of racism as was the case in Zambia and Zimbabwe or even in apartheid South Africa. At the level of personal benefit, Senghor had lied that he was a French citizen in order to graduate and obtain his diploma at the Sorbonne. But even before that, he had wrestled with the racial attitude of Father Lalouse and with the disappointing aspects of French cultural life.

Thus, intellectually, Senghor found himself within the narrow path of navigating through the stormy waters of assimilation in order to arrive at the "calm" beach of political independence. And this path, in Senghor's mind, was to be by "cultural liberation." In 1956, four years after he was appointed to be Secretary of State, he explained what this cultural liberation was all about.

At the First Congress of Black Writers and Artists held in Paris in September 1956, Senghor delivered an address titled "The Spirit of Civilisation, or the Laws of African Negro Culture." This address was Senghor's theological anthropology, not based on the doctrines of the Bible, but rooted in the African culture. The essence of it was a plea for an African cultural renaissance as a pre-condition for "political liberation" from colonial rule.

Senghor contended that "cultural liberation is an essential

condition of political liberation."[13] He emphasized what he termed the African's "existential ontology" and argued that "in order to exist, man must realize his individual essence by the increase and expression of his vital force."[14]

He noted that the African "has drawn up a rigid hierarchy of Forces." At the summit of these forces is "a single God, uncreated and creator."[15] He believed that it was the link with these forces that provided the dynamic power for cultural reformation and that it was expressed through the arts and literature. Senghor believed that an African cultural renaissance "will be the doing not so much of the politicians, as of the Negro writers and artists."[16]

The sum of his thesis was this: the African can find real and true freedom if his culture was "liberated" through the arts and literature. Since "Man [is] at the center" of this "existential ontology,"[17] we may safely state that Senghor was advocating a kind of humanism nearly similar to that held by Kenneth Kaunda of Zambia.

Senghor had become aware that "[The Frenchman] wants bread for all, culture for all, liberty for all; but this liberty, this culture, and this bread will be French. The universalism of this people is French."[18] Also, he probably understood, as Kaunda did, that violent resistance to French colonialism, even if he was inclined to go that way, would be suicidal.

Senegal could not beat France on the battlefield in order to be free from colonial rule and domination. Besides, as a practical man, Senghor believed that for an independent Senegal, "[w]e shall not scorn private capital; instead, we shall seek it, whether it comes from France or elsewhere, provided it does not alienate [our] rights."[19]

Also, in 1956, Senghor had said: "We wish ... to liberate ourselves politically in order to express our Negritude, that is, our true black values."[20] It is apparent, then, that for Senghor,

African freedom was intricately tied to his concept of negritude, or vice-versa. So, what was so wonderful about this negritude that consumed and dominated Senghor's mind and literary commitment?

According to Senghor himself, negritude was "the whole complex of civili[s]ed values – cultural, economic, social and political – which characteri[s]e the black peoples, or, more precisely, the Negro-African world."[21] This was the definition he gave during an address delivered at Oxford University in England.

Negritude was brought about as "we had become aware within ourselves that assimilation was a failure; we could assimilate mathematics or the French language, but we could never strip off our black skins nor root out our black souls." He continued: "Its whereabouts was pointed out to us by that handful of freelance thinkers – writers, artists, ethnologists, and prehistorians – who bring about cultural revolutions in France."[22]

The essential elements of negritude were "the sense of communion, the gift of myth-making, [and] the gift of rhythm." Senghor stated that negritude was an "anti-racial racialism," which satisfied "our need to love."[23] Anthropologists had taught the African that "there is no such thing as a pure race: scientifically speaking, races do not exist."[24]

In this case, Senghor was echoing the view of Ashley Montagu who had said the same thing in several of his publications. But, with regard to African freedom, Senghor pointed out that through negritude, "we remain wholly free to cooperate or not, to provoke or prevent the synthesis of cultures. This is an important point,"[25] he insisted.

Senghor added that negritude was the black man's "contribution to the Civili[s]ation of the Universal." His vision was that through negritude "the (African) will have contributed with other peoples, to reforging the unity of man and the world; linking the flesh to the spirit, man to fellow man, the pebble to God."[26]

At the time that Senghor offered the above definition, he conceded that "our Negritude no longer expresses itself as opposition to European values, but as a complement to them …" He added that "its militants will be concerned …, *not to be assimilated, but to assimilate.* They will use European values to arouse the slumbering values of Negritude, which they will bring as their contribution to the Civili[s]ation of the Universal."[27]

However, Senghor did not wholly endorse European values. Indeed, he disagreed with Europe "not with its values any longer … but with its theory of the Civili[s]ation of the Universal." He contended that the Europeans often presumed that Africans "have no idea of the pre-eminent dignity of the human person."

The Europeans forget, he argued, that the free enterprise, democracy, and communism are myths (speaking not in a pejorative sense) and that their myths are "monstrously anti-humanist."[28] Conversely, negritude, though also itself a myth, is "a living, dynamic one, which evolves into a form of humanism."[29]

Author Sylvia Washington Ba, who painstakingly examined Senghor's ideas in terms of the basis, experience, expression, fundamental traits and future of negritude, cited one of his poems as follows:

My Negritude is no slumber of the race but sun of the soul.
My Negritude is a trowel in the hand, a spear in the fist.
Scepter. It is not to eat and drink the fleeting moment.[30]

Senghor's biographer, Janet G. Vaillant argues that negritude first began as a young African's search for self-discovery in a foreign country. Senghor, the young African in question, came into contact with Aime Cesaire, another young man from Martinique, who had come to France to study. It was Cesaire who had coined the word "negritude."

The idea of negritude developed slowly to become an intellectual concept. "For Cesaire Negritude was primarily an attitude," Vaillant wrote, but, "for Senghor it was an objective reality."[31] Eventually, negritude became Senghor's political ideology alongside African socialism.

As I had already indicated, the political career of Senghor began in 1945 after World War II. In August 1946, he publicly declared his dissatisfaction with the French colonial rule when he stated:

> We do not wish any longer to be subjects nor to submit to a regime of occupation ... I would like ... to assure the whites of our unshakable will to win our independence and that it would be stupid as well as dangerous for them to wish to make the clock march backwards. We are ready, if necessary as a last resort, to conquer liberty by any means, even violent ones.[32]

These were harsh words for the colonialists to hear. But, he was not yet a political star nor the leader of any political party or organization. But his words reveal the general mood of discontent toward colonialism in the post-war era. Senghor was still a firm believer of the role of the arts and literature in the evolution of African civilization. He was still guided by his notions of negritude.

He had been molded by the concept and was not yet ready to become a firebrand anti-Westerner or a radical revolutionary like Kwame Nkrumah. Therefore, between 1945 and 1948, he was willing to remain under the tutelage of Lamine

Gueye, a successful lawyer, trained in France, who had become an influential politician in Senegal.

On September 9, 1946, one month short of his fortieth birthday, Senghor married his first wife, Ginette Eboue, the daughter of the legendary Felix Eboue. Two sons were born to him between 1946 and 1948. Sadly, this marriage ended in the 1950s. It was at this time that Senghor began to sever his political ties with Gueye.

The break-up actually began in September 1947 when Senghor appraised himself of the worsening conditions of the local people outside of the *communes*. In addition, Senghor had come into contact with Ibrahima Seydou Ndaw, a self-trained lawyer, who was interested in the well-being of his local people of Kaolack and Sine-Saloum. Ndaw was a staunch Muslim with a deep interest in local economics.

Senghor also came into contact with Mamadou Dia, a local young teacher gifted with organizational skills. Dia had organized a friendship society which had a newspaper. The three men – Senghor, Dia, and Ndaw were not the product of the *communes* and were linked to a common cause: the dissatisfaction with and improvement of the lot of ordinary Senegalese.

Thus, in September 1947, at a local branch meeting of the Socialist Party which Gueye led, Senghor took the floor and delivered a blistering attack on the leadership of the party for what he called "its excessive centralization, nepotism, and habit of clan politics."[33] That same year, Senghor was allowed by the party to publish his own newspaper, *The Human Condition*, which became his political mouthpiece.

This newspaper set a different tone to Senegalese politics. It focused on Senghor's interest in negritude. But, it also provided space for discussions on educational reforms, the liberation of Africa within a French framework, rapid autonomy (not independence) of all French Africa, and improvement of the welfare of Senegal's rural population. In October 1948, Senghor resigned from Gueye's party and formed his own party – the Bloc Democratique Senegalais (BDS).

Senghor, Ndaw and Dia were the foremost members of the new party. These three friends worked very hard to consolidate political grounds. They brought their party to the point where the BDS won the two seats of Deputies allotted to the colony in the French National Assembly in 1952. The BDS "was to be democratic and socialist, against nepotism and the politics of clan, and for the interests of Senegal and West Africa within the French Union."

Also, the BDS "would respect religion and traditional leaders. It would also act in accord with the principles of scientific socialism."[34] The personal character of Senghor played an important role for the survival of the BDS. Senghor was a man of sterling qualities and talents. An excellent teacher, he was friendly, yet cautious; he was conciliatory and possessed the ability to persuade and mediate between people.

He could compromise in order to reach a shared common goal. He had the ability to take on those who disagreed with him as a challenge. He would not use his power to crush his opponents. His being part of an ethnic and Christian minority had taught him the value of tolerance. Thus, in 1957, he was able to seek out and persuade Gueye, whom he had defeated in 1952, to join him by uniting with the BDS in order to negotiate with the French.[35]

The Senghorian era, which actually began in 1952 and lasted up until 1980, when Senghor voluntarily retired from active politics, is now to be analyzed in order that we may discover how it fared in terms of the exercise and promotion of human freedom and liberty. Words are one thing; but actions often speak louder than words.

In terms of autocracy, despotism, dictatorship, and downright tyranny, what was it like to be under President Leopold Senghor? To be sure, Senghor was no Idi Amin nor a Thomas Jefferson. In politics, he was still guided by his belief in negritude. In economic matters, he chose the path of African socialism. And, he kept close ties with France.

Senghor believed that African socialism was the middle road between the two evils of communism and capitalism. "We are not Communists," he once replied to his political opponents. Then he added: "We stand for a middle course, for a democratic socialism, which goes so far to integrate spiritual values, a socialism which ties in with the old ethical current of the French socialists."[36]

"This thirst for freedom," Senghor maintained, "this hunger for spiritual nourishment, strengthened by the moral tradition," was what made French socialism appealing or attractive and which he wanted to transform into a Senegalese socialism. Thus, in his book, *On African Socialism* (1964), Senghor totally rejected "atheistic materialism."[37]

He also took the time to expose what was wrong with Russian revolutionaries: Karl Marx, Vladimir Lenin and Josef Stalin, whose ideas were incompatible with Senegalese socialism. He asked: "What good is our independence if it is only to imitate European totalitarianism, to replace external colonialism by domestic colonialism?"[38]

However, Senghor failed to offer any succinct definition for his African socialism. Was it an amalgam of negritude and humanism? One may answer, "yes." What is clear is that he sought for "a community of free and equal peoples with the mother country,"[39] France. He endorsed the concept of freedom which was held by Gaston Berger (1896-1960), a famous Senegalese philosopher.

Berger had said that "liberty is a right; it is the absence of shackles, the possibility of acting as one wishes. A people is free when no other people can dictate its decisions ... Independence is quite another thing."[40] Though brief, this is the clearest statement on freedom which, it appears, Senghor would have made. He was a man of few words.

The political scientist, Irving Leonard Markovitz, rightly stated that "Senghor rejected both the Western capitalist and Eastern communist camps, and affirmed that he and his people were both African socialists and adherents of democratic socialism."[41] Markovitz also contended that Senghor emphasized economic development and efficiency.

Senghor's application of negritude to economics helped to expose some crucial questions, such as, "does materialism provide a powerful enough spur for individual and social advancement and, if so, is a society built on this basis morally worthwhile?"[42] Senghor's answer would have been a firm "no" and he would have recommended a return to African values and culture.

The Nigerian author, Ihechukwu Madubuike noted that Senghor was not a literary pacifist, since he was part of the majority of Senegalese writers who challenged "the tenets of the politics of assimilation."[43] But, at the same time, Madubuike added that Senghor had "argued against national independence and favored adherence to France."

In 1950, Madubuike said, Senghor had written that "Europe is not being faithful if it considers the thought of excluding the people of overseas countries from the Community." Senghor "condemned nationalism and reduced the practical utility of political independence to a minimum."[44]

Senghor believed that "nationalism ... appears out-of-date

and independence is nothing but illusion. And in this absurd world ridden with anxiety, men, if not nations, prefer liberties to Liberty; to the independence of their country they prefer the material and moral independence of each of their compatriots."[45]

Even back in 1937, Senghor had stated that "the cultural problem in French West Africa is the most serious problem of the hour."[46] The point that Madubuike made was that, while decolonization was about to take off, Senghor worried about culture instead of political freedom from foreign rule. For Senghor, as I had stated earlier on, cultural liberation was much more important than political liberation.

In 1946, Senghor had threatened that unless Africans had equal rights within the French Union, African territories would become independent, even by violence; but he soon changed his opinion on this matter and opposed those who demanded national independence. This change of opinion may have been because he was more of a "French black man." By 1958, Madubuike said, Senghor was dead set against independence.

Also, Madubuike argued that even Senghor's position on national sovereignty was at variance with the tenets and some cardinal principles of the negritude movement. For example, Senghor wrote that "to speak of independence, is to reason with the head downwards and with legs in the air. It is not reasoning but creating a false problem."[47]

Madubuike concluded that Senghor had an anti-independence mentality which he expressed in one of his poems, *Chaka*. Madubuike also noted that in *Chaka*, "negritude takes over from the struggle against colonization."[48] Paradoxically, Senghorian negritude prepared the way for Senegal's independence by emphasizing what was unique about the African.

Of this independence, Senghor had written that it "is only a myth devised to keep alive an outdated nationalism." But ironically, this same man who seemed to have been a stumbling block to Senegalese nationalism and independence became its president in 1960. It is clear, therefore, that Senghor regarded politics as a means to an end; not the end itself, as it was with most African leaders of his time. The end was cultural liberation.

So, Senghor emphasized "the primacy of culture over politics."[49] According to Madubuike, Senghor's African socialism "is ... a theory of collaboration of independent Africa with the dominant class of Western countries."[50] Two other keen analysts of Senghor will bring to an end this attempt to understand him.

Robert H. Jackson and Carl G. Rosberg, in their book, *Personal Rule in Black Africa* (1982), observed that Senghor's ruling strategy was never to close the polity entirely – to completely deprive individuals and groups of their liberties and opportunities to express their opinions and engage in politics. He permitted intellectual and press freedom during his rule.[51] This strategy allowed him to stay on in power for a total of twenty years.

President Senghor sustained the lively activity of one of Africa's leading intellectual centers. Political freedom was more subject to State control, but never with the aim of restricting it entirely during his presidency. Senegal began as a democracy in 1960, then became a de-facto one-party State (1963-1978) until the re-introduction of multi-party politics in 1976 and 1978. Senghor enjoyed "presidential royalism."[52]

Jackson and Rosberg concluded:

> During the course of Senghor's political career, other important Senegalese politicians have been

defeated, outmaneuvered, or subordinated, and had their parties banned; some who have persisted in their rivalry have been excluded from the dominant party (and therefore the polity); and a few have been forced into exile or have had their civil and political liberties curtailed.[53]

Examples of such abuses of political rights under the Senghor regime included the case of Mamadou Dia who was defeated in a power struggle over the leadership of the country in 1962; Lamine Gueye who lost his paramount position as leader of the Socialist Party; and Cheikh Anta Diop, the famed historian, who suffered a similar fate as Gueye. "Over the years," Jackson and Rosberg averred, "corruption ... emerged as Senegal's national political style."[54]

So, it was not hard for Jackson and Rosberg to include Senghor among the "princes and oligarchic ruler(s)" of Africa. In this group belong also the late Jomo Kenyatta, William Tubman and William Tolbert of Liberia; Emperor Haile Selassie of Ethiopia; King Sobhuza II of Swaziland; and Gaafar Mohamed Numeiri of Sudan. This was no group for ardent libertarians.

We may summarize by stating that Senghor belonged to the class of moderate political leaders of modern Africa. He, like some of the others already examined, provided no masterly thesis on the African concept of freedom. As an African statesman married to a white Frenchwoman, a Christian leader in a predominantly Muslim country, a member of the Serer minority ethnic group, it was no easy road for Senghor to walk toward freedom.

Nevertheless, I agree with Sanford J. Unger when he wrote that Senghor's "truly unique contribution to African political history" (and, perhaps, vicariously, to the cause of the promotion of freedom) "was in becoming the first leader of an independent black nation on the continent to relinquish power voluntarily and turn it over to a constitutional successor."[55] This he did when he handed his presidency over to Abdou Diouf on December 31, 1980.

The significance of what Senghor did lies in the fact that since 1957 there have been more than 150 African heads of State. Only seven in the history of postcolonial Africa up to 1999 have relinquished political power voluntarily. These include: Olusegun Obasanjo and Abdulsalami Abubakar, both of Nigeria.

The other five were El Hadj Ahmadou Ahidjo of Cameroon, Abdul al Dahab of Sudan, Julius Nyerere of Tanzania, Siaka Stevens of Sierra Leone, and Leopold Senghor. The rest have either stayed on until death or were pushed out in a violent coup d'etat.[56] They have been able to hang on to power because, in Africa, freedom is always under fire. President Senghor died at his home in France on Thursday, December 20, 2001, at the age of 95.

CHAPTER ELEVEN

AFRICAN FREEDOM: NELSON ROLIHLAHLA MANDELA

To men, freedom in their own land is the pinnacle of their ambitions, from which nothing can turn men of conviction aside.

— Nelson Mandela

Four months before World War I ceased in 1918, another freedom fighter was born in the Republic of South Africa. His name was Nelson Rolihlahla Mandela. And, whoever doubts that Africans have a knack – a love and a passion – for human freedom should first have a talk with Mandela, a man who spent 27 of his 83 years of life in an apartheid prison because of his total commitment to true liberty and human freedom.

Nelson Mandela is the truest personification of the African struggle for freedom and the struggle to receive respect as persons worthy of human dignity. And he earned it. The son of a Xhosa-speaking Thembu chief, Mandela was born on July 18, 1918, in "a tiny village on the banks of the Mbashe River in the district of Umtata, the capital of the Transkei."[1]

His mother's name was Nosekeni Fanny Nkedama. A woman whose hut was always filled with the children of her other relations, Nosekeni was the third wife of Mandela's father. She was a Christian (Fanny was her adopted Christian name) and she sharpened Nelson's imagination with the stories she told of Xhosa legends and fables that contained moral lessons for the young Mandela. In time, she became his first friend.

Mandela's father, Gadla Henry Mphakanyiswa, was a tall, dark-skinned man with a straight and stately posture which Mandela inherited. A chief at Mvezo town, Gadla was often referred to as "the prime minister of Thembuland."[2] He received government stipends under the British colonial rule. He had four wives and thirteen children, four boys and nine girls. He was influential in the social and political life of Thembuland.

Gadla was a noble and wealthy man by the standards of his time. He had no Western education but had a great respect for it. He did not subscribe to the local tribal prejudices of his day. Neither was he a Christian. He followed after the African traditional religion and served as an "unofficial" priest of his community.

Also, Gadla "possessed a proud rebelliousness, a stubborn sense of fairness"[3] which he passed on to his son, Nelson. Due to this "rebelliousness," Gadla fell out of favor with the local white colonial magistrate who stripped him of his status and wealth. As a result, Nelson and his mother moved to a nearby village called Qunu, close to Umtata. It was at Qunu that Mandela's boyhood began.

In 1927, two years after Mandela had begun elementary school, his father, Gadla died suddenly of some kind of lung disease. He had been a tobacco-pipe smoker for quite some time. Mandela, the eldest son of his mother, and the youngest of his father's four sons, was to be raised and nurtured by Nosekeni, now a single mother. Thus, at an early age, Nelson came to believe that "nurture, rather than nature, is the primary molder of personality."[4]

Mandela's three brothers died when he was young. He grew up with his sisters, all three of course were his mother's daughters. He did not inherit any landed property since all the Africans had been dispossessed and paid rents as tenants annually to the government. So, he did not grow up in affluence nor opulence. To put it mildly, he was poor in his boyhood, even though he could have inherited an aristocratic status.

He wrote that "Qunu was a village of women and children."[5] Most of the men worked at remote farms and mines. They would only return twice a year to the village to plow their fields. Soon, Mandela learned how to hoe, weed, and harvest. Fetching of water from the streams and springs were part of women's work, with the children assisting.

In Qunu, there were only two primary schools, though many children did not attend them. Few knew how to read and write. Without a father to look up to for direction and guidance, Mandela had much time to play and fight with the boys. "A boy who remained at home tied to his mother's apron strings was regarded as a sissy."[6]

Therefore, like King David described in the Bible, Mandela was no more than five when he became a "herd boy," looking after some sheep and cattle in the field. Out there, he learned the ruggedness of the countryside, knocking the birds out of the sky with his catapult. He also gathered wild honey, fruits and edible roots for food.

In his autobiography, *Long Walk to Freedom* (1994), Mandela claims that he drank warm, sweet milk "straight from the udder of a cow," swam in the clear, cold streams, and caught fish "with twine and sharpened bits of wire."[7] He was practically left alone to his own devices. This was a great type of freedom. But, this freedom helped him to acquire knowledge mainly by observation.

Mandela learned by imitation and emulation, with no questions asked. In his home as in many of the traditional African families back then, questioning by children was regarded a nuisance. A child was better seen than heard. Mandela wrote that his life "was shaped by custom, ritual, and taboo. This was the alpha and omega of our existence, and went unquestioned."[8]

Regarding his religious life, Mandela was exposed to the Christian faith quite early in his life. This was so, in part, because of his mother. But, in part, it was due to the influence of George and Ben Mbekela, two brothers at Qunu who were educated Methodists. Mandela was baptized into the Wesleyan Church.

By the advice of George Mbekela, Mandela's parents agreed to send him to study at the local school in 1925. He was seven at the time. No one in the Mandela family had ever been to school. It was at school that Mandela received the name, Nelson, from his teacher.[9] After his father had died, Mandela left Qunu at the orders of his mother.

Nosekeni, his mother, needed a man who would be responsible for her young son. Traveling by foot, she took Mandela to Mqhekezweni, the provisional capital of Thembuland where the royal palace of chief Jongintaba Dalindyebo was located. Dalindyebo was the "acting regent of the Thembu people."[10] Also, he had been recommended for this post by Mandela's father. Dalindyebo was now returning the favor he had received. Thus, he became Mandela's guardian and benefactor for a decade.

It was at Dalindyebo's palace that Mandela was introduced to the world of politics, money, class, and power. Puerility would soon come to an end. He quickly adapted to the new life at the palace. He continued with his education, studying English, Xhosa, history, and geography. One of the books he read was *Chambers' English Reader*. He did well at school. His aunt, who also resided at the palace, supervised his homework nightly. This education was of the British type.

Mandela soon became fond of Justice, a son of the regent. Four years older than Mandela, Justice played with Mandela often. Dalindyebo ensured that Mandela was brought up as if he were one of his own children. The two boys became best friends and Mandela looked up to Justice as his first hero "in every way."[11]

There were two "principles," as Mandela calls them, that greatly influenced him at this time. These were chieftaincy and the Church. The first was about the manner by which the political, economic, and social matters of Thembuland were handled. The second was the Christian Methodism as reflected in the personal life of Reverend Matyolo, who was the spiritual counselor of the regent. It all seemed like fate had brought Mandela there to be an apprentice by observation.

In the daily devotional life of the regent's family, and in Reverend Matyolo, Mandela found "all that was alluring in Christianity."[12] Back in Qunu, religion for Mandela had been merely a ritual and an indulgence which he engaged in for his mother's sake. It was meaningless. But, now, in the regent's home, Mandela discovered that Christianity had brought "virtually all of the achievements" which the Africans aspired to.

Such achievements included some Africans who had become clerks, interpreters, and policemen. Christianity had brought freedom from the fear of dangerous ghosts.

Dalindyebo also took his religion seriously. All members of his family were to do the same. So, Mandela regularly went to Church and taught Sunday school as a teenager. He rarely missed the services.

Chieftaincy gave to Mandela his first notions of leadership. In time, his conception of freedom would be rooted in the principles of leadership which he had observed very carefully. He wrote: "I watched [everything] and learned from the tribal meetings that were regularly held ..." He saw "democracy in its purest form." He described what this democracy was like in these words:

> There may have been a hierarchy of importance among the speakers, but everyone was heard, chief and subject, warrior and medicine man, shopkeeper and farmer, landowner and laborer. People spoke without interruption and the meetings lasted for many hours. The foundation of self-government was that all men were free to voice their opinions and equal in their value as citizens.

Regrettably, Mandela acknowledged that women were deemed as second-class citizens. But, he added:

> I was astonished by the vehemence – and candor – with which people criticized the regent. He was not above criticism – in fact, he was often the principal target of it. But no matter how flagrant the charge, the regent simply listened, not defending himself, showing no emotion at all....
>
> The meetings would continue until some kind of consensus was reached. They ended in unanimity or not at all.... Democracy meant all men were to be heard, and a decision was taken together as a

people. Majority rule was a foreign notion. A minority was not to be crushed by a majority....

Only at the end of the meeting, as the sun was setting, would the regent speak. His purpose was to sum up what had been said and form some consensus among the diverse opinions. But no conclusion was forced on people who disagreed. If no agreement could be reached, another meeting would be held.[13]

What Mandela describes here is nearly true of all traditional African political systems. I personally observed this same method of deliberation in my village as a young boy. In sad retrospect, the Western form of representative democracy has replaced our purest form of participatory democracy. This has created room for modern dictatorships in Africa. Also, one should not fail to notice the existence of the freedom of speech inherent in this piece by Mandela.

Besides these two principles of Church and chieftaincy, Mandela was also exposed to African history and culture. By intentionally listening to the oral narrations by members of the regent's council, Mandela learned that South African history went far beyond 1652 when Jan Van Riebeeck first arrived from Europe to the Cape of Good Hope.

Mandela learned that "the history of the Bantu-speaking peoples began far to the north, in a country of lakes and green plains and valleys."[14] He understood that his history did not begin with the advent of whites to South Africa. He learned how the Europeans and European colonialism had devastated African civilizations and societies.

He learned how, in Chinua Achebe's words, the white man had put a knife into the things that held Africans together and caused them to fall apart. And, speaking of Riebeeck, the name reminded the South Africans of the fateful day in April 1652 when some two hundred Europeans, led by Riebeeck, arrived in three ships as part of the Dutch East India Company.

The aim of these original arrivals was not to colonize but to establish "a refreshment station" for themselves on the East India trade route. They were uninvited to South Africa. They arrived as squatters. Had they all passed on to India, the history of black South Africa probably would have been different. But in 1657, five years later, nine of the two hundred arrivals decided to settle down at the Cape.

The following year, 1658, some Africans attempted to repel the encroachers. But their effort was unsuccessful. From that year of defeat onwards, the Europeans began to regard themselves as superior and masters over the native population. By 1875, the Dutch policy of refreshment station had changed to colonization.

Much of the lands owned by the Africans were seized. The discovery of gold and diamonds led to increased white immigration, domination and power. The Europeans expanded the original territory around the Cape Coast and claimed the Transvaal, Natal, the Orange Free State, and Transkei (Mandela's home state).

Leonard Thompson, a Yale University Professor of History Emeritus, has done a marvelous work in his book, *A History of South Africa* (2001) by painting a picture of South Africa before the second decade of the twentieth century.[15] In 1910, when the Union of South Africa was formed, there were four million Africans, half a million Coloreds, 150,000 Indians, and 1,275,000 whites.

By 1967, six years after South Africa had declared itself a Republic, there were 68% Africans, 19.3% whites, 9.8% Coloreds, and 3.0% Asians. Of the national population of

18.7 million, there were 12.75 million Africans, virtually without any rights in their own country. There were only 3.56 million whites in absolute control of everything. These whites called themselves "Afrikaners" and referred to Africans as "Kaffir," a Boer derogatory term for an infidel.[16]

In Qunu, however, Mandela had only a distant relationship with whites. For example, the local magistrate as well as the nearest shopkeeper were whites. The many travelers and policemen were also white. He was unaffected by them nor by the tribal rivalries of the time. But, at the home of Dalindyebo, Mandela was learning more and more about white people. And, this new knowledge was making him angry.

First, Mandela had to cross the road from boyhood to manhood. This crossing was through a rite of passage by circumcision at the age of sixteen in 1934. At the end of the celebration of this rite, Mandela heard a speech which painfully brought him face to face with the harsh realities of colonialism. The speech was made by chief Meligqili, the son of the regent.

Among other things, Meligqili had said:

> We have just circumcised [these boys] in a ritual that promises them manhood, but I am here to tell you that it is an empty, illusory promise. ... For we Xhosas, and all black South Africans, are a conquered people. We are slaves in our own country. ... The abilities, the intelligence, the promise of these young men will be squandered in their attempt to eke out a living doing the simplest, most mindless chores for the white man. These gifts today are naught, for we cannot give them the greatest gift of all, which is freedom and independence.[17]

Initially, Mandela was disappointed and unimpressed by "the abusive comments of an ignorant man who was unable to appreciate the value of the education and benefits that the white man had brought to our country."[18] Mandela had not yet been mentally de-colonized. But as the words of Meligqili began to sink deeper into him, Mandela realized that a seed had been sown in him, a seed that would one day germinate to make Mandela one of the greatest freedom fighters of our time.

Second, Mandela knew that he had to prepare himself educationally if he were to become a great leader. He attended the Clarkebury Boarding Institute. It was both a secondary school as well as a teacher training college. It was a Thembu college headed by Reverend C. Harris, "a white Thembu."[19]

The courses of instruction included carpentry, tailoring, and tinsmithing. The school functioned more like a military academy than a teacher training college. Here, Mandela learned discipline, a requisite for leadership, and excelled. He completed the program in two rather than the usual three years. He graduated with a junior certificate.

In 1937, at the age of nineteen, Mandela was admitted into the Wesleyan College in Fort Beaufort, "the largest African school below the equator." Dr. Arthur Wellington, an Englishman, headed this college which "provided a Christian and liberal arts education based on an English model." The school was supposed to produce "black Englishmen." Here, Mandela discovered his true identity as "an African, not just a Thembu or even a Xhosa."[20] It was an important step in his intellectual development.

During his final year at Wesleyan College, Mandela again came into contact with a famous Xhosa poet named Krune Mqhayi who visited the college and deeply touched his mind with his oral presentation. In his dramatic and poetic performance, Mqhayi said:

I predict that one day, the forces of African society will achieve a momentous victory over the interloper. For too long, we have succumbed to the false gods of the white man. But we will emerge and cast off these foreign notions.[21]

Mandela was astonished that an African was boldly protesting against colonialism publicly and in the presence of whites! He was aroused and motivated by the speech. His perception of whites began to change. "I saw that an African might stand his ground with a white man,"[22] Mandela noted in his autobiography. His racial inferiority had nearly been erased. He was done with secondary education and was now ready for the university.

Mandela was twenty-one in 1939 when he enrolled at the University College of Fort Hare, "the only residential center of higher education for blacks in South Africa." The university was located about twenty miles east of Fort Beaufort. World War II was just beginning.

Also, Mandela came under the academic influences of many African intellectual activists such as Professors Z. K. Matthews, who taught social anthropology and law, and D. D. T. Jabavu, who taught Xhosa, Latin, history, and anthropology. Jabavu was "a persuasive spokesman for African rights."[23] He had also founded the All-African Convention in 1936.

Mandela took courses in English, anthropology, native administration, law, physics, and interpretation. At the time, he aspired to be a civil servant. For extra-curricula activities, he engaged in cross-country running and soccer. He also learned ballroom dancing for the opportunity to meet and mingle with the who's who of that society.

He did not abandon his Christian faith. Instead, he seems to have made much progress by joining the Students

Christian Association which aided him in making "missionary" trips to the neighboring villages to teach Bible classes. One of the "missionaries" whom Mandela came to know was Oliver Tambo, a serious young science scholar, destined for great things.

Another organization which Mandela joined was the dramatic club. Once, he played the role of John Wilkes Booth, the man who assassinated Abraham Lincoln. Mandela regarded Lincoln's Gettysburg Address as "one of the greatest of all speeches."[24] Before his first year at the university ended, Jan Smuts, the former South African prime minister, visited the college to speak.

Mandela admired Smuts for being one of the pioneer leaders of the League of Nations. Smuts promoted freedom around the world, though he failed to stop the repression of black freedom at home in South Africa. Over the radio, Mandela would often listen to Winston Churchill's "stirring speeches" against Adolf Hitler. But he confessed that, at the time, he had only vaguely heard of the African National Congress (ANC) which had been founded in 1912.

In his second year at the University College of Fort Hare, Mandela's continuance at the college took a serious and different turn due to the events that will be discussed hereafter. He was nominated to stand election into the Student Representative Council (SRC). The student elections were held toward the end of the year. But, before the elections were held, all the students voted to boycott it in protest of the unsatisfactory quality and quantity of the food served at the college.

Dr. Alexander Kerr, the head of the college, would not tolerate the boycott. He threatened to expel the SRC members. Mandela wrote: "I was beginning to realize that a black man did not have to accept the dozens of petty indignities directed at him each day." When Mandela stood his ground, Dr. Kerr expelled him.

Mandela maintained that he "found it difficult to swallow the idea that I would sacrifice what I regarded as my obligation to the students for my own selfish interests." He added: "I resented his absolute power over my fate."[25] Mandela was the only student expelled because he refused to mortgage his conscience and his loyalty to the students

Thereafter, Mandela conspired with Justice, son of Dalindyebo, in order to escape to Johannesburg where he completed his degree work by correspondence with the University of South Africa. He received his Bachelor of Arts degree in 1942. At the beginning of 1943, he enrolled at the University of the Witwatersrand for a Bachelor of Laws degree.

The racist professors at this university made it impossible for Mandela to succeed in his academic career. After failing his exams several times, he opted to take the qualifying exam so that he could practice law and begin to support his family. Eventually he passed and, in August 1952, opened his own law office.[26]

Mandela's conception of freedom was linked to his political struggles against the oppressive government policies in his country. We have seen the many influences that led to his philosophy of freedom. But now with his academic pursuit completed and his law career in sight, Mandela could not turn a blind eye to the sufferings of his people.

Black South Africans had been waging a desperate struggle for freedom from 1658 when they tried to repel the white interlopers in their country. In the early twentieth century, their efforts were galvanized into the founding of the ANC, with stalwarts like Albert Luthuli, Robert Sobukwe and Walter Sisulu as their guiding lights.[27]

Mandela was introduced to the ANC in 1942 by Gaur Radebe, a law office colleague in Johannesburg. Gaur was a clerk, an interpreter and a messenger when Mandela was an apprentice in the law firm. Also, he was a firm believer in the work of the ANC. By August 1943, Gaur had convinced Mandela to march with Gaur and ten thousand others in a public demonstration.

Therefore, to understand Mandela's commitment to the ANC, one must understand the ideological origins of the ANC. The ANC was a non-racialist organization. Its leaders had come from different tribal groups. It advocated non-violent resistance to oppression. It preached full citizenship for all Africans in South Africa. On the other hand, the white regimes in South Africa made the work of the ANC very difficult, if not impossible.

Mandela painted a picture of what it was like to be an African in South Africa in the 1940s:

> An African child is born in an Africans Only hospital, taken home in an Africans Only bus, lives in an Africans Only area, and attends Africans Only schools, if he attends school at all.
>
> When he grows up, he can hold Africans Only jobs, rent a house in Africans Only townships, ride Africans Only trains, and be stopped at any time of the day or night and be ordered to produce a pass, failing which he will be arrested and thrown in jail. His life is circumscribed by racist laws and regulations that cripple his growth, dim his potential, and stunt his life. This is the reality, and one could deal with it in a myriad of ways.
>
> I have no epiphany, ... but a steady accumulation of a thousand slights, a thousand indignities, a

thousand unremembered moments, produced in me an anger, a rebelliousness, a desire to fight the system that imprisoned my people. There was no particular day on which I said, from henceforth I will devote myself to the liberation of my people; instead, I simply found myself doing so, and could not do otherwise.[28]

The first two paragraphs of the above quotation represents black life during the years 1910 to 1948 which historian Leonard Thompson called "the segregation era." It was followed by three decades (1948-1978) which he termed "the apartheid era." The third paragraph illustrates the spontaneous response by Mandela and his fellow black South Africans to white oppression.

And, lest anyone should think that Mandela had exaggerated the situation, I would refer them to Alan Paton's popular novel, *Cry, the Beloved Country* (1948), which depicted the true picture of the penal system in apartheid South Africa. The victims of that system were Africans. And, what was their crime? The color of their skin. I challenge such a thinker to opt to live all of his or her life under such a "wonderful" system!

It has been said that apartheid was merely about discrimination, segregation, and separation of the races. I beg to differ. Apartheid was much more than discrimination and segregation by whites against blacks. It was the dehumanization of black life. It was tyrannical, despotic, dictatorial, and in fact, a camouflage for "ethnic cleansing." Life for Africans was a living-hell. Naked power and the absolute corruption of that power had reached its zenith. Its destruction had become a sine-qua-non.[29]

With unmatched resoluteness against such monstrosity,

Mandela declared: "The struggle is my life." No threats, no bodily injuries, no incarcerations, not even the possibility of assassination or any kind of murder was going to deter Mandela from the struggle for the truest freedom for black South Africans. This was a noble commitment to liberty in its purest sense. The ANC was only a platform for the execution of his plans against white tyranny and oppression.

Mandela had learned that there was no easy walk to freedom from India's first prime minister, Jawaharlal Nehru. In 1952, Albert Luthuli, after being stripped of his status by the government, declared: "The Road to Freedom Is via the Cross."[30] This was a statement of principles for the ANC. It preceded the Defiance Campaign protest against apartheid laws held that year and in which Mandela was an important participant. For this, he was arrested on July 30 at his office by the state police. The struggle had really heated up.

Mandela believed that "apartheid is the rule of the gun and the hangman" and "was a war against the people." He declared "death to racism" and added: "I detest racialism, because I regard it as a barbaric thing, whether it comes from a black man or a white man." He contended that "racism pollutes the atmosphere of human relations and poisons the minds of the backward, the bigoted and the prejudiced."[31]

In his "No Easy Walk to Freedom" speech in 1953, when he was thirty-five, Mandela had stated that "To overthrow oppression has been sanctioned by humanity and is the highest aspiration of every free man." On June 26, 1961, during his press statement titled "The Struggle Is My Life," Mandela said that "No power on earth can stop an oppressed people determined to win their freedom."[32]

Mandela believed that "to men, freedom in their own land is the pinnacle of their ambitions, from which nothing can turn men of conviction aside." He said: "We do not want freedom without bread, nor do we want bread without freedom." And, "freedom cannot be given in doses: one is either free or not free – not half free."[33]

For holding to these convictions and practicing them, Mandela was harassed and arrested, on at least four separate occasions (1952, 1956, 1962, and 1963). He was imprisoned more than once and banned from seeing his wife; his writings and speeches were banned; he was banned from holding any kind of meetings; and on October 9, 1963, after having served nine months of a five year term, he was rearrested while in jail and tried again.

This trial lasted for about nine months. At the end of it, Mandela made one of his most memorable speeches:

> During my lifetime I have dedicated myself to this struggle of the African people. I have fought against white domination, and I have fought against black domination. I have cherished the ideal of a democratic and free society in which all persons live together in harmony and with equal opportunities. It is an ideal which I hope to live for and to achieve. But if needs be, it is an ideal for which I am prepared to die.[34]

The white South African Justice Quartus de Wet, who presided over the case, was unmoved. On June 12, 1964, de Wet sentenced Mandela and his ANC colleagues to life imprisonment for sabotage! This was the Afrikaner punishment on Mandela for daring to demand freedom and justice for himself and for his fellow black South Africans. Mandela spent 27 years in prison until he was released at 4:16 p.m. on February 11, 1990. He was 72 at the time of his release.

When word reached Mandela that he was about to be set free, he did a most surprising thing. On February 9, he met with a smiling president F. W. de Klerk who told Mandela that he would be released the following day. Thereupon, Mandela objected and said that he ought to be given a week's notice before the release in order that his family and the ANC could be better prepared.

Since he had been in prison for twenty-seven years, Mandela argued, he could wait a few more days. De Klerk was astonished. But, clearly, this action revealed how much Mandela was still in control of himself and of the ANC. Prison had not imprisoned his mind and spirit. Mandela insisted that he wanted to walk out of jail and be able to thank those who had cared for him and greet the people of Cape Town.

This was the kind of spirit with which Mandela left Victor Verster prison and re-entered the free society. A moment after he had left prison, Mandela "was greatly vexed by the fact that [he] did not have a chance to say good-bye to the prison staff." Imagine that! Among the things Mandela said in his first speech out of prison were:

> Friends, comrades and South Africans. I greet you all in the name of peace, democracy and freedom for all! I stand here before you not as a prophet but as a humble servant of you, the people. Your tireless and heroic sacrifices have made it possible for me to be here today. I therefore place the remaining years of my life in your hands.[35]

In April 1994, the ANC won the first nonracial election ever held in South Africa. It was the first time that Mandela had voted in his life, at the age of seventy-four. On that occasion, he recalled the words of Martin Luther King, Jr., and declared: "We can loudly proclaim from the rooftops – Free at last! Free at last!"[36] The week following, on May 10, the entire world celebrated the inauguration of Nelson Mandela as the first African president of the Republic of South Africa.

Freedom under president Mandela (1994-1999) was maintained, in keeping with his beliefs and convictions. Nobody was deprived of his life because of Mandela's need to seek revenge against his former enemies. He stunned the world when, on December 10, 1993, he shared the Nobel Peace Prize with F. W. de Klerk, the former state president who had released him from prison.

He said: "I wanted South Africa to see that I loved even my enemies while I hated the system that turned us against one another."[37] He publicly complimented de Klerk for his courage and admission that "a terrible wrong" had been done to black South Africans by the imposition of apartheid. He established The Truth and Reconciliation Commission which began its work in February 1996.

In an interview with *The New York Times* in March 1997, Mandela said: "You can't build a united nation on the basis of revenge."[38] So, he took time out to have tea with the widow of Dr. Hendrik F. Verwoerd, the architect of apartheid who resided in the all-white Boer enclave of Oranje. He also met with Dr. Percy Yutar, the state attorney who prosecuted him at the Rivonia Treason trial.

Unlike many of the other African leaders of his era, Mandela did not hunt down his former political rivals or opponents such as Mangosuthu Buthelezi, head of the Inkatha Freedom Party. He did not hang Lucas Mangope, the brutal dictator of Bophuthatswana, who insisted that he would keep the "independence" he had been given by the apartheid regime. Lucas even banned the ANC from campaigning in his area.[39]

Mandela negotiated with his enemies, including persons in the security forces, for a smooth transition of power. In the words of the Archbishop Desmond Tutu, the Nobel Peace Prize winner in 1984, "the nadir of despair"[40] occurred between 1989 and 1994, reaching its zenith in March 1990 just about when Mandela was released from prison. But Mandela advocated for peace, forgiveness, reconciliation and hope. In June 1999, he voluntarily relinquished power, having served for only one term in office.

Regarding how he thought of himself, Mandela said: "No single individual can assume the role of hero or Messiah." He added: "I'm an ordinary person, I have made serious mistakes, I have serious weaknesses." When asked what he wished for after death, he replied that "it would be very egotistical of me to say how I would like to be remembered. I'd leave that entirely to South Africans."

Furthermore, Mandela characteristically said: "I would just like a simple stone on which is written, 'Mandela'."[41] This is the kind of man whom I believe is the truest personification of the struggle for African freedom. Africa badly needs many Mandelas in positions of national leadership. May it be so with Thabo Mbeki, Mandela's successor and the current President of the Republic of South Africa.

Mandela did not write volumes on the African conception of freedom; but he lived and exemplified that concept. By his example, he totally conveyed to many that quality of human life which can rise above selfishness, meanness, revenge, and all that is contrary to human decency, harmony, and peaceful co-existence. This is not to say that he is flawless or an angel.

Desmond Tutu stated that Mandela's life and contribution is significant because Mandela "has articulated the aspirations of blacks in a particularly eloquent manner and been prepared to pay the price of his commitment. Twenty-seven years in jail is no plaything. And he has remained, even on the testimony of people who would have been his enemies, a gracious person."[42]

It should not be forgotten that Mandela was offered release from prison on conditions that would have jeopardized his honest commitment to the cause of black freedom in South Africa. But he deliberately rejected those offers. He is truly a great man. As news anchorman Ted Koppel has publicly acknowledged, when you stand in the presence of Mandela, you feel that you are standing in the presence of greatness.

Therefore, it is not surprising that David Aikman, a former senior correspondent for *Time* magazine, has included Mandela in his list of the six great souls who changed the twentieth-century.[43] Mandela is held in highest esteem and placed among people like Billy Graham, Mother Teresa, Aleksandr Solzhenitsyn, Pope John Paul II, and Elie Wiesel.

Africa will greatly miss this great son that God has given to her the day Mandela passes into the great beyond. He will ever remain one of the greatest champions of human freedom and liberty that this world has ever produced.

CHAPTER TWELVE

THE EIGHT MORAL
IMPERATIVES FOR FREEDOM

You shall know the truth, and the truth shall set you free.

— Jesus Christ

We come now to a discussion of the moral imperatives for freedom to thrive in Africa. Freedom, without morality, is an illusion. Like human rights, freedom has its moral imperatives. Freedom is not simply an "immunity from coercion," to use the phraseology of Reverend Father J. Bryan Hehir, author of "Human Rights From A Theological and Ethical Perspective."[1]

Freedom is an inalienable, universal, moral good which ought to be desired by all persons in all societies. Our concern here is not just with the "freedom from" State coercion and unnecessary intrusions into our personal lives. It is also with our deepest involvement with the "freedom for" the survival of African civilization in particular, and with human civilization, in general.

Therefore, I believe that intrinsic in any consideration of the idea of the quality of freedom must be the morality question. Freedom, I insist, is a supernatural gift of such inestimable value higher than anything that any human government may offer. Given this premise, I must attempt to examine the moral fulcra upon which freedom will stand.

I believe that there are eight such moral foundations for freedom. The first fulcrum is Truth. Others are Justice, Righteousness, Honesty, Faith, Hope, Love, and Equality. Without these foundations, freedom would perish or fail.[2] Let us analyze each of these in some detail.

1. Truth

What is truth? This is the 2,000-year-old question put forward by Pontius Pilate, the Roman proconsul of Judea about 30 A.D. I do not pretend here to have a definitive answer to Pilate's question. Many wise and insightful men and women, ancient and modern, have attempted to answer the question, however, and I will at least ateempt to share my thoughts regarding truth.

Ptah-hotep, a 24th century philosopher before Christ, stated that "truth is great and its effectiveness endures."[3] But this statement does not go very far at really defining truth. The Carpenter of Nazareth, Jesus Christ, made one of the most stupendous statements ever credited to man when he said: "I am ... the Truth" and later, as recorded in the Bible, added: "The Truth shall set you free."[4]

The English writer and critic, Samuel Butler (1612-1680), also thought of truth in terms of divine freedom when he said that "truth is precious and divine – too rich a pearl for carnal swine."[5] Butler's contemporary, Blaise Pascal (1623-1662), wrote that "we know the truth, not only by the reason, but by the heart."[6] Also, Henry Frederic-Amiel (1821-1881) observed that "truth is the secret of eloquence and of virtue, the basis of moral authority; it is the highest summit of art and of life."[7]

The imperishability of truth was set forth by author William Cullen Bryant (1794-1878) when he made those oft-quoted and immortal words which ring through the annals of history: "Truth, crushed to earth, shall rise again."[8] Such an imperishable good is found when people search for it.

Hence President Franklin Roosevelt told an impressive Temple University audience in Philadelphia, on February 22, 1936 that "truth is found when men are free to pursue it."[9] The philosopher, Mortimer J. Adler, listed truth, along with goodness, beauty, liberty, equality, and justice, as one of the six great ideas which have shaped history.[10] Sadly, in contemporary African life, few people cherish truth as a precious commodity.

In his book, *The Blessings of Liberty*, first published in 1956, Zechariah Chafee, Jr. (1885-1957) analyzed the relationship which exists between truth and freedom. First, he carefully examined John Milton's contention that truth generally emerges from the clash of ideas in a culture that exercises the freedom of expression. Chafee argued that those who opposed Milton's stance have often done so from an authoritarian perspective.

Chafee noted that Milton's opposers often believe that "truth is already possessed by those in authority." He responded by stating that there are a few men "good enough to decide what is bad for a great many people."[11] The perspective that the State already knows what is true and good enough for the people seems to persist in the minds and attitudes of State officials in much of Africa. This is a mindset that limits freedom.

The antagonists of Milton's view may argue that the

multiplicity of ideas in a culture of freedom does not produce truth. Discussion, they may further say, often leads to arguments and deadlocks, rendering the entire exercise worthless. Chafee refuted this charge by pointing out that "it is almost impossible to find men with the wisdom and incorruptibility which are essential for the task of controlling the minds of everybody else and killing bad ideas *en masse*."

In addition, Chafee said that "men in authority are tempted to identify their own policies with truth and to make opposing ideas criminal as a means of perpetuating those policies and their control of the government."[12] He maintained that when we speak of truth, we are often thinking of "the ultimate good desired" in three respects: purposeful existence, accurate facts, and choice.

Purposeful existence deals with "the existence and nature of God, the purpose of the universe, our relations to God and the universe and our fellowmen, [and] our reasons for living."[13] The second respect is about "those stubborn things in the external world;" for example, that the sun exists and shines each day is a truth.

The evidence to support this fact may be mistaken or deliberately falsified. Yet, the fact remains that the sun shines daily and exists. The third respect, choice, deals with the manner in which men and women can safely say what they wish or believe without governmental attack.

This choice allows for intellectual diversity rather than conformity or uniformity. It also allows for the weighing of matters before reaching a decision. Among the Ibibios of Nigeria, we say that he who prejudges a matter without first hearing from both sides of the case is a fool. Such a person has not properly weighed the matter. Truth can emerge from this "weighing" of matters. And freedom is connected to this search for truth.

Chafee noted that there are, at least, three obstacles to the automatic emergence of truth from the clash of ideas. The first obstacle, he said, is the possibility of the manipulation of ideas by those who own or control the organs of communication. Such owners determine what kind of information may reach the public. They decide on what is "true" information.

The second obstacle is the multiplicity of issues and arguments. One requires a deliberate calmness and care to sift the truth from the flux of opinions and ideas. Chafee conceded that, sometimes, this calmness is beyond human attainment. The third obstacle is with the age-old problem of our basic human nature. Chafee stated that the task of attaining truth in a culture of freedom is generally harder than we think.

He wrote: "Reason plays a smaller part in human affairs than we used to believe, but it still remains the best guide we have – better than any few men in places of authority, however exalted."[14] In the African situation, the words and insights of Chafee become very relevant and significant. Freedom must be founded upon the solid rock of truth.

Truth must be regarded as the moral basis of State governments desirous of freedom and universal liberty for all its people. A lying, conniving, and manipulative government which continues to presume that it possesses a few good men who are best endowed to think and act for all the citizenry cannot endure long. Soon it looses its credibility. The distrust and public contempt for its policies and officers will soon become evident.

African politicians must, therefore, understand that telling the truth is not necessarily just an aid to one's entry into heaven. It is a vital element for the survival of freedom, social progress, and economic development. When government records are wrong, deliberately falsified, or are deemed to be unreliable by the general public, how can such governments succeed? How can the public continue to have faith in such governments?

When election results are falsified, should an aggrieved opposing political party not protest? When census figures are manipulated and are falsified, how can the statisticians do their work correctly? When a Central Bank lies about the state of a national economy, would a government not be misled? If scientists deliberately lie about the results of their research, would not the entire medical apparatus suffer and even collapse?

And, if, for instance, the airport-controllers were to deliberately lie and deceive the pilots, would there not be major national air-traffic tragedies? Thus, in all these cases, we see the necessity, and indeed, the moral imperative to tell the truth. When, and if, we don't, we court trouble and do terrible harm to our countries. Eventually, our freedoms will come under fire!

Therefore, truth is not just a mere abstraction. It is an important fulcrum, a pillar which upholds our collective capacity to trust one another. It upholds our collective freedoms and enhances our progress. We cannot maintain freedom in Africa without a culture of truth-telling.

2. Justice

Benjamin Disraeli once observed that "Justice is truth in action."[15] Amos, the prophet who wrote a book of the Bible, said: "But let justice roll down as waters, and righteousness like a mighty stream"[16] Adler said that justice has a sovereignty unique to itself. He added that justice "regulates our thinking about liberty and equality. Without its guidance, certain errors are unavoidable and certain problems insoluble."[17]

Think about justice as truth in action. Adler argues that justice is, in fact, "the supreme value, a greater good than either liberty or equality."[18] Also, he insists that "only justice is an unlimited good."[19] It is justice which controls the extremities of liberty and equality and harmoniously allows the two to function in any society.

Without justice, Adler contends, there would be extreme egalitarians and libertarians fighting each other for supremacy and domination. He argues that our moral law "commands us to act for the common good or general welfare of the community of which we are members." "This," he insists, "is the contributive aspect of justice."[20] Hence, without justice, our freedom is impaired.

For me, I do not quarrel with Adler. In a world nearly gone mad with oppression, tyranny, and despotism, the issue is not about "extreme egalitarians and libertarians." For, how long have African peoples enjoyed extreme egalitarianism or libertarianism? Have they not been out of slavery and colonialism barely forty years ago?

However, what Adler says about the role of justice in any civic society is of paramount importance. It is the issue of fairness in human affairs. It is a matter which relates to equity. We are to stride toward freedom and liberty. We are also to strive toward equity. "Those who come to the Bar of Justice must approach it with clean hands," we are often told in a court of law. The Court of morality and justice is intolerant of corruption and favoritism.

In Africa, many horrendous wrongs and crimes have been perpetrated against some individuals and against some ethnic groups. I am thinking of the Ogonis in the delta region of southern Nigeria who have suffered so much mistreatment from the government and from the foreign oil companies because of their opposition to the pollution of their land.

I am also thinking of political domination by some oligarchic governments throughout Africa and the religious intolerance and destruction of lives and property in many countries such as the Sudan. In the Sudan, even children are sold into slavery and, often, such children belong to parents from the Christian south. I discussed this matter in Chapter Two.

Adler writes that justice is much more than fair play. The least that a wronged person or community expects is an acknowledgement of the wrong done and restitution for the wrong. Certainly, there can be no progress of freedom where injustices prevail. It is morally imperative that those who govern in Africa must "let justice roll down as waters" over the continent.

Contemporary Africa is a land plagued by many injustices. Therefore, righteousness must flow through their complex socio-political and economic structures like a mighty stream. Very little meaningful reconciliation and harmony among the African peoples can occur without justice. Without this justice, there can be no enjoyment of freedom. African leaders must remember this: oppression does not always last forever.

3. Righteousness

King Solomon of ancient Israel said that "righteousness exalts a nation; but sin is a reproach (disgrace) to any people."[21] He added: "It is an abomination for kings to commit wickedness; for the throne is established by righteousness."[22]

Since righteousness appears to be such an important element for the sustenance of political power, then it is stupidity for African leaders not to consider carefully the role of righteousness in the maintenance of such political power. To analyze this matter further, let us step back and examine briefly what we mean by "right" and "right doing."

Generally, people often think and talk in terms of the "good" and the "right." The concept of right is part of our human experience and reality. According to one scholar, the idea of right presupposes that "men carry on their lives in groups that require some modes of organization and regulation involving practices, rules, and institutions."[23]

Right falls within the juridical framework in our thinking and involves a system of laws or rules enjoined upon human beings and constituting our moral law. It would be meaningless or even nonsensical to say that an action is right if there is no such thing as rightness or if the opposite sense was implied.

Laws are codified morality. They constitute a body of rules and regulations regarding what is right conduct or right doing. For the ancient Hebrews, it was the Decalogue which fulfilled this purpose. For the Greeks, the *nomos* "had an incipient juridical character."[24]

Since that time, every society of man has developed its *nomos* which is binding upon all, whether the individuals belonging therein agree to it or not. This is often done in the name of utilitarianism. In this way, the *nomos* becomes the normative moral code for that community. So we had the Code of Hammurabi, King of Babylon (1792-1749 B.C.), for an example.

In pre-colonial times, Africa had its own *nomos* and there are many examples that can be cited. Professor Chancellor Williams spent over sixteen years studying such indigenous African constitutions derived from customary law and practices. The Fanti Constitution has been mentioned already. But we can also cite the Kano Chronicle which offered the political and constitutional history of the city.

Early Christian theology held that the *nomos* was derived from God and that all right doing was part of man's obedience to God. In Islamic thought, there is a parallel belief that man must live in submission to the will of God. Christians received their ideas of right and right doing from the Judeo-Hebraic tradition and ethics.

I believe that the modern and secular idea about what is right centers around the views of Jeremy Bentham (1748-1832), who first coined the term utilitarianism. Here, right actions are those which maximize the general good or welfare and reduce negative consequences. In the nineteenth century, this notion of right was furthered by John Stuart Mill, Bentham's disciple.

Even at the time of Bentham, the utilitarian notion of what is right was opposed by his contemporary, Immanuel Kant (1724-1804). Kant believed in an *a-priori* conception of right in which man was assumed to possess an inherent sense of what was right or wrong. Kant called this the "categorical imperative."

Every person, Kant argued, has the inherent desire to be respected and be treated properly. In the early years of the twentieth century, Kantianism and utilitarianism came under fire. They were vehemently opposed by the English philosopher William David Ross (1877-1971) who, in his book, *The Right and the Good*, argued that utilitarianism was an inadequate moral theory "because it is inconsistent with the moral convictions of the ordinary man."[25]

Ross said that what is right for an individual may not be necessarily right for the society and vice-versa. He argued that this was the problem with utilitarianism: the submerging of individual rightness for society's rightness. His central thesis was that "right acts can be distinguished from wrong acts only as being those which of all those possible for the agent in the circumstances, have the greatest balance of *prima facie* rightness ... over *prima facie* wrongness."[26]

In my view, Ross only complicated matters through some intellectual jargon. He failed to solve the basic problem of why the "thoughtful and well-educated" often fail to do the right things. Author Clarence Irving Lewis serves us better when he insists that "every man can know his duty."[27] This takes us back to the Kantian view that the sense of rightness or wrongness is ingrained in each of us.

As Victor Grassian had suggested, we can combine the theses of Kant and Bentham and say that whatever the case, the necessity of right doing exists for the survival of an orderly and civic society. It is at this juncture that freedom serves the cause of rightness by allowing each of us to do the right thing.

Freedom speaks to our consciences and our will impels us to do the right things. Freedom, however, implies that we have the choice to do wrong. But doing the right thing also serves freedom by preserving it from corruption. In the theological jargon of King Solomon, righteousness (that is, doing the right thing) exalts (that is, uplifts) a nation.

The opposite sense (that is, sin or doing the wrong things) brings about catastrophic results leading to national degradation (reproach). Political leaders who ignore this truth do so at their own peril. In the African situation, we have tended to be at the opposite spectrum of this equation.

See what Africa has become in these past forty years! A land where many of her brave and brightest ones have fled from the oppressors in black skins. A land inundated with economic and political woes. A land where political leaders seem to know nothing about fairness, rightness, and decency. A land where the government leaders appear not to have learned anything from history. They seem to be totally lost about rightness and wrongness.

The tragedy is that anyone who dares to speak out for rightness is persecuted, demonized, and even slaughtered.

The unnecessary shedding of innocent blood is no longer deemed to be a grave error by the despots. Our sensitivity toward *a-priori* rightness appears to have been blunted. We have no prophets to denounce this trend. Those who attempt to do so are roundly apprehended and incarcerated into where they often are murdered in their dungeons.

Without righteousness, freedom is bound to come under fire. Therefore, it is imperative that African nations seek to uphold righteousness in order that freedom may flourish. The African El-Dorado must include righteousness. Africans must heed the words of Henry David Thoreau who said: " It is not desirable to cultivate a respect for the law, so much as for the right."[28] A people that fail to heed this solemn admonition will certainly perish.

4. Honesty

I was reared up in the days when, at the Secondary school level, I was taught to believe that honesty is the best policy. As a young boy, my father reinforced this belief at home, rigidly forbidding theft and dishonesty. To tell a lie was a very serious punishable offence.[29] For several years, I wondered who made the statement that honesty is the best policy. Now, I know that it is attributed to author Miguel de Cervantes (1547-1616).

Authors Shailer Mathews and Gerald Birney Smith define honesty as "the disposition to deal uprightly and justly, having especial regard for the rights and property of others; a virtue based on a recognition of the social order."[30] What this implies is that honesty provides the basis for contractual obligations and agreements. The parties to such contracts do so in good faith and believe that they will not be defrauded or duped.

There would be no sense to contract where there is the slightest likelihood for dishonesty. Men and women simply do not enter into such contracts unless they are under some duress or hallucination. Freedom of action is enhanced where honesty prevails. Conversely, dishonesty leads to mistrust, contentions, a demand for redress and justice; and when justice is denied, sometimes, violence occurs as a result.

No society can function smoothly where people always feel that they are about to be cheated in business transactions. Hence, the goal of many governments is to promote the virtue of honesty. This is one reason why there are courts of law. The legal system is built upon the premise that men and women prefer honest deals and the courts are meant to enforce this rule. They are duty bound to uphold equity, justice and honesty.

There is a desperate need to inculcate the habit of transparent honesty among Africans if freedom will prevail. Over the past forty years, Africans have tended to run amok after the god of materialism. Rather than pursuing what is preeminent in life, that is, the development of the soul and the preparation of that soul to meet its maker, modern Africans have become drunk with the wine of greed, avarice, and covetousness.

Africa cannot continue to tolerate a society of dishonest public servants, fraudulent businessmen, and amoral political leaders. We cannot continue to tolerate a socio-political system that is more and more advancing the fortunes of the kleptocrats. We cannot continue to promote national heroisms based upon the cult of persons who become wealthy by dishonest means. We must root out corruption at all cost.

The place to begin this exercise is not at the State level but in the home. Then comes the school level. Parents who desire and love freedom must no longer take it for granted that their children will grow up to become honest and law-abiding citizens without this ethical instruction in the home. I believe that a time should come when we ought to hold parents responsible for the crimes of their minors. Somebody has to pay for the cost of the crimes of these juvenile delinquents.

There should be a return to rigorous discipline. The religious bodies throughout Africa have a duty to re-dedicate themselves to the cause of ethical and moral renaissance. If we fail in this pursuit, we shall surely reap the whirlwind of social, political and economic unrests. African freedoms cannot survive without the virtue of honesty.

5. Faith

The fifth moral imperative for freedom is faith. An old Jewish writer defined it as "the substance of things hoped for, the evidence of things not seen."[31] He went on to catalog the things which faith can accomplish.

John W. Gardner, who served under six American presidents and was once the Secretary of Health, Education and Welfare, wrote in his book, *On Leadership* (1990), that faith is the vital vehicle for the release of our human possibilities. "When the faith is present in the leader," he said, "it communicates itself to followers with powerful effect."[32]

In *Wealth 101: Getting What You Want – Enjoying What You've Got* (1992), John Roger and Peter McWilliams insist that faith is a generative factor, a catalyst for success. They preferred to use the term "faithing" to portray the "action to the concept of faith."[33] In the matter of freedom, faith is what makes it work. It is always what has made it work. It is what will always make it work.

Without faith, it is nearly impossible to count on man to allow the free exercise of liberty. Without faith in the value of freedom, it will never persist. Faith is what lifts the eyes of freedom to see the triumph of good over evil, the triumph of democracy over oligarchy, and the victory of liberty over tyranny.

Faith is a very powerful force in our human experience. Faith does not cohabit with fear under the same roof. One is positive and productive. The other is paralyzing and destructive. Faith promotes freedom. And, Africa desperately needs men and women of faith who love freedom and will advance its cause.

If the leaders of Africa truly had faith in their peoples, they would promote the peoples' freedoms. But, if African leaders are men and women driven by fear and paranoia, men and women who, at the least instance of a dilemma, sneak by night to the witch doctor to seek counsel from the occult, they will become misguided, paralyzed in terms of their leadership abilities, and eventually, cruel and autocratic. Such has been the case in many parts of Africa.

It should become evident to modern African leaders that fear enhances oppression and tyranny. Barbara Ward, author of the book, *Faith and Freedom* (1954), wrote that "fear alone is a poor counselor because it is essentially negative." She added that fear is the open path to "the line of least resistance in politics [which] tends toward the full apparatus of totalitarian rule."[34]

Faith, however, is a positive response to crippling fear. The Bible says that fear brings torment. St. Paul, the apostle, stated that we live by faith, not by sight.[35] For example, we take the medicine prescribed by a doctor by faith in the belief that the doctor knows what he is prescribing. We travel by air by faith in the expertise of the pilot. We rarely question the pilot's credentials before hopping into the aircraft.

And even if the pilot were to satisfy our querulous minds and showed us his or her certificate of flying, we would still need some measure of faith in the ability of the aircraft to lift up and zoom into the cloudy, blue or stormy skies. Every day, we are always exercising some amount of faith in something. Faith always demands some amount of risk-taking.

Faith looks steadfastly far beyond the risks of an action and on to the visions, dreams, and the expected ends of it. Barbara Ward insightfully said that faith also leads to material achievements and not the other way around. The contemporary idea of the reduction of man to a mere thing or property is rooted in fear and often prepares the ground for our surrender to dictatorship and slavery.

Ward noted that this reduction of man to the level of a mere thing is the hard lesson to be learned from the history of Anglo-American slave trade and slavery. But faith raises man up to the summit of his inherent greatness and grandeur. Man is always yearning to be free and creative. Man always aspires to succeed in life. Faith will help freedom to accomplish these expectations. But a government guided by fear and suspicion cannot realize the people's potential because the people would soon have left all their initiatives and creativity behind.

If you asked me why Africa is still backward and poor and lags behind in the advance toward prosperity and progress, compared to other countries, my answer is that there is an acute poverty of thought, initiative, and creativity because of the prevailing clouds of dictatorship and tyranny throughout the continent. After forty years, Africa seems to have lost her vision and dreams. It is a ship marooned on the high seas of misdirection and despair. Who will save her?

Africa is being run by a cabal of visionless men in army uniforms. An ideal State is usually run by wise men and philosopher-kings, not by men whose only training is to fight and destroy. Africa's current rulers are heartless military autocrats. They are liliputians in matters of faith and leadership.

They ought to step aside and let the people save themselves from the nightmare of hopelessness. The people can reclaim their faith in their God-given right of freedom. It is their birthright. Faith and freedom can lead Africa on to a new renaissance. Unless there is a re-birth of genuine interest in letters and the arts, Africa is doomed!

Barbara Ward, already cited, reminds us that faith always rebels against meaninglessness. She says that "faith is not a matter of convenience ... It is a question of conviction and dedication and both spring from one source only ... from the belief in God as a fact, as a Supreme Fact of existence."[36]

She adds that "a recovery of faith in God is necessary as a safeguard of ... freedom."[37] She points out that the fundamental root of Western freedom lies in "the infinite value of each human soul before God and the infinite respect each man owes to his neighbor's liberty and well-being."[38] I may safely say that what Ward states here is not peculiar nor unique to Western culture.

As Dr. Ayittey has shown in his writings, it is a universal phenomenon that African peoples also desire dignity and respect. Man constantly longs for a higher, nobler calling in life. No one wants to be debased. Those who deny this are often the apostles of oppression. However, the contours and progress of history teach us otherwise.

Yet, man will often return to his right track, looking beyond the present and the mundane, preparing to meet his maker as he draws closer to death. He religiously exercises faith in this pursuit. He cannot but be a religious animal of faith. He was born with faith. And he dies hopeful that by faith he has made peace with his maker.

Ward also made the sweet remark that "religion is not abolished by the 'abolition' of God; the religion of Caesar takes its place."[39] When religious faith vanishes due to man's rebellion against God, he still wants something upon which to hang his faith. Rather than continue in a vacuum, man usually returns to a political faith.

A charismatic, political demagogue may emerge to channel such a faith toward some selfish ends. This is what happened in Germany in the 1930s. Nazism represented such political faith in Germany. German nationalism became the religion for the propagation of their new political faith. And Hitler was the god of this cult and State religion. Africans should never forget the lessons from German history.

Elsewhere, I have argued that authentic Christian faith promotes the separation of Church and State.[40] It prevents the deification of the State. I also believe that authentic Christian faith is intolerant of any political apotheosis. Now, I may say that even our African traditional religion is intolerant of atheism and the deification of the State.

This is what Professor John Mbiti meant when he wrote that Africans are notoriously religious and that, in African traditional belief, there were no atheists. So, even our traditional religious mode of thinking about the universe is undergirded by faith. Yes, Africans may be notoriously religious; but they are not without faith.

This faith must be an authentic faith, not the present kind of Westernized faith, corrupted and aimed at the commercialization of the sacred and the merchandization of religion. The kind of faith which I insist upon is that which loves God for His own sake, which loves man for his worth's sake, and which respects man for his potential.

As Barbara Ward best puts it, "God is known by means of love. Love in this sense has nothing to do with emotion or sentiment. To love is to desire the Good."[41] There is no doubt in my mind that many Africans desire "the Good." All they ask for is to be left alone to exercise their freedom in creativity and, thereby, bring about progress and prosperity for themselves and others.

6. Hope

Dr. Billy Graham, the greatest American evangelist of our time, has said that "perhaps, the greatest psychological, spiritual, and medical need that all people have is the need for hope."[42] He adds that "hope is both biologically and psychologically vital to man. Men and women must have hope."[43] In Africa's Nigeria, the greatest casualty of the Sani Abacha regime from 1993 to 1998 was hopelessness.

Robert E. Luccock, the Emeritus Professor of Social Ethics at Union Theological Seminary, included hope in his list of the seven "great resources to live from."[44] Hope, therefore, is a very important element in our human experience. But, what really is hope?

Author Jill Haak Adels, offers a description of its essential characteristics in his book, *The Wisdom of the Saints: An Anthology* (1987). He writes:

> The virtue of hope has the possession of God and eternal happiness as its object. Its grounds are God's goodness, his power, his faithfulness, and, most specifically, the resurrection of Christ. Without hope, faith is weakened or disappears.[45]

Here, Adels's description of hope would not satisfy the secularist. But, what do most hardcore secularists know about hope, anyway?

Let us look at the statement by Gregory Nyssa (330-395 A.D.) who was the brother of St. Basil the Great, a fourth-century bishop of Caesarea. Nyssa wrote that "hope always draws the soul from the beauty that is seen to what is beyond, always kindles the desire for the hidden through what is perceived."[46]

Author Aly Wassil provided us with an insight about the relationship that exists between hope and freedom when he wrote, in his book, *The Wisdom of Christ* (1965), that "the chained intellect of man sees merely the past fragments of history; his free spirit alone can glimpse eternity."[47] Thus, there are two important things about hope that should be borne in mind.

First, the Christian author Hy Pickering made the point that "in the Scriptures hope simply refers to the future, never to the uncertain,"[48] which is the more common to conventional thinking. Hope is often linked to religious faith and makes sense to many only in that context.

The second thing that we must note also is the futility of hoping *only* in this present world. St. Paul, the author of about two-thirds of the New Testament books in the Bible, ably argued the point when he repudiated this kind of mundane faith. About 55 A.D., he wrote that "if in this life only we have hope in Christ, we are of all men most miserable," and to be pitied.[49] Why? Because mankind apart from God is doomed. The "positivists" cannot change this verdict.

Hope, therefore, always points to a future reality, to a certainty of better conditions. As the apostle Paul once asked: "Who hopes for what is already attained?" While faith provides the fuel which sustains us in our present need to press on with life, it is hope that greases the engines of our drive toward a future reality.

While faith says: "Freedom is attainable," it is hope which assures us that freedom is awaiting us if we persevere to the end. We cannot quit. Faith and hope always work hand in hand to sustain freedom. Despair will not lead us to the freedom-land. Africans must remember that the freedoms which the Western countries seem to have today were not won in a day, in a decade, nor in a century. Hope sustained the freedom-fighters of the past.

Therefore, Africans must believe not only that they will overcome the present state of oppressions and tyrannies, but also know that freedom is an attainable reality. It is not yet *uhuru*. Keeping this kind of hope in mind, they should not be easily intimidated by the brutal iron of despotism. Hope will eventually win the day.

7. Equality

The seventh moral imperative for freedom is equality. Those who love freedom and yet despise equality are fools. For freedom cannot be sustained in a culture of inequalities. "What is good for the goose is good for the gander." An example of the inconsistency between freedom and inequality can be seen in the evolution of the American Republic. Americans fought a terrible civil war from 1860 to 1865 because of inequality among the races in the Republic.

The much maligned Thomas Paine, author of *The Age of Reason* (1793), an equally despised book by some Christians, wrote: "I believe in one God and no more, and I hope for happiness beyond this life. *I believe in the equality of man*; and I believe that religious duties consist in doing justice, loving mercy, and endeavoring to make our fellow creatures happy."[50]

Contrary to the popular Christian view which assumed that Paine and all his writings were atheistic, Paine had a religious conception of equality. Also, Robert Maynard Hutchins (1899-1977) believed that "equality and justice, the two great distinguishing characteristics of democracy, follow inevitably from the conception of men, all men, as rational and spiritual beings."[51]

Thomas Jefferson, who is credited with the writing of the Declaration of American Independence, stated: "We hold these truths to be self-evident; that *all men are created equal* ..."[52]   But, in his book, *The Love of Liberty* (1975), Leonard E. Read distanced himself from this popular Jeffersonian creed.

Leonard E. Read argued that "everything in the Cosmos ... is unique; things are neither identical nor equal; even for a single instant." He added: "Women are no more equal to men than any woman is equal to any other woman or any man equal to any other man."[53]   So, then, what is equality? How is it related to freedom?

Mortimer J. Adler, already mentioned, analyzed three aspects of equality which can help us understand more clearly the kind of equality which is necessary for freedom. The three aspects were: personal and circumstantial equality, declarative and prescriptive equality, and equality in kind and degree.[54]

Adler argued that the first aspect refers to "the endowments that persons bring into this world at birth and that which derives from their attainments."[55]   This kind of equality relates to the levels of intelligence, education, ability, disposition and environment in a person's life. Two people, he said, may be equal in these respects.

Adler maintained that circumstantial equality or inequality refers to the degree of opportunity which a person may have. For example, two people may start a race at the same points but the speed by which they run may differ. Circumstantial equality relates to the matter of competition, *ceteris paribus*. Equality before the law, without favoritism, is another example of this first aspect of equality.

The second aspect is about the equality *that is* or *is not*, namely, "declarative" equality. Adler termed the equality which *ought to be* as "prescriptive" equality and contended that the social contract theory is a myth. Accordingly, he wrote that "nature is neither just nor unjust in the gifts it bestows. Only human beings can be just or unjust in the proposals they advance with regard to an equality of conditions."[56] Leonard Read put it this way: "Let men and women find their place according to the merit of each individual person."[57]

I believe that the main problem with Adler's and Read's positions regarding equality is that they do not support the right to justice for past wrongs or exploitations. They would not support the right to reparations for the injustices suffered during slavery and colonialism. And merit is not often distributed justly or equally within any social order or community. There are always some people capable of having more than the lion's share of a society's amenities and benefits.

This criticism brings us to the third aspect of Adler's notions of equality which is about the equality in kind and degree. Adler believed that this third aspect is the most difficult and most important aspect of equality to be considered when defining equality. As an example, Adler pointed to the equality of citizenship. This is the equality which flows out of one's political liberty. Here, unjust conditions can be rectified.

But, Adler cautioned that there can still be inequality which flows out of the *status* of office, for instance, the President or Minister of the State. He emphasized that the equalities which we are entitled to are basically those that justice allows or requires, no more and no less.[58] Since human beings are naturally endowed with freedom of the will and the power of free choice, they have the right to such equalities but only of the kind which justice allows.

Because we are all human beings, we are equally entitled to dignity and respect for our life. In all other respects, our entitlement to equality is only circumstantial.[59] Adler's central point is this: "To say that all human beings are equal in their common humanity is ... to say that all have the same species-specific properties."[60] Slavery and oppression negate the entitlement to a common equality.

It is interesting to note that Leonard E. Read was opposed to the kind of equality which negates competence and merit and promotes quotas and mediocrity. In his book mentioned earlier, he gave the example of situations where women were being employed *simply* because they were women. Another example was a situation where a student was admitted into a university, not because of good grades, but *simply* because of the race of the student.

He upheld the kind of equality which was based upon the uniqueness of the individual, but not that based upon preferential treatment. In all likelihood, Read would not have approved of affirmative action programs intended to ameliorate for the injustices of the past. I am not sure what Adler's position would have been. Both men have to be clear on their solutions for historical injustices and inequalities. It is not enough to say: "let bygones be bygones."

Having learned what we mean by equality, we may affirm that we are all born with the common gift of thinking. Adler contends that apart from this common endowment, "there is no other respect in which all human beings are equal."[61] Thus, Jefferson's assertion that we are born equal is not as self-evident as it might purport to be. The assertion does not take care of the equality of conditions or circumstances.

Adler himself stated that, "individual members of the [human] species differ from one another either by innate endowment, genetically determined, or by voluntary attain-ment."[62] He concluded that "more liberty than justice allows is possible in society, but more equality than justice requires cannot be sustained."[63]

As we have seen, no society can have the extremes of libertarianism and egalitarianism. The equality which sustains freedom is that which has a balance. It is the equality or even the inequality which respects our humanity. The current situation in Africa is corroding and corrupting our basic humanity. It is one which treats Africans as unworthy or undeserving of this basic humanity.

Nobody is asking for the political, economic, religious and intellectual freedoms and equalities from these African despots in the absolute sense. The ordinary African is simply asking for the equality of humanity, for the liberty which justice allows. We demand no more and no less.

In my Secondary school days, I read a book called *Animal Farm*, in which a supposed condition of equality was to be enjoyed by all the animals on the farm. But, as it turned out, some animals were "more" equal than others. This is the picture of today's Africa. Decolonization was supposed to bring to all Africans a new birth of freedom from the imperialists.

But, alas, alas, a new kind of "animal farm" has emerged in Africa. For how long shall the common man continue to tolerate this kind of situation? The conditions of life have almost become worse than when the colonialists were in charge! I have lived through both worlds and I know that I am not alone in making this verdict.

Africans leaders must promote equality in order that the people may be free to join in the global march toward progress and prosperity. They must remember the words of Barbara Ward when she said that "no work of civilization is possible without the cooperation of more than one human group."[64] Treating people as equals will make this successful in Africa.

8. Love

The last and eighth moral imperative for freedom is love. Emerson once said that "the power of love, as the basis of a

State, has never been tried."[65] Love is an important fulcrum for freedom. We shall examine its meaning and relationship to freedom.

Let us begin with an observation by Sir Philip Sidney (1554-1586), the English patron of scholars and poets. Sidney wrote that "to define love is impossible, because no words reach to the strange nature of it: they only know it, which inwardly feel it."[66] In spite of this apparent difficulty in defining love, it still remains the sweetest word in the languages of world culture.

In all societies, and at different times in world history, great minds, thinkers, and seers have sought to define love. The literature in every land and culture is replete with the sentiments and actions of men and women who profess to love or are in love. Therefore, we can begin by asserting that there is such a thing as love which many have fought and died for throughout history.

If there is no such reality as love, then, how did it ever come to be invented or invoked? Men do not spend their lives wrestling with the nonsensical or with that which is not real unless they are thoroughly demented. But, we know that many people have paid the supreme sacrifice(s) for Cupid's sake. The 33-year-old carpenter of Nazareth did give his life for love's sake. Human beings have never had too much of love!

This complex term which we call love in the English language, (*ima* in the Ibibio), has three important descriptive aspects: *agape*, *philia*, and *eros*, all Greek words. The first represents the divine love of God made manifest to man by his mercy and grace. The second is that which friends or families, mothers, fathers, sons, and daughters can share with one another. This is another level of love, often motivated by a sense of altruism and generosity.

The third represents the carnal and erotic desire for gratification of the flesh and is directed toward a perceived object of beauty. Often, this is the kind promoted by Hollywood enthusiasts in America. Much of the contemporary usage of the term love refers to this third aspect.

It is a sad commentary on our modern civilization that the nobler aspects of our highest emotion have been corrupted in the fashions we find today. But, J. Bruce Long writes that "love is the single most potent force in the universe, a cosmic impulse that creates, maintains, directs, informs, and brings to its proper end every living thing."[67] Obviously, Long is here describing the functions of love. According to him, Plato's concept of love was in terms of immortality when he wrote:

> Love ... is the quest for the knowledge of the good, the true, and the beautiful that is transformative. It is the veneration of wisdom ... love procreates things immortal within the realm of mortal existence, which arises out of the desire for supreme embodiments of immortality, the good, the true, and the beautiful. Love is the quest for the possession of the good for oneself for eternity.[68]

The Christian concept of love embraced both the Hebraic and Greek notions of the term. The Christian teaching on love is that God is LOVE Himself. Because God is love, He is able to exude love to His creatures and, in turn, expects them to love Him back "for his own sake," as Barbara Ward has insisted in her book.

The famed carpenter from Nazareth, Jesus, taught that the greatest responsibility which any man has is two-fold. There is the vertical dimension to love God with all of our heart, soul, and ability. There is also the lateral or horizontal dimension, a social dimension, to love our fellow man as we love ourselves.

This second part is difficult for most people who have never loved themselves. So, they go about hurting other people.

Jesus said that there were no other human responsibilities in moral law which surpassed these two responsibilities. By example, he showed that love always involves sacrifice and caring. Love involves servanthood. Love thinks, considers, and *acts* for the best interests of the other fellow first.

The best explication of love in the religious literature is to be found in the Bible, in St. Paul's first letter to the Corinthians, chapter thirteen, verses one through thirteen. The most excellent way for any man to live is by the way of love. It is only love which can and will move us beyond the limits of our comfort zones in human relationships.

In Christian theology, *agape* is the ultimate spiritual response of man to his God. It is the sublimest motivating factor in spiritual endeavor. We are to be like God, our heavenly father and creator, in our dealings with our fellow man in the socio-political and economic realms of life. We find then that because we must love our fellow man as God loves us, we cannot (indeed, dare not) terrorize, tyrannize, or oppress any member of God's creation.

Love will compel us to seek their best interests. This is something much more than philanthropy allows. Love will restrain us from harming His dear ones. Thus, those who love in this way can only be the true champions of freedom. The truest fulfillment of ourselves will find expression in the maximization of *agape* (love).

The Bible says: "We love him because he first loved us." We care for our fellow man because God has first cared for us. We respect other people because God first respected us by giving to each of us the freedom of choice to do right or wrong. As for *philia*, we enhance it when we aim at the excellence of *agape*.

I need not say much about *eros*. Those who love only for the gratification of themselves at this level will tell, regrettably, how this exercise and experience perverts. Perhaps, only Sigmund Freud can best help us here. But, I am for the highest elevation of man by that which is noble, meaningful, and immortalizes. I agree with what Emerson said, that the power of love, as the basis of a State, needs much of our attention today.

Therefore, African Churches and mosques have much work to do in the teaching of our people the art of love for one another. This is the essence of all true religions. Unfortunately, they have woefully failed in this respect. We have now so-called religious gurus who have committed apostasy by politicizing the sacred.

These blind religious gurus have carried their evils to the level that they have led the people to commit genocides and pogroms and indescribable barbarities in Rwanda and Burundi in 1994. In Kaduna, such barbarities shocked President Olusegun Obasanjo during his visit to that Nigerian city in February of 2000. Afterwards, Obasanjo told the nation: "I could not believe that Nigerians were capable of such barbarism against one another."

There is so much religious hostility in Africa which seems to make nonsense of the essence of any true religion and one's participation in it. But, real love promotes true patriotism, nationalism, and respect for the sanctity of human life. No true worshipper of the true God will engage himself in the wanton destruction of life. Love will protect our African freedoms.

In the foregoing paragraphs, I have attempted to show that freedom is preserved by the eight moral imperatives of truth, justice, righteousness, honesty, faith, hope, equality and love. If, as Plato once said in his book, the *Republic*, that "freedom

... is the glory of the State,"[69] then African leaders must promote freedom in order to have that kind of glory.

Freedom, individual or corporate, will not be preserved until Africans and their leaders rise up to embrace these eight moral imperatives. Then, and only then, shall we assure to ourselves and to our posterity the freedoms which we desperately need.[70]

CHAPTER THIRTEEN

TEN CHALLENGES
TO AFRICAN FREEDOM

If the Son of Man shall set you free, you shall be free indeed.

—- Jesus Christ

In this chapter, I want to examine ten challenges to African freedom. For so long we have been feeding at the junkyard of ethical relativism. And now, the consequences of the paralysis of morality is upon us. Who can we blame? Let me begin with a situation which prevailed in the United States in the early years of the twentieth century. This will provide a background for our understanding of the challenges to African freedom.

The United States emerged from its civil war in 1865, not to an arsenal of freedom for all her citizens, but to a relative state of unfreedom. For, although the war had been fought to free about four million of her people from slavery, a great number of Americans, especially the African-Americans, were not ushered into a new era of true freedom.

Many white Americans were not ready to accept the equality of the races.

The thirty-five years following the end of the civil war, just before 1900, have been described as "the nadir" of American history. They were characterized by Jim Crow, segregation, discriminations, prejudice, and the lynching of African Americans. Some scholars have referred to that era as the American apartheid. The era included the 1930s and ended with the rise of the Civil Rights Movement in the 1960's.

It was with that era in mind, which included the "Great Depression" years, that Herbert Hoover, the thirty-first president of the United States, wrote and published his book, *The Challenge of Liberty*. Hoover had become "anxious for the future of freedom and liberty of men."[1] American political, social, economic, intellectual and spiritual freedoms faced the threat of an eclipse due to the dislocations which accompanied World War I.

World War II was looming in the horizon. Greed in economic matters and greed for political power and for "the spoils system" seemed to rock the very foundations of American democracy. There were voices raised that called for Americans to abandon liberalism and to change their conceptions of government and of society.

In response to such calls and voices, Hoover released his book to emphasize that "liberty is a thing of the spirit – to be free to worship, to think, to hold opinions, and to speak without fear – free to challenge wrong and oppression with surety of justice." Hoover added:

> Liberty conceives that the mind and spirit of men
> can be free only if the individual is free to choose his
> own calling, to develop his talents, to win and to
> keep a home sacred from intrusion, to rear children

in ordered security. It holds he must be free to earn, to spend, to save, to accumulate property that may give protection in old age and to loved ones.[2]

Thus, Hoover defended American freedoms and democratic capitalism. He argued that the very foundations of modern civilization rested upon freedom and upon the free exercise of fundamental human rights. Hoover pointed out that there were some challenges to freedom and that such challenges were often violations to the American system and naturally led to the stifling of initiative and creativity.

Hoover concluded that "no country or ... society can be conducted by partly acknowledging the securities of Liberty and partly denying them, nor by recognizing some of them and denying others." "That," he wrote, "is part democracy and part tyranny."[3] What Hoover observed as challenges to American freedoms are no less true of the African situation.

There are many challenges to African freedom. One such challenge is the intolerable mindset of moneymania which tends to subvert the very essence or meaning of life. If unchecked, the ten challenges that I am about to highlight can and will forever destroy African liberty. I believe an anarchy is coming upon their heels which will be hard to prevent.

1. Hamartiology

I believe that one of the most serious challenges to freedom in Africa is the lack of a proper understanding of hamartiology. The Christian doctrine of hamartiology posits that man is a sinner, that he continues to sin irrespective of his status, and that he will eventually face God's righteous indignation and judgment *unless* he truly repents and is saved by the mercy and grace of God.

This doctrine is not hard for anyone to understand and accept. One only needs to look at the moral condition of the world today. There is only one reason why people will not accept this biblical truth – ego or pride. But this doctrine is a universalism which transcends nationality, class, ethnicity and gender.

The doctrine unapologetically insists that all men and women are sinners in the sight of God, irrespective of their religion. S. G. F. Brandon, the author of several books on comparative religions, held that the belief in sin and salvation dates back to 2400 B.C. in ancient Egypt.

Huston Smith, the author of *The World's Religions: Our Great Wisdom Traditions* (1991), stated that "the basic theological concepts of Islam are virtually identical with those of ... Christianity."[4] But, although this may be true, Islam does not seem to have a concrete doctrine of hamartiology. "The closest Islam comes to the Christian doctrine of original sin," Smith wrote, "is in its concept of *ghaflah*, or forgetting."[5]

But even Brandon agreed that the Koranic term *najah*, for salvation, implies the presence or acknowledgment of sin. The founder of Islam had come to warn men and women against the heinous sin of idolatry. However, Muhammad "did not regard mankind as being in a state of perdition owing to some original defect or sin, as in Christianity."[6] Nevertheless, Islam believes in a final Judgment in which there will be rewards and punishments.[7]

The application of the doctrine of sin is very important to political science and to freedom. It relates to the issue of political ethics and morality. (I do not believe in the secular notion of "ethics without God.") The doctrine implies that human governments can err and do err. They are not perfect political orders but imperfect.

Governments are made up of fallible human beings who are

prone to err. They are not sinless. Every constitutional arrangement and law must be understood within the context that they are not flawless. Therefore, no one person, not even a king in a monarchy, is flawless. Consequently, there must be checks and balances within the constitutional arrangements.

More importantly, however, the rulers under such constitutions must accept the fact that they are not sinless but are human beings who can make grave mistakes with grave consequences. They should not rule arbitrarily nor despotic. It seems that the leaders in modern Africa have forgotten this vital ingredient in the human experience.

The best intentions of human governments still leave room for errors and mistakes. The challenge, therefore, is for African leaders to earnestly "seek to do justly, to love mercy, and to walk humbly before God," their maker (Micah 6:8). This is the best way to insure a harmonious socio-political and economic order, one that constantly strives toward excellence, peace and freedom.

The opposite end which pretends to deny personal sinfulness or ignores its serious implications in governance is simply a delusion. This group of African leaders must stop pretending that they are political angels who can do no wrong. This mindset is at the root of the intolerance, despotism, and tyranny present in many African countries. African politicians must see themselves as others see them – comrades in human frailties.

But, much more important than this, I believe African leaders must also see themselves as God sees them, to whom they are accountable in the ultimate sense. Whether as civilians or military men and women, African leaders must bear in mind that one of the worst political philosophies which anyone can hold is one which has the self-assurance that he or she can never do wrong.

This kind of philosophy is also one that presumes that the leader is unaccountable to anyone. This is simply the grossest kind of political myopia and hypocrisy. Sooner or latter, such a leader comes to the bar of justice through death or a political overthrow. But, freedom is best enhanced by a just, moral, political process where the game is freely played on the green lawn of ethical and moral considerations.

2. Human Greed

On January 3, 1936, President Franklin Roosevelt told Congress that the Americans had "earned the hatred of entrenched greed."[8] And, centuries before Roosevelt, the ancient Chinese philosopher, Lao-tzu, said that "there is no greater disaster than greed."[9]

One may safely say that in today's Africa, politicians have not only entrenched greed as a national lifestyle; they have also courted no other social disaster than that which accompanies greediness. This is a sickening thought. The new generation has well emulated the older ones who were never the apostles of contentment.

During the brief period of my life, which has now run for more than half-a-century, I have witnessed men and women live as if greed had no costly repercussions! When I was a student at the Polytechnic at Calabar, Nigeria, I met such people. Then I became a civil servant, and met such people again. In my twenty-one years abroad, I have observed that such people are everywhere.

It seems to me that young Africans have no other nobler aspirations to live by than the multiplication of wives and children, an insatiable desire for the accumulation of material things, and ostentatious living. Even church-going people are increasingly imbibing this obnoxious "prosperity" theology. Recently, in America, there was even a television program called "greed!"

The challenge of greed to African freedom lies in the fact that life has been reduced to the level of sheer aggrandizement. In the craze competition thereof, there is bound to come a time of nemesis, of retributive justice, of social upheaval because the economic pie is just not large enough for everyone. Such an upheaval often brings social unrest that does not promote freedom but autocracy bolstered for the sake of law and order.

As long as the consciences of Africans are not directed away from greediness, and as long as the leaders do not set the example, there is bound to be a future fulfillment of the prophecy of Lao-tzu, that there is no greater disaster than greed. For, greediness is the twin brother of exploitation and oppression. In fact, greed neither cares for brotherliness nor for economic justice.

3. Inordinate Political Ambition

The author Donald Robert Perry Marquis (1878-1937) made two poignant statements which connect inordinate political ambition to our discussion. First, he stated that "ours is a world where people don't know what they want and are willing to go through hell to get it."[10]

Second, Marquis said that "there is bound to be a certain amount of trouble running any country; if you are president the trouble happens to you; but if you are a tyrant you can arrange things so that most of the trouble happens to other people."[11] What a fitting or apt description of presidential politics in modern Africa, especially during the military interregnums!

Many politicians in Africa want to lead their countries. But few of them know precisely what their countries really need; but they are willing to go through hell to get into political offices. They often have no tested political agenda nor philosophies. For example, in Nigeria, nearly every politician wants to be president. In the advanced countries, people give much thought to the idea of running for the presidential office.

In the advanced countries, party philosophies and manifestos are clear and generally understood by the populace. For example, in the United States, the Democrats are known for their liberalism and the Republicans are known for their conservatism. In Africa, political parties often seem to have only one objective – the presidential office and ministerial portfolios. The most ignorant and stupid politician may become the country's leader.

Even where there are party manifestos, these are sheer rhetoric and empty propaganda, to be discarded as soon as the elections are over. The winners of the elections then go on a binge of loot and plunder of the national treasury, the extent of the plunder and looting depending upon the personal ambitions and greed of the winning candidate.

Anyone who thinks that I am exaggerating should recall what happened in Nigeria soon after Shehu Shagari's government was sworn into office in 1979. Regarding that regime, a noted Nigerian scholar has stated that "the Second Republic was consumed by its own inadequacies, by the failure of the political actors even to work for their own survival."

This scholar concluded that "the performance of the Second Republic was a dismal failure, although large amounts of funds were expended on agriculture, shelter, and education."[12] The "predatory rule" by the military which lasted from 1983 to 1999 was no better. Ordinary Nigerians almost lost total confidence in the politics of their country.

The mistakes, failures and evils of the First Republic, which led to a terrible civil war in 1967, were quickly forgotten. The causes and lessons that should have been learned from the war were discarded. Inordinate political ambition took over the spirit of selfless national service and patriotism. The military came in again in 1983 and made things worse.

Even today, what one reads about the activities of politicians in the Third Republic in Nigeria does not offer much hope or comfort. The Umaru Dikkos are alive and well. In Nigeria, politics means more than life itself. Why? Because politics is a very lucrative business. The super-politicians know how to swindle and defraud the country. That is the real challenge to freedom.

Some may be tempted to say: "Farewell to freedom. Welcome, lasting plutocracy!" But let us not continue to deceive ourselves anymore. Either Africans really want freedom and would be ready to die for it, or we must submit to the dictatorship of the kleptocrats or of the plutocrats.

The incipient inadmission by African politicians that governments are human creations for the general good and not the tinker-houses for the robber barons constitutes one of the greatest challenges to the exercise of freedom on the continent. Inordinate political ambition is at the root of these affairs in African politics.

For the sake of the survival of the African republics, each of us must re-consider what should be the main motivating factor for those who yearn for political office: inordinate political ambition or service to mankind. We must decide when we shall cease to elect men of inordinate ambition to run our public affairs. The sooner Africans make this decision, the better the chances for the survival of freedom.

4. Betrayal of Public Trust

Politicians and preachers have something in common. Both function best under a climate of trust – public or private. Betray this trust and you are finished. The reason why African politicians who betray public trust are never finished with is that they often resort to mindless brutality. But it is true that when trust is violated, the proper running of the State becomes difficult.

In a true democracy, the people would vote out politicians who betrayed public trust from office. Or, the particular public servant caught in this act of betrayal would resign. In an autocracy, the ruler(s) sit(s) tight, ready to destroy everything. The consequence of this unwillingness to resign is popular discontent and a gradual descent into chaos and anarchy. In Africa, corrupt public leaders rarely resign.

In Nigeria, the civilians enjoyed power for only ten years, from 1960 to 1966 and from 1979 to 1983. The military ruled for a total of 29 years (1966-1979 and 1983-1999). As at the end of 2001, the civilians have been back for a little more than two years. How much of the public trust is there? Does anyone in government even care about this notion of public trust?

I believe that many African leaders know something of the importance of public trust. But I believe that they simply disregard it because **they think that the people are stupid**. They believe that the populace are weak enough not to hold them accountable or demand justice. But they have not learned anything from history. They do not understand the power of the powerless.

The ordinary people of Africa are not stupid. Neither are they altogether powerless. They know of the peoples' revolution in the Philippines where the people overthrew an evil government. They are aware that the mighty Soviet Union collapsed. Common sense tells them that nothing lasts forever in this world. It appears that they are patiently waiting for the right time to strike back.

Therefore, it is high time that there be a revival of the political principle of public trust in Africa. This principle would hold public servants and leaders accountable for their actions while in office. This is particularly needed to hold former military leaders accountable since they were never elected and seized power by the barrel of the gun.

In Nigeria, it is high time to require that Muhammed Buhari and Ibrahim Babangida should give an account of their stewardship. A thorough house-cleaning is necessary if we ever expect or desire a return to political stability. The tendency to shield these men from accountability will only increase national contempt, distrust, and apathy. In the end, there will be a significant threat to peace and freedom if African leaders continue to betray their public trust.

5. Intolerance

Thomas Paine once said that "toleration is not the opposite of intolerance, but is the counterfeit of it. Both are despotisms: the one assumes to itself the right of withholding liberty of conscience, the other of granting it."[13] In Africa, there are five kinds of intolerance that come to mind: political, religious, economic, intellectual and social. I shall endeavor to analyze each of these.

Also, author Maurice Cranston said that "toleration is a policy of patient forbearance in the presence of something which is disliked or disapproved of."[14] Intolerance is, therefore, the opposite of this patient forbearance. Cranston argued that toleration must thus be distinguished from freedom or liberty "precisely because it implies the existence of something believed to be disagreeable or evil."[15] He maintained that we do not tolerate what we enjoy.

Toleration also means "to put up with." Cranston stated that alternatives to toleration are persecution and suppression.

"Intolerance in private life," he maintained, "is considered a moral defect or weakness, a defect allied to arrogance, narrow-mindedness, and impatience." He insisted that human freedom and variety cannot flourish in a repressive atmosphere.

Although some have argued that intolerance can serve as a necessary preservative of society, Cranston pointed out that "the toleration of intolerance" can become an acute problem.[16] For me, political freedom implies a democratic society where a person is freely able to vote for the candidate of his choice without any intimidation or coercion.

It implies the holding of peaceful elections without resort to thuggery and threats to one's personal life and safety. In Africa, elections are rarely peaceful. An atmosphere of political freedom is also one where an individual is free to hold membership in any political party of his own choice and can change his party affiliation without terrorism or persecution. Gangsterism is excluded as part of the political process. Political freedom also means that there is no dictatorship of the majority.

Majoritarian rule can be oppressive and tyrannical. This is what Plato alluded to when he said that "dictatorship naturally arises out of democracy, and the most aggravated form of tyranny and slavery out of the most extreme liberty."[17] Political freedom implies that the rights of minorities are respected because they are human beings. On the other hand, minorities should not dominate the majority groups of any society.

Political intolerance is a serious challenge to African freedom since it frustrates the goal of a just social order. The bloody barbarism in Rwanda and Burundi are cases in point. Had the leaders there cultivated a culture of peaceful human co-existence, the Rwanda-Burundi debacle may have been averted. Also, Nigeria would not have lost about one million lives in the so-called Ojukwu's or Biafran war of 1967 to 1970 if there was political freedom.

The second type of intolerance we shall discuss is religious intolerance. It arises when religious freedom has been denied or the right to such freedom is violated. Religious freedom has been described as "a matter of high religion as well as sound government." Professor Franklin H. Littell called it "soul liberty" and stated that it "is a right and a truth which is not government's to deny or grant: government may only recognize it and protect it, for it stands upon higher ground."[18]

Anson Phelps Stokes, an expert on religious liberty, wrote that:

> Liberty or freedom means the unfettered right – as far as the civil law and its administration are concerned – to believe what one wishes, to worship God alone or with others as one sees fit, to be a member of any religious organization which is not illegal, or of none, and to follow such practices as one's religious convictions dictate, as long as these are not clearly inconsistent with the fundamental moral ideals, peace, and safety of the State.[19]

Obviously, here Stokes' definition must be understood within the American context. But, it is nonetheless, a useful definition. It is important to note that this definition makes room for the irreligious. Religious freedom is the right to worship (or not to worship) and pray as a person deems fit.

Religious intolerance has led to the massacre of many innocent persons in Africa. Blinded by fanaticism and stupid zealotry, these perpetrators of intolerance have forgotten that the true essence of any religion is the betterment of the individual's soul and worship of his chosen deity. No amount of State-sanctioned coercion can satisfactorily perform this role. In fact, it is not the State's business to dictate where, when or how people should worship. The State is not in the business of saving souls!

I have suggested that a Christo-Islamic convergence of thought is necessary for religious freedom to thrive in Africa. This means that Christians and Muslims must *honestly* dialogue with each other and build trust as it was before religion was politicized after the 1960's. This is the way to strive forward.[20] The vexatious matter of the *sharia* can only be solved through dialogue.

The challenge before us is that any other way will continue to encourage the present state of rivalry and tension. Do the Muslims really believe that they can win in any efforts to islamize all of Africa through a 21st century jihad? Does the Christian faith allow for a future inquisition against Muslims? Time will tell.

Economic intolerance is our next subject of discussion. It is the denial of the liberty of a person to use God's natural resources for the production of goods and services for his benefit and the benefit of his fellow man. There is an implied mutuality of benefits. It should be noted that I said: "God's natural resources" not the State's. The State creates nothing; it never created any minerals.

Economic freedom involves one's "economic theology" or a "theology of money."[21] Here, I am not concerned about capitalism, socialism, communism, or welfarism. I am concerned with a *prima facie* freedom which allows an individual to use his creative energies, talents, and skills to bring about economic productivity that benefits his fellow man. It is about the freedom to maximize such skills, talents, and creativity.

God did not create us as capitalists, socialists, Marxists, or Communists, but as free human beings endowed with His creative capabilities to take care of our needs. Such capabilities are not inherent in the State but in individuals who constitute the State. The State ought to hunt for and encourage such individuals.

African leaders ought to understand that historical slavery and colonialism had done much damage to Africa's initiative and creativity. The leaders should have been up front motivating the people and reviving the work ethic. It is their selfishness that has hindered this possibility which, in turn, has kept many Africans poor.

It is economic intolerance, and indeed arrogance, when a government presumes that it is the sole agency that can solve all the economic needs of a country. This mindset is rooted in colonialism. Before the colonial masters came, Africans assumed ownership of everything that nature's God provided within the realms of their proprietary rights. Colonialism abrogated such claims. Now, it is time to re-visit this issue.

Just as a State may not take one's property, even by the power of eminent domain, without payment of full and adequate compensation, a State that corrupts and defrauds her people in the allocation and distribution of essential economic resources is a robber State. It should be vigorously resisted. No State has a right to deprive a man of his God-given inheritance.

Africans should reframe the principle: "No taxation without representation," to read "no taxation without proper economic justice." An oppressive government does not deserve my taxes. After all, taxes represent the best of our collective energies and labors. When a government allowed $3 billion to "disappear" from its coffers in 1992 in Nigeria, should it be rewarded with more taxes and money from the citizens, money that would end up in the Swiss banks?

Intellectual intolerance is our next subject. This type of intolerance involves the hinderance to the profusion of ideas which are cherished, not stifled, and are always on their march. But intellectual freedom deals with the right to the free use and exercise of one's faculties. It is the free application of one's inert talents, intuitions, and skills of creativity in the direction and promotion of ideas. In the words of the martyred South African, Steve Biko, intellectual freedom means that you write what you like.

An intellectual deals with abstract ideas that could become concrete technologies, propositions, and formulas. He deals with concepts, philosophies, and phenomena. Professor Ali A. Mazrui defined the intellectual as "a person who has the capacity to be fascinated by ideas and has acquired the skill to handle some of those ideas effectively."[22]

When a State takes an anti-intellectual stance, as in the banning of books and the persecution of authors, it has dabbled into intellectual intolerance. It is on its way to destroy intellectual freedom. This kind of State intolerance often leads to the flight of the intellectuals and to brain-drain. Intellectual intolerance curtails creativity, the precursor of inventions. But intellectual freedom leads to the flourishing of experiments, which, in turn, leads to inventions and technological breakthroughs.

I, for one, do not hold to a narrow definition of the term intellectual. For me, an intellectual need not be the possessor of a Ph.D. James Watt, the inventor of the steam engine, had no Ph.D. Neither did Matthew Boulton, Watt's business partner. And, George Stephenson, of the railway fame, was a self-made engineer who did not know how to read until he was seventeen.

However, Stephenson was given full liberty to carry out his plans and thus the first locomotive engine appeared in the 1820s. Stephenson and Thomas Brassey, his colleague, are not known to have read for the Ph.D. in locomotive engineering. Thomas Alva Edison who gave to the world the electric light, the phonograph, and the moving picture camera, did not have a Ph.D. either.

I could go on and on to mention others like Eli Whitney who revolutionized the cotton industry in 1793. The point is that Africans today do not need so-called intellectuals who cannot manufacture a pin or intellectuals whose ideas are out-dated and dysfunctional. Africa needs intellectuals whose ideas can solve our myriad problems. Any action that frustrates this objective is tantamount to intellectual intolerance.

Social freedom means the right to freely associate with other members of one's community, without discrimination. It includes the right to hold meetings, to intermarry, and to reside wherever one may choose to. It means a right to the sanctity of life, a right not to be unnecessarily arrested, detained, harassed, or tortured. It also includes a right to privacy. Any violations of these rights would represent a form of social intolerance.

Anyone who has lived in Africa since 1960 knows that the above rights are barely protected by African governments. A person can be abducted from his residence at gunpoint at midnight and taken to prison without due process. He can be held *incommunicado* for as long as the leader of a government may choose. This is social intolerance.

6. Coups and Dictatorships

The sixth challenge to African freedom is the illegal usurpation of political power through military coups and dictatorships. When coup d'etats first began in Africa, they were welcome and popular because the people thought that the military were corrective regimes. They were meant to be temporary measures in political engineering.

Major Chukwuma Kaduna Nzeogwu, the Nigerian coup leader of 1966, told a frustrated nation that his coup was intended to "bring an end to gangsterism and disorder, corruption and despotism." He added: "My compatriots, you will no longer need to be ashamed to be Nigerians."

The enemies of the coup plotters were not the Nigerian citizenry; for he also said that,

> Our enemies are the political profiteers, swindlers, the men in high and low places that seek bribes and demand ten percent, those that seek to keep the country permanently divided so that they can remain in office as Ministers and VIPs of waste, the tribalists, the nepotists, those that make the country look big for nothing before international circles.[23]

The pioneer coup plotters in Africa may have had good intentions at first. But after 30 years of military barbarism in some countries, like in Nigeria, and life-presidencies in some others, what does the ordinary African do to sustain his freedom? Without a constitutional right to bear arms like in the United States, what is his last resort?

Let me say without equivocation that, in the matter of the progress of liberty and of fundamental human rights, the introduction of a military presence into African politics has been a terrible mistake, a total curse, and an abysmal failure. God forgive anyone who would say that Sani Abacha was a blessing to Africa. The challenge is with what to do if another Idi Amin or Sani Abacha should reincarnate in any country of Africa.

7. Regimentalism

Writing in 1913 about a regimented mentality, Justice Oliver Wendell Holmes, Jr. stated that "the only prize much cared for by the powerful is power. The prize of the general is not a bigger tent, but command."[24] Holmes' statement aptly describes the regimented mindset in post-colonial Africa.

A political climate has emerged in Africa which may best be termed *regimentalism*. This regimentalism knows nothing of persuasion, which is the language of true democracy – but of coercion. Consequently, Africa is breeding a new generation of people who know nothing of civics, tolerance, humility, and persuasion. Africans of this new generation are being bred in a culture of violence.

All that this new generation has heard, seen and learned from their leaders in the past thirty years has been shaped by a regimented mindset. They have known and witnessed the exercise of brute force meted out to the people. They have heard and seen their leader speak to the people as if the people were his servants or slaves. They have seen nothing of civility or courtesy in the public arena. This is the sad specter of neo-colonialism.

The new generation of Africans have rarely witnessed humility manifested in the public discourses and manners of their heads of States. A psychological orientation based upon rudeness and forceful language has permeated the minds of the youth. It is no wonder that they are also rude to parents, restless, arrogant, and violent. They have emulated very well what they have seen on their national political landscape. Once, a Nigerian military governor humiliated some revered traditional rulers by whipping them publicly!

This psychological orientation (or, should I say, disorientation) is, perhaps, the worst legacy of the military regimes in Africa. Africans had suffered from this sort of mistreatment from the European colonialists. Then the military came and perpetuated it. The outcome is a new generation of Africans who think that the appropriate response to everything is brute force and rudeness. Thanks to the military!

These kinds of Africans, should they ever become leaders, would not be able to stand tall in the great halls of international politics and economic competition. Why? Because they had been raised with inferiority complexes through the doctrine of imperialism. They were bred in the schoolhouse of colonialism. Hence, lacking self-esteem, they could not stand tall. They had been psychologically cowed by the colonial military colossus which had made them think that they could get whatever they wanted by force.

A regimented mentality is also noticeable in the "immediate effect" approach of the military to intricate and complex legal, economic, moral, spiritual, and political matters. The watch-word here is statism. Africans should understand that the central philosophy underlying statism is that man is a pawn and a product of the State. Therefore, he can be ruled arbitrarily. Statism often violates the principle of **habeas corpus**.

Regimentation usually begins with the concentration of power into the hands of an individual. With such powers, a dictatorship emerges. The dictator could suspend the constitution and all freedoms within a particular State. Sometimes, this regimentation begins with a response to "a state of emergency." This then usually leads to a suspension of the freedom of the press.

In economics, regimentation manifests itself in the arbitrary acts of the State against workers and labor unions. A minister of the State may refuse to issue licenses to corporations and other business agencies not liked by the minister. Strikes are ruthlessly crushed without regard to loss of lives. Certain amenities may be denied to some districts not in favor of the ruling party or political leader.

In education, the regimented mindset would not tolerate student complaints, demonstrations and protests. Neither would it try to understand the students nor negotiate with them. Even the complaints of academic staff and university authorities may be treated with slight. Often, a regimented State would respond with the closure of these institutions "indefinitely."

In the area of the judiciary, a regimented State would attempt to influence and control the decisions of the courts. It does not promote an independent judiciary. It threatens the judges with dismissals if they don't rule as the authorities like since the State hires and appoints them to their duties. It is no wonder that justice is bound to suffer. Thus, regimentation is a challenge to the free exercise of freedom.

African educators must boldly embrace the re-introduction of programs and courses that teach ethics, morality and leadership, and which lead ultimately to the cultivation of a true civic culture. I repeat what I have already suggested, that a civilization based upon immorality or upon amoral governments will not endure long.

8. Mafiaism or Personality Cults

I come now to a very strange and yet important challenge to African freedom. This is the matter of mafiaism and personality cults. This challenge is a direct consequence of regimentalism which breeds a false sense of security in a leader who thinks that only he alone is fit to run a country and no one else. In practice, such a leader would surround himself with sycophants.

Until I read *The Kaduna Mafia* (1987) edited by Bala J. Takaya and Soni Gwanle Tyoden, I knew little or nothing of mafiaism and how this concept prevails in African politics. The *Webster's Ninth New Collegiate Dictionary* definition of the term mafia is "a secret society of political terrorists."[25]

In 1994, Colonel Abubakar Dangiwa Umar, a former

military governor of Kaduna state in Nigeria, revealed that there were many mafia groups in that country which were involved in many adverse activities in the northern part of Nigeria. He spoke of the economic and political manipulations and domination by these mafia groups. He hinted that the "spoils system" in Nigeria promoted the evolution and growth of such mafia groups.[26]

According to Takaya and Tyoden, the mafia originated in the city of Sicily in Italy and then spread to Spain, America, and to some Latin American countries like Columbia. Today, the mafia is a world-wide network. Like all bad things from Africa's colonial past, the mafia arrived in Nigeria from Europe and established itself in certain Nigerian cities like Ikenne, Langtang, Bida, and Nsukka. The most well known of these mafia groups is the Kaduna mafia.[27]

The mafia operates in disguise and secrecy. It is a politico-economic pressure group struggling for power and legitimacy. It carries on its activities through undemocratic means such as violence, intimidation, intrigue, corruption and even murder. When necessary, it may collaborate with State agencies.

The mafia is the strongest where the government is the weakest and has failed to provide security and adequate means for livelihood. In other words, the mafia exploits any conditions of poverty. But, the mafia is not a defender of the poor. To survive, the mafia works very hard to permeate all segments of the society: military, government, religious and economic bodies. Its basic goal is the quick accumulation of wealth by illicit and dishonest means.

Takaya believes that the Kaduna mafia had its roots in the Fulani domination of Northern Nigeria since the days of Usman Dan Fodio of the nineteenth century. Through the British-Fulani conspiracy, this domination was sustained up to the days of Ahmadu Bello, the former premier of Northern Nigeria.[28]

One of the contributors to *The Kaduna Mafia*, S. A. Ochoche revealed that the mafia was behind the political executions of 1976 and 1986. For instance, during the 1976 Nigerian coup, when Major-General I. D. Bisalla was publicly executed, Ochoche tells us that only four Muslims compared to **thirty-five** Christians were executed as coup-plotters!

In the 1986 coup in which Major-General Mamman Vatsa was publicly executed, only one Muslim compared to **nine** Christians were executed as coup plotters. The disparities in the numbers suggested the question whether the mafia was waging a secret "religious cleansing" war through the Nigerian military.[29]

Takaya and Tyoden contended that the former head of State of Nigeria, Muhammed Buhari, came to power because of "the apparent marginalisation of the Kaduna mafia." They added that "when Babangida displaced Buhari, ... the mafia was furious."[30] Thus, clearly, the mafia had been playing a role in Nigerian politics.

There is no doubt that what happens in Nigeria is not unique to that country. I believe that there are pockets of mafiaism in all the fifty-three countries of Africa. The challenge to freedom by the mafia lies in the fact that it is self-seeking and does not serve the interest of the nation. Neither does the mafia adopt peaceful and democratic means to achieve its aims.

In another context, since some members of the mafia, like those in Nigeria, have a religious intention to forcibly islamize all of Africa, the stability of Africa and the safety of Africans who are not Muslims come into question. How can freedom thrive in such an atmosphere?

For me, I rest my case in the words credited to Austin Ezeanya, the Coordinator of the International Igbo Congress when he wrote in 1994:

> And let the word go out from this time and place, that the generation of Igbos that saw the humiliation of their fathers, mothers, sons and daughters, has warned that, never again shall the blood, property, and honor of the Igbos be the solution to the Nigerian political, economic, and religious settlement.[31]

I hope that Umaru Dikko and his cohorts, who believe in another jihad in Nigeria, are listening. I hope that the mafia in Nigeria are not taking the Christian community's desire to live in peace and safety for granted. The Christians may be peace-loving and non-violent, but they are not pacifists!

I hope that in the rest of Africa, no member of the mafia will be silly enough to think that a legitimate State apparatus will become their possession. The mafia must first be like any other political organization that will use legitimate means to seek power. The challenge to freedom by the mafia is a very serious threat to the future political survival of Africa as a whole, and of Nigeria, in particular.

9. Ethnicity (Tribalism).

H. O. Davies, a prominent Nigerian politician, defined "tribalism" as the notion that "an ethnic group wants to isolate itself from other groups and enjoy separate autonomous existence." In 1961, in his view, "tribalism" was not altogether a bad thing. Nigerian leaders had seen its usefulness in the days before independence.

Davies argued that in 1943, when Azikiwe published his book, *Political Blueprint For Nigeria*, Azikiwe "proposed the division of a self-governing Nigeria into eight 'Protectorates'" along the lines of ethnic groupings. Four years later, in 1947, when Awolowo published his book, *Path To Nigerian Freedom*,

Awolowo also proposed a federation based upon ethnic lines.[32]

Thus, tribalism was not a bad idea, although recent scholarship has tended to give this word a bad name. Tribalism was considered a means to achieving equal development at the grassroot level. On May 15, 1964, during an address at the University of Nigeria, Nsukka, Azikiwe equated nationality and community with the word tribe.

In that speech, Azikiwe attempted to "demonstrate how tribalism can become a pragmatic instrument for national unity." Drawing inferences from the tribes in Britain, Switzerland, Germany, and the United States, he concluded that "if the concept and practice of tribalism would be a mode of adaptation to reality, then tribalism is an instrument for national unity."[33]

People who believe that tribalism is a destructive element tend to ignore Azikiwe's and Davies' propositions. As Azikiwe had pointed out, everyone belongs to a community or an ethnic group to which one owes his or her loyalty. Such groups come close to what he called nationalities. The colonial masters ignored this important factor. In Nigeria alone, there are about 250 such "nationalities." Azikiwe said that there were about 400 in Nigeria.

In Africa, it is not tribalism or ethnicity which destroys a country and its freedoms. What destroys a country are economic and political injustices, distrust and domination. People in other countries, like America, have become the "melting pot" and have learned to live together in spite of their ethnicities. Nigerians had lived together since 1914 in relative peace until the civil war in 1967. They had inter-married across ethnic lines.

Inter-tribal or ethnic marriages and relationships in Nigeria are also true of the other African countries. The challenge, then, is not to de-ethnicize African States but to successfully create political communities where peace, justice and freedom are not always under fire. There is absolutely nothing wrong with my *Ibibioness*. There is nothing wrong with my being a Kikuyu or a Yoruba or an Ibo.

However, there is everything wrong when I am persecuted and oppressed because I am an Ibibio, an Ibo, a Hutu or a Tutsi. There is also something wrong when I am discriminated against solely because I am an Ibibio. And, there is everything wrong when I am denied my fundamental human rights simply because I am an Ibibio.

Africans have to review their conception of the idea of man if they sincerely believe in the brotherhood and sisterhood of men and women. Then, there will be hope for freedom in Africa. The challenge is for Africans to repudiate, in the strongest terms, any kind of man's inhumanity to man perpetrated in the name of ethnic solidarity!

10. Exploitation (Abuse of the Powerless)

For most Africans, the bottom line in their struggle for survival is economic exploitation because they are powerless to fight against it. They really do not care who is in power as long as they can have the barest necessities of life: food, clothing and shelter. Regrettably, in many parts of Africa, these are denied to so many people because their freedom is often under fire.

Truly, no African likes to be exploited. Therefore, anyone who convinces himself that there are a set of Africans marked for exploitation and who enjoy being mistreated must be actually demented. Exploitation usually leads to resentment and a demand for restitution and justice. When these are denied, the outcome is violence.

No nation or people can afford to allow itself or her people to be perpetually exploited. Those who do so stand the risk of annihilation or extermination. A nation or people cannot survive for too long without economic progress and prosperity. Many Africans have been exploited severely for too long, especially the minority groups of the continent. It is time for domestic reparations to be paid.

I am not an advocate for the destruction of any African State. But if any State has to survive on the backs of the oppressed minority groups, as Nazi Germany did with the Jews, would this not warrant a call for throwing off the yoke? Should the oppressed not resist and seek economic self-determination?

There can be no mincing of words here. Those who would oppose my remedy have only one challenge. My children and grandchildren will hereby be reminded that they must never let the exploiters go unpunished in their time. Africa is a rich continent. Those who feel that we do not all possess the right to enjoy God's wonderful bounty have to read the handwriting on the wall: "mene, mene, tekel upharsin."

CHAPTER FOURTEEN

FREEDOM OR SLAVERY:
WE MUST CHOOSE NOW!

If you love freedom, you must hate slavery.

— Menachem Begin

In the preceding 13 chapters, I have sought to emphasize that human freedom is vital to African prosperity and progress. It is a sine-qua-non. I have argued that the average African is a freedom-loving person. However, it has been the elites in politics and the military who have created such a terrible situation and hardship for the Africans.

I conclude this study by referring to an interesting book entitled *Generation of Vipers* (1942), written by Philip Wylie. In it, he states that,

> It has been fairly fancy of me ... to write so long and noisy a book just to say that if we want a better world, we will have to be a better people.[1]

In the same manner, I wish to say that if Africans want to

have a better continent, they must begin to have some committed and freedom-loving people and leaders. There is no doubt in my mind that Africa is going through a transition, a process of evolution and transformation from traditionalism to modernity, and in some areas, from feudalism to a freer democratic society, and from political experimentation to a hopeful state of perfection.

But, as Professor Donald W. Treadgold asserted in his book, *Freedom*, "attaining freedom ... is extremely difficult and has eluded the best efforts of many a would-be liberator or liberating army or party or group." And, he added this advice: "For those who would undertake the task, study and reflection on the past ought to be the bedrock on which the edifice rises."[2]

The fulfillment of Treadgold's advice is at the heart of the study in this book. It is my hope that my labor will provide the basis for the reflection and further study which Treadgold wrote of. This study is not the last word on the concept of freedom in Africa nor for the advocacy for the resurrection of the freedom spirit in Africa.

I believe that it is not a mere coincidence or accident that while I was engaged in this task, two notable magazines about Africa carried front-cover pictures of a black man shackled in chains. The first picture appeared on the cover of *News Africa*, dated October 23, 2000, with the headline: "Freedom: 40 Years After." The editors of this magazine analyzed "forty years of freedom," which, apparently, they meant freedom from colonial rule in Africa.

Isaac Umunna, one of their editors, concluded that the celebration of that freedom was "amid feelings of disappointment over unfulfilled dreams and aspirations." But, also, Umunna was quick to add this ray of hope: "that the future will usher in a rebirth for the continent."[3] This rebirth or renaissance must come with an enlightenment in the direction of improvements in the condition of human freedom in Africa.

The second magazine that had a cover picture was the *NewAfrican* dated July/August 2001, with a shackled African, on bended knees as if he was pleading against contemporary slavery. The headline read: "Slavery: Greatest crime against humanity."[4] This magazine came out at the same time that the United Nations "World Conference Against Racism, Racial Discrimination, Xenophobia and Related Intolerance" was meeting at Durban in South Africa.

The editors of this magazine dedicated a 13-page analysis to the African struggle for human freedom. Therefore, no one in his or her right mind can say that Africa is truly free today. As of this writing in December 2001, America is reeling from the September 11, 2001 terrorist attacks in New York and in Washington, D.C. The media in Africa has been quick to connect the attacks with the brutalities rampant in many parts of Africa.

The week following those attacks in the United States, I traveled to Nigeria, specifically to see things for myself. What I saw in Nigeria further convinced me that freedom is currently under fire. The degree of lawlessness and confusion is nondescript. A national newspaper, the Nigerian *Vanguard*, wrote about the "violent clashes that threaten democracy under Obasanjo."[5]

The clashes were described as ethno-religious. Fanatical Muslims were attacking and burning down Christian churches! These attacks were serious enough to warrant official action and concern at the highest level of government. Thousands of Nigerians have perished as a result of those clashes. There is a growing feeling of uneasiness because of the religious terrorism that is occurring all over the country.

Paul Marshall, a Senior Fellow at the Center for Religious Freedom in Washington, D.C. and Nina Shea, also an expert in this field of study, have revealed that religious persecutions and terrorism against Christians are not unique to Nigeria. Terry Madison, the president of *Open Doors* ministry in the U.S., reported in its September 2001 newsletter that "a total of 294 churches [were] burned in Kaduna city" in northern Nigeria during the clashes which took place on May 20, 2000.

Do these religious and ethnic clashes speak of the prevalence of freedom in Africa? Certainly not. Rather, in many Islamic countries, like the Sudan, Mali and Egypt, Christians are routinely persecuted and even martyred. The Christians are terrorized as "infidels" in their own native lands. Many of these cases are well documented.[6]

Africans can no longer pretend ignorance concerning a growing religious terrorism engendered by a nascent fundamentalism and an advancing twenty-first century Islamic jihad that may engulf all of Africa. If that were to succeed in Nigeria today, there would be a terrible war between Muslims and Christians.[7] Can such a war be averted? Time will tell. But one thing is certain: freedom is seriously under fire.

There is yet another kind of uneasiness in the continent and that is: the fallout from years of military dictatorship and tyranny in Africa during the last four decades. In many African countries like Nigeria, this fallout has led to a high level of juvenile delinquency and lawlessness. It has also introduced State-sponsored terrorism in the form of brutal political assassinations.

For example, in Nigeria, Dele Giwa, the founder of a national magazine, was murdered by a State-sponsored act of terrorism. It was believed that a parceled bomb killed him at his home on Sunday, October 19, 1986, from the Cabinet Office, Office of the President, Lagos.[8] General Ibrahim B.

Babangida was at the time the President. Fifteen years later, the Nigeria Police Department has still not solved the crime!

To make matters worse for the course of truth, justice and reconciliation in Nigeria, when the time came in 2001 for Babangida to refute the allegations that he was implicated in the brutal crime, he spurned the important opportunity to appear before the Justice Chukwudifu Oputa Human Rights' Violations Investigating Commission (HRVIC). Since that murder, "bomb-throwing has proliferated exponentially,"[9] writes Ray Ekpu, the Chief Executive Officer of Newswatch Communications who succeeded Giwa as editor of the *Newswatch* magazine.

Dele Giwa is not the only person who has fallen victim to State-sponsored terrorism. Napoleon Ovie Igbuku-Otu, an environmentalist and political activist, was also murdered at his home in Lagos on November 23, 2000. This Nigerian was stabbed several times and his murderers finished him off by slashing his throat. Like Giwa, the police have yet to discover who did it. Add to all these the problems of nepotism, corruption, poverty, and money-mania, and you get a picture of where contemporary Africa is headed.

Before his murder, Igbuku-Otu had penned these words:

> Since the colonial masters left us, my government has been engulfed in a far more gruesome battle for the control of this nation. I believe today as I believe[d] yesterday and will believe tomorrow that the freedom of our people from all forms of slavery was the supreme reason for our fight for freedom. We didn't fight for freedom because we wanted a few people committed to the spiritual worship of demonism to enjoy the privileges of the whole society.[10]

Igbuku-Otu probably died for writing these words. And, if so, he died for the cause of freedom in Africa. Therefore, the freedom-lovers in all of Africa must arise. They must rise up now and choose freedom or liberty as a precious value to be cherished far above crass materialism. Or, they must choose slavery. There is no middle road.

Dr. Myles Munroe, the multi-gifted international motivational speaker from Nasau, Bahamas, has said that "more men are afraid of freedom than they are of slavery and oppression."[11] If this is true of Africans, then the future is really hopeless and bleak. But my religious orientation inspires me to believe in the one who said, centuries ago, that "the truth shall set you free." And, He also said: "If the Son of Man shall set you free, you shall be free indeed."[12]

I earnestly hope that the Africans and lovers of Africans will seek Him and find out that He can set them free, too. Any other kind of searching is simply an exercise in futility which will lead us to a dead-end road – to slavery. Africans must put out the fires that burn under freedom and choose liberty, now!

NOTES

Preface:

1. William Ebenstein, "Liberty," in *The Encyclopedia Americana*, vol. 17 (Danbury, CT: Grolier, 2000), 303.

Chapter 1:

1. Joseph E. Harris, *Africans and Their History* (New York: New American Library, 1972), 210; Sanford J. Ungar, *Africa: The People and Politics of An Emerging Continent* (New York: Simon and Schuster, 1986), 58; and Basil Davidson, *The Black Man's Burden: Africa and the Curse of the Nation-State* (New York: Times Books, 1992), 180.

2. In 1963, there were 32 independent African states.

3. Chancellor Williams, *The Destruction of Black Civilization: Great Issues of a Race From 4500 B.C. To 2000 A.D.* (Chicago, IL: Third World Press, 1987), 158. See also Bernard Lewis, *Race and Slavery in the Middle East: An Historical Enquiry* (New York: Oxford University Press, 1990).

4. See Paul E. Lovejoy, ed., *The Ideology of Slavery in Africa* (Beverly Hills, CA: Sage Publications, 1981).

5. See Herbert Aptheker, *Abolitionism: A Revolutionary Movement* (Boston, MA: Twayne Publishers, 1989); Benjamin Quarles, *Black Abolitionists* (New York: Oxford University Press, 1969); and Shirley J. Yee, *Black Women Abolitionists: A Study in Activism, 1828-1860* (Knoxville: University of Tennessee Press, 1992). These books deal with American abolitionism.

6. See K. Onwuka Dike, *Trade and Politics in the Niger Delta 1830-1885: An Introduction to the Economic and Political History of Nigeria* (Oxford: Clarendon Press, 1956), 204-207.

7. [Frederick] Lugard, *The Dual Mandate in British Tropical Africa* (Hamden, CT: Archon Books, 1965), 613, 615-617. See also Ronald Robinson and John Gallagher, *Africa and the Victorians:*

The Official Mind of Imperialism (London: Macmillan and Co., 1961), 1-26.

8. Emile Banning cited in Raymond F. Betts, ed., *The "Scramble" For Africa: Causes and Dimensions of Empire* (Lexington, MA: D.C. Heath and Co., 1966), 1.

9. King Leopold cited in Kwame Nkrumah, *Challenge of the Congo* (New York: International Publishers, 1967), 5.

10. Edmund D. Morel, *The Black Man's Burden: The White Man in Africa From the Fifteenth Century to World War I* (New York: Monthly Review Press, 1969), 109 and Chinweizu [Ibekwe], *The West and the Rest of Us: White Predators, Black Slavers and the African Elite* (New York: Random House, 1975), 55-72.

11. G. N. Uzoigwe, *Britain and the Conquest of Africa: The Age of Salisbury* (Ann Arbor: The University of Michigan Press, 1974), 89-90.

12. Brian Lapping, *End of Empire* (New York: St. Martin Press, 1985), 353.

13. A. P. Thornton, *Imperialism in the Twentieth Century* (Minneapolis: University of Minnesota Press, 1977), 73.

14. Ibid., 147.

15. Charles Reynolds, *Modes of Imperialism* (New York: St. Martin's Press, 1981), 1.

16. Jomo Kenyatta, *Facing Mount Kenya: The Tribal Life of the Gikuyu* (London: Secker and Warburg, 1953), 318.

Chapter 2:

1. Elizabeth Isichei, *A History of Nigeria* (London: Longman, 1983), 372.

2. Theo Ayoola cited in Sanford J. Ungar, *Africa: The People and Politics of an Emerging Continent*, 125.

3. Ibid.

4. James S. Coleman, *Nigeria: Background to Nationalism* (Berkeley: University of California Press, 1971), 220. This book was first published in 1958. The *Pulse* magazine of August 1947 regarded Azikiwe as the African Gandhi.

5. Nnamdi Azikiwe, *My Odyssey: An Autobiography* (New York: Praeger, 1970), 161-162. See also Emma S. Etuk, *Destiny Is Not A Matter of Chance: Essays in Reflection and Contemplation on the Destiny of Blacks* (New York: Peter Lang, 1989), 123.

6. Etuk, *Destiny*, 127-128.

7. Ibid., 127.

8. Ibid., 126.

9. Mbonu Ojike, *I Have Two Countries* (New York: The John Day Company, 1947), 37.

10. Karl Borgin and Kathleen Corbett, *The Destruction of A Continent: Africa and International Aid* (San Diego, CA: Harcourt Brace Jovanovich, Publishers, 1982), 188, italics added for emphasis.

11. Etuk, *Destiny*, 18.

12. George B. N. Ayittey, *Africa Betrayed* (New York: St. Martin's Press, 1992), 121 and 279.

13. Ibid., 120.

14. Ibid., 65.

15. Ibid., 107. See also 145-146.

16. Ibid., 145.

17. Ibid., 131, italics added for emphasis.

18. See "National Broadcast By His Excellency, President Olusegun Obasanjo On the Occasion of the 40th Anniversary of Nigerian Independence, October 1, 2000," http://www.nigeriaworld.com, October 18, 2000, pages 2-3.

19. See "Sharia's Speech About the Disturbances in Kaduna," www.africanews.org, March 2, 2000, p. 1.

20. See "National Broadcast," 5 and 7-8.

21. Joseph E. Harris, *The African Presence in Asia: Consequences of the East African Slave Trade* (Evanston, IL: Northwestern University Press, 1971). See also John Ralph Willis, ed., *Slaves and Slavery in Muslim Africa*, vol. 1: *Islam and the Ideology of Enslavement* (London: Frank Cass, 1985), Shaun E. Marmon,

ed., *Slavery in the Islamic Middle East* (Princeton, NJ: Markus Wiener Publishers, 1999), and J. E. Inikori, ed., *Forced Migration: The Impact of the Export Slave Trade On African Societies* (New York: Africana Publishing Co., 1982).

22. See Ayittey, *Africa Betrayed*, 5.

23. Ibid.

24. Ibid., 6.

25. Ibid., 124. See also Ayittey, *Africa In Chaos* (New York: St. Martin's Press, 1998), 288 and 298-299.

26. Ayittey, *Africa Betrayed*, 125 and "Special Report: A Country In Crisis – The Forgotten Children of Sudan," *Friends in the West*, Arlington, Washington, undated, p. 4.

27. "Special Report," 4.

28. Ibid.

29. Ibid.

30. Ibid.

31. Ibid.

32. See his "Slavery in Modern Ghana?" *The African Shopper* (December 1997): 1 and 23.

Chapter 3:

1. Rayford Logan, *The Betrayal of the Negro From Rutherford B. Hayes to Woodrow Wilson* (New York: Collier Books, 1965). See also Charles F. Darlington and Alice B. Darlington, *African Betrayal* (New York: David McKay Co., 1968).

2. Joyce Cary, *The Case For African Freedom* (New York: McGraw-Hill Book Co., 1964).

3. Azikiwe cited in Etuk, *Destiny Is Not A Matter of Chance*, 124.

4. Akweke Abyssinia Nwafor Orizu, *Without Bitterness: Western Nations in Post-War Africa* (New York: Creative Age Press, 1944), 99-100.

5. George B. N. Ayittey, *Indigenous African Institutions* (Ardsley-on-Hudson, NY: Transnational Publishers, 1991). This book

deals with African indigenous institutions before the colonial era. I have already cited two of his other books.

6. Yoweri K. Museveni, *What Is Africa's Problem?* (Minneapolis: University of Minnesota Press, 2000). Museveni, who is the president of Uganda, writes that many of the post-colonial African leaders took the ideological position that there was nothing to be changed in Africa, (page 147).

Chapter 4:

1. This poem is taken from John Bartlett, *Familiar Quotations* (Boston, MA: Little, Brown and Co., 1980), 936.

2. Menachem Begin cited in *Familiar Quotations*, 881.

3. Jefferson cited in *Familiar Quotations*, 387. See also Suzy Platt, ed., *Respectfully Quoted: A Dictionary of Quotations* (New York: Barnes and Noble, 1993), 131.

4. Oscar and Mary Handlin, *The Dimensions of Liberty* (Cambridge, MA: Harvard University Press, 1961), 5.

5. Herbert J. Muller, *Issues of Freedom: Paradoxes and Promises* (New York: Harper and Brothers Publishers, 1960), 3.

6. Jean Jacques Rousseau cited in *Familiar Quotations*, 359.

7. John Milton cited in *Familiar Quotations*, 282.

8. Johann von Schiller cited in *Familiar Quotations*, 413.

9. Herbert Spencer cited in *Familiar Quotations*, 579.

10. Abraham Lincoln cited in Platt, *Respectfully Quoted*, 127.

11. John Stuart Mill cited in Platt, *Respectfully Quoted*, 127.

12. Handlin, 9.

13. Ibid.

14. Ibid., 16. See also J. Melvin Woody, *Freedom's Embrace* (University Park: The Pennsylvania State University Press, 1998), 21-63 and 69-112.

15. Muller, *Freedom in the Western World From the Dark Ages to the Rise of Democracy* (New York: Harper and Row, 1964), xiii.

16. Friedrich A. Hayek, *The Constitution of Liberty* (Chicago, IL: The University of Chicago Press, 1960), 11.

17. Isaiah Berlin, *The Power of Ideas*, ed., Henry Hardy (Princeton, NJ: Princeton University Press, 2000), 15-18 and 111-114.

18. Randy E. Barnett, *The Structure of Liberty: Justice and the Rule of Law* (New York: Oxford University Press, 1998), 2. Compare his arguments with those by Christian Bay, *The Structure of Freedom* (Stanford, CA: Stanford University Press, 1970), 83-101.

19. David C. Cochran, *The Color of Freedom: Race and Contemporary American Liberalism* (New York: State University of New York Press, 1999), 41.

20. Ibid.

21. Mortimer J. Adler, *The Idea of Freedom: A Dialectical Examination of the Conceptions of Freedom* (Garden City, NY: Doubleday and Co., 1958), 585-600 and Muller, *Issues of Freedom*, 17-18.

22. Adler, 585-600.

23. Ibid.

24. Adler, 586.

25. Ibid., 614 and Muller, *Issues of Freedom*, 18.

26. Orlando Patterson, *Freedom*, vol. 1: *Freedom in the Making of Western Culture* (New York: Basic Books, 1991), 3.

27. Ibid., 3-4.

28. Ibid., 4.

29. Ibid.

30. Ibid., 5. Compare his ideas with those of Samuel Fleischacker, *A Third Concept of Liberty: Judgment and Freedom in Kant and Adam Smith* (Princeton, NJ: Princeton University Press, 1999), 243-278.

31. Muller, *Freedom in the Western World*, xix, and Patterson, *Freedom*, vol 1, 20-63. See a challenge to these views in W. E. Abraham, *The Mind of Africa* (Chicago, IL: The University of Chicago Press, 1962), 142-159.

32. Donald W. Treadgold, *Freedom: A History* (New York: New York University Press, 1990), 81-82. See also Patterson, *Freedom*, vol 1, 23-28 where he suggests that Africans had no notion of personal freedom.

Chapter 5:

1. Dr. George Ayittey's ideas on the African conception of freedom are scattered throughout his book, *Indigenous African Institutions*. For example see pages 3-4, 75, 265, 451-454, 494-514.

2. Julius K. Nyerere, *Freedom and Unity* (London: Oxford University Press, 1964), *Freedom and Socialism* (London: Oxford University Press, 1968), and *Freedom and Development* (New York: Oxford University Press, 1973).

3. Nyerere cited in A. B. Assensoh, *African Political Leadership: Jomo Kenyatta, Kwame Nkrumah, and Julius K. Nyerere* (Malabar, FL: Krieger Publishing Co., 1998), 5-6.

4. Personal telephone interview with Dr. Chim Ogbonna dated July 6, 2001. Dr. Ogbonna is an Igbo from Nigeria.

5. R. F. G. Adams, Etim Akaduh, and Okon Abia-Bassey, *English-Efik Dictionary* (Oron, Nigeria: Manson Bookshop, 1981), 83 and 199.

6. Personal interview with the Reverend Stephen Gyermeh, senior pastor of the Church of the Living God, Hyattsville in Maryland dated December 23, 2001. Pastor Gyermeh is a Ghanaian.

7. Personal interview with Mr. Peter Nudomesi dated December 23, 2001. Peter is an Ewe.

8. Personal interview with Dr. Sulayman Nyang, a professor of Howard University dated February 10, 2001. Dr. Nyang is originally from the Gambia.

9. Personal interview with Rhoi Wangila dated December 6, 2001. Rhoi is a Ugandan.

Chapter 6:

1. Etuk, *Destiny Is Not A Matter of Chance*, 105-115.

2. Hans Kohn and Wallace Sokolsky, *African Nationalism in the Twentieth Century* (Princeton, NJ: D. Van Nostrand Co., 1965), 31.

3. Kwame Nkrumah, *Ghana: The Autobiography of Kwame Nkrumah* (New York: International Publishers, 1984), 69. This book was first published in 1957.

4. Ibid., 76.

5. Ibid., 91.

6. Ibid.

7. Ibid., 96-99.

8. Ibid., 100-101.

9. Ibid., 111.

10. Ibid., 111-112.

11. Ibid., 112.

12. Ibid., 141.

13. Ibid., 185.

14. Ibid., 186 and 199.

15. Ibid., 190.

16. Ibid., 192.

17. Ibid., 201.

18. John G. Jackson, *Introduction to African Civilizations* (Secaucus, NJ: The Citadel Press, 1970), 31-32.

19. Nkrumah, *Ghana*, 192.

20. Ibid.

21. Ibid., 202.

22. Ibid. See also his book, *Towards Colonial Freedom: Africa in the Struggle Against World Imperialism* (London: Heinemann,

1962). This 45-page booklet, first published in 1945, was an essay on the liberation of Africa from foreign rule.

23. Nkrumah, *Ghana*, 202.

24. Ibid., 201. See also his book, *I Speak of Freedom: A Statement of African Ideology* (New York: Frederick A. Praeger, Publisher, 1961), 175, where he stated: "When I talk of freedom and independence for Africa, I mean that the vast African majority should be accepted as forming the basis of government in Africa."

25. Nkrumah, *Ghana*, 232 and 268.

26. Nkrumah, "What Nkrumah Said to the U. S. Senate," in Langston Hughes, *An African Treasury: Articles/ Essays/ Stories/ Poems By Black Africans* (New York: Pyramid Books, 1961), 80-81.

27. Tom Mboya, *Freedom and After* (Boston, MA: Little, Brown and Co., 1963), 208-211.

28. Ibid.

29. Ibid., 137-142.

30. Kohn and Sokolsky, 19, and Ralph Uwechue, *Makers of Modern Africa: Profiles in History* (London: Africa Books Ltd., 1991), 473-474.

31. Mboya, *Freedom and After*, 55-59.

32. Ibid., 61.

33. Ibid., 62.

34. Ibid., 75.

35. Ibid., 79.

36. Mboya, "African Freedom," in Hughes, *An African Treasury*, 39-44.

37. Mboya, *Freedom After*, 47-48.

38. Ibid., 48.

39. Jomo Kenyatta, *Facing Mount Kenya: The Tribal Life of the Gikuyu*, 186. For biographies of the *Mzee*, see Jeremy Murray-

Brown, *Kenyatta* (London: George Allen and Unwin, 1972), George Delf, *Jomo Kenyatta: Towards Truth About "The Light of Kenya."* (New York: Doubleday and Co., 1961), and A. B. Assensoh, *African Political Leadership*, 31-68.

40. Kenyatta, *Facing Mount Kenya*, 197-198.

41. Ibid., 318.

42. Fred Majdalany, *State of Emergency: The Full Story of Mau Mau* (Boston, MA: Houghton Mifflin Co., 1963), 221. See also Richard Cox, *Kenyatta's Country* (New York: Frederick A. Praeger Publishers, 1965) and B. A. Ogot and W. R. Ochieng,' *Decolonization & Independence in Kenya 1940-93* (London: James Currey, 1995).

43. Kenyatta, *Suffering Without Bitterness: The Founding of the Kenya Nation* (Nairobi: East African Publishing House, 1968), 213.

44. Ibid.

45. Ibid., 219.

46. Ibid., 227.

47. Kenyatta, *Harambee! The Prime Minister of Kenya's Speeches 1963-1964: From the Attainment of Internal Self-Government to the Threshold of the Kenya Republic* (Nairobi: Oxford University Press, 1964), 23 and 96-104.

48. Ogot and Ochieng, 17-18 and 91-109; Assensoh, 66-68.

49. Ajuma Oginga Odinga, *Not Yet Uhuru: The Autobiography of Oginga Odinga* (New York: Hill and Wang, 1967).

50. Kenyatta cited in Ayittey, *Indigenous African Institutions*, 237.

Chapter 7:

1. Judith Listowel, *The Making of Tanganyika* (London: Chatto & Windus, 1965), 43.

2. Ibid.

3. Ibid., 177. See also Leonard Kenworthy and Erma Ferrari, *Leaders of New Nations* (Garden City, NY: Doubleday and Co., 1968), 10.

4. Kenworthy and Ferrari, 11.

5. Ibid.

6. Listowel, 201-202.

7. Ibid., 204.

8. Ibid., 203.

9. Julius K. Nyerere, *Freedom and Unity/Uhuru na Umoja: A Selection From Writings and Speeches 1952-65* (Dar Es Salaam: Oxford University Press, 1966), 35-39.

10. Ibid. See also Listowel, 248-251, and Kenworthy and Ferrari, 13.

11. Nyerere, *Freedom and Unity*, 40-44.

12. Ibid., 44.

13. Ibid., 45-47.

14. Ibid., 59-60.

15. Ibid., 67-68.

16. Ibid., 103- 104.

17. Ibid., 53.

18. Ibid., 69-71.

19. Kenworthy and Fearrari, 15.

20. Nyerere cited in Kohn and Sokolsky, *African Nationalism in the Twentieth Century*, 17.

21. Nyerere, *Freedom and Unity*, 138-141.

22. Ibid., 116-117.

23. Ibid., 145-147.

24. Ibid., 157-158.

25. Nyerere, *Freedom and Development/Uhuru na Maendeleo: A Selection From Writings and Speeches 1968-1973* (London: Oxford University Press, 1973), 58-71.

26. Nyerere, *Freedom and Socialism/Uhuru na Ujamaa: A Selection From Writings and Speeches 1965-1967* (London: Oxford University Press, 1968), 136, and 316-317.

27. Nyerere, *Freedom and Development*, 372-373. See also chapter 7 therein and William Redman Duggan and John R. Civille, *Tanzania and Nyerere: A Study of Ujamaa and Nationhood* (Maryknoll, NY: Orbis Books, 1976), 98-104.

28. Duggan and Civille, 172.

29. William Edgett Smith, *We Must Run While They Walk: A Portrait of Africa's Julius Nyerere* (New York: Random House, 1971), 216.

30. Duggan and Civille, 42.

31. Sanford J. Ungar, *Africa*, 407-408.

32. William Edgett Smith, 23-25.

33. Robert H. Jackson and Carl G. Rosberg, *Personal Rule in Black Africa: Prince, Autocrat, Prophet, Tyrant* (Berkeley: University of California Press, 1982), 219-220.

34. Ibid., 221-222.

35. Ayittey, *Indigenous African Institutions*, 420 and 428.

36. Sanford J. Ungar, *Africa*, 410.

37. Ibid., 411 and 415.

38. "Albright Remarks At the Julius Nyerere Memorial," *Internet* printout dated January 24, 2001.

Chapter 8:

1. See Andrew Roberts, *A History of Zambia* (New York: Africana Publishing Co., 1976), 149-173. See also Brian M Fagan, *A Short History of Zambia From the Earliest Times Until A. D. 1900* (Nairobi, Kenya: Oxford University Press, 1966).

2. Kenneth D. Kaunda, *Zambia Shall Be Free: An Autobiography* (London: Heinemann, 1979), 5. See also John J. Grotpeter, *Historical Dictionary of Zambia* (Metuchen, NJ: The Scarecrow Press, 1979), 123-126 and Geoffrey J. Williams, *Independent Zambia: A Bibliography of the Social Sciences, 1964-1979* (Boston: G. K. Hall and Co., 1984), 100-102.

3. Kaunda, *Zambia*, 9.

4. Ibid., 10.

5. Ibid., 22.

6. Ibid., 146-147.

7. Roberts, 197.

8. Ibid., 198.

9. Kaunda, *Zambia*, 21.

10. Ibid., 31.

11. Ibid., 33.

12. Ibid., 52-54.

13. Ibid., 40-41.

14. Ibid., 166-167.

15. Ibid., 168. See also 168-176.

16. Ibid., 56-57.

17. Ibid., 57.

18. Ibid., 58 and 59.

19. Ibid., 62-65.

20. Ibid., 34-35.

21. Ibid., 89. For an excellent description of the personal character of Kaunda, see Richard Hall, *The High Price of Principles: Kaunda and the White South* (London: Hodder and Stoughton, 1969), 36-51. See also John Hatch, *Two African Statesmen: Kaunda of Zambia and Nyerere of Tanzania* (Chicago, IL: Henry Regnery Co., 1976).

22. Kaunda, *Zambia*, 120. See also Thomas Patrick Melady, *Kenneth Kaunda of Zambia: Selections From His Writings* (New York: Frederick A. Praeger, 1962), 156.

23. See Robert Garfield, "Kenneth Kaunda," in *The Encyclopedia Americana*, vol. 16 (Danbury, CT: Grolier, 1999), 334.

24. Kaunda, *Zambia*, 132.

25. Ibid., 138-139. See also David C. Mulford, *Zambia: The Politics of Independence 1957-1964* (London: Oxford University Press, 1967), 142.

26. Kaunda, *Zambia*, 141. See also his book, *Black Government? A Discussion Between Colin Morris and Kenneth Kaunda* (Lusaka: United Society For Christian Literature, 1960). This book seems to be Kaunda's political manifesto.

27. Colin Legum, ed., *Zambia: Independence and Beyond. The Speeches of Kenneth Kaunda* (London: Thomas Nelson, 1966), 3 and 64. See also Roberts, 195-252.

28. Melady, 3.

29. Sanford J. Ungar, *Africa*, 418. For more on this humanism, see Kenneth D. Kaunda, *A Humanist In Africa: Letters To Colin Morris* (London: Longmans, 1966), which is his philosophical contribution, and J. B. Zulu, *Zambian Humanism: Some Major Spiritual and Economic Challenges* (Lusaka: Neczam, 1970). See also Henry Meebelo, *Main Currents of Zambian Humanist Thought* (Lusaka: Oxford University Press, 1973) and Timothy K. Kandeke, *Fundamentals of Zambian Humanism* (Lusaka: Neczam, 1977).

30. Kenneth Kaunda, *The Riddle of Violence* (New York: Harper and Row, 1980).

31. Kenneth David Kaunda, *Letter To My Children* (London: Longman Group Ltd., 1973), 85-92 and *A Humanist In Africa*, 55.

32. Unger, 418 and 419.

33. George Ayittey, *Africa Betrayed*, 120 and 338; *Africa In Chaos*, 92 and 206; and *Indigenous African Institutions*, 122, 454-455 and 503.

Chapter 9:

1. Obafemi Awolowo, *Awo: The Autobiography of Chief Obafemi Awolowo* (Cambridge: The University Press, 1960) was dedicated to "a new and free Nigeria where individual freedom and a more abundant life are guaranteed to all citizens." The book was revised and republished in 1968 by John West under the title *My Early Life.*

2. Awolowo, *Path To Nigerian Freedom* (London: Faber and Faber Ltd., 1947), 23.

3. Ibid., 102-111.

4. Awolowo, *Voice of Reason: Selected Speeches of Chief Obafemi Awolowo, vol. 1* (Akure, Nigeria: Fagbamigbe Publishers, 1981), 160. This lecture was titled "Education As A Means To National Freedom."

5. Francis Ishola Ogunmodede, *Chief Obafemi Awolowo's Socio-Political Philosophy: A Critical Interpretation* (Rome: n.p., 1986), 78.

6. Awolowo, *Voice of Reason*, 162.

7. Ibid., 165.

8. Ibid., 93.

9. Ibid., 131.

10. Awolowo, *Freedom and Independence For Nigeria: A Statement of Policy* (Ibadan: PDA, 1958), 4. See also his other book, *Thoughts On Nigerian Constitution* (Ibadan: Oxford University Press, 1966), 114-122 and 150-154 which deal with his views on human rights.

11. Awolowo, *Voice of Reason*, 17. I have deliberately excluded Ahmadu Bello from this analysis because I believe that if he ever wrote anything on freedom or liberty, it was a typographical error. See his autobiographical book, *My Life* (Cambridge: The University Press, 1962).

12. Ibid., 26-35.

13. Awolowo, *Awo: The Autobiography*, 294 and 299.

14. See Colin Legum and Marion Newson, eds., *Africa Contemporary Record: Annual Survey and Documents 1987-1988* (New York: Africana Publishing Co., 1989), B109.

15. See "Chief Awolowo's Legacy," *West Africa* (May 18, 1987): 947.

16. Ibid.

17. See Ad'Obe Obe, "Succeeding Oduduwa," *West Africa* (May 18, 1987): 951. For another view of the struggle for political power in Africa, see Samuel Decalo, *Psychoses of Power: African Personal Dictatorships* (Boulder, CO: Westview Press, 1989).

18. Azikiwe, *Zik: A Selection From the Speeches of Nnamdi Azikiwe* (Cambridge: The University Press, 1961), 2 and 8.

19. Awolowo, *Awo: The Autobiography*, 86-87.

20. Azikiwe, *Zik: A Selection*, 23. See pages 24-47 for his educational views.

21. Coleman, *Nigeria: Background To Nationalism*, 215-216.

22. Awolowo, *Awo: The Autobiography*, 87.

23. Coleman, 220.

24. Anthony Enahoro, *Fugitive Offender: The Story of A Political Prisoner* (London: Cassell and Co., 1965), 67-68.

25. Azikiwe, *Zik: A Selection*, 154.

26. Ibid., 158. See also Elizabeth Isichei, *A History of Nigeria*, 403.

27. Azikiwe, *Zik: A Selection*, 154-155.

28. Ibid., 50.

29. Etuk, *Destiny*, 126.

30. Ibid.

31. Ibid., 129.

32. Azikiwe, *Zik: A Selection*, 51.

33. Ibid., 52.

34. Ibid., 139.

35. Ibid., 13.

36. Ibid., 147-153. This is on his racial views. For his views on democracy, see pages 82-99.

37. Ibid. 20.

38. For example, see Chinweizu, *The West and the Rest of Us*, 80-100. Note particularly pages 98-99 therein.

39. Richard L. Sklar, *Nigerian Political Parties: Power In An Emergent African Nation* (Princeton, NJ: Princeton University Press, 1963), 143-189. Zik was found guilty of misconduct but not of theft.

40. Sklar, 121-124 and 160. Sklar wrote that Mbonu Ojike was responsible for the overthrow of the Eyo Ita government. But was Zik quite unable to thwart the actions of Ojike?

41. Azikiwe, *Zik: A Selection*, 306-307.

42. H. O. Davies, *Nigeria: The Prospects For Democracy* (London: Weidenfeld and Nicolson, 1961), 95.

43. Azikiwe, *Zik: A Selection*, 91-94.

44. Davies, 92.

Chapter 10:

1. Hubert Deschamps, "France In Black Africa and Madagascar Between 1920 and 1945," in L. H. Gann and Peter Duignan, eds., *Colonialism In Africa*, vol. 2 (Cambridge: Cambridge University Press, 1982, 1970), 226. See also Robert L. Delavignette, "French Colonial Policy In Black Africa, 1945 To 1960," L. H. Gann and Peter Duignan, eds., *Colonialism In Africa*, vol. 2 (Cambridge: Cambridge University Press, 1982, 1970), 251, and Norman R. Bennett, *Africa and Europe From Roman Times To National Independence* (New York: Africana Publishing Co., 1984), 98-99.

2. Andrew F. Clark and Lucie Colvin Phillips, *Historical Dictionary of Senegal*, 2nd. ed., (Metuchen, NJ: The Scarecrow Press, 1994), 146-148.

3. Ibid., 9. See also pages 7 and 8; Benneth, 52-53; and John W. Blake, *European Beginnings In West Africa 1454-1578: A Survey of the First Century of White Enterprise In West Africa, With Special Emphasis Upon the Rivalry of the Great Powers* (Westport, CT: Greenwood Press, 1937), 121.

4. Robert W. July, *The Origins of Modern African Thought: Its Development In West Africa During the Nineteenth and Twentieth Centuries* (New York: Frederick A. Praeger, 1967), 240. See also pages 67-84 and 234-253 for an analysis of colonial Senegal.

5. Ihechukwu Madubuike, *The Senegalese Novel: A Sociological Study of the Impact of the Politics of Assimilation* (Washington, D.C.: Three Continent Press, 1983), 3.

6. Clark and Phillips, 65.

262

7. Janet G. Vaillant, *Black, French, and African: A Life of Leopold Sedar Senghor* (Cambridge, MA: Harvard University Press, 1990), 9.

8. Ibid., 6. See *The Encyclopedia Americana*, vol. 24 (Danbury, CT: Grolier, 1999), 556; Mark R. Lipschutz and R. Kent Rasmussen, *Dictionary of African Historical Biography*, 2nd ed., (Berkeley: University of California Press, 1986), 212-213; Clark and Pillips, 239-245 and 278-279. For analyses of the impact of Islam upon Senegal, see Martin A. Klein, *Islam and Imperialism in Senegal: Sine-Saloum, 1847-1914* (Stanford, CA: Stanford University Press, 1968), Sheldon Gellar, *Senegal: An African Nation Between Islam and the West* (Boulder, CO: Westview Press, 1982), 1-27, and J. Spencer Trimingham, *A History of Islam in West Africa* (London: Oxford University Press, 1959).

9. Vaillant, 19 and 29.

10. Ibid., 29-31.

11. Ibid., 64-88.

12. Leonard Kenworthy and Erma Ferrari, *Leaders of New Nations*, 92-105 and Vaillant, 89.

13. Leopold Sedar Senghor, "The Spirit of Civilisation, or the Laws of African Negro Culture," cited in Hans Kohn and Wallace Sokolsky, *African Nationalism in the Twentieth Century*, 154. The essay was first published in *The First Conference of Negro Writers and Artists* (Paris: Presence Africaine, 1956), 51-64.

14. Senghor, "The Spirit of Civilisation," 155.

15. Ibid.

16. Ibid., 153-154.

17. Ibid., 155 and 156.

18. Vaillant, 37. See also Senghor, *Liberte 1: Negritude et humanisme* (Paris: Le Seuil, 1964), 98.

19. Senghor cited in Kohn and Sokolsky, *African Nationalism in the Twentieth Century*, 103.

20. Vaillant, 287.

21. Senghor, "What Is Negritude?" *Negro Digest* (April 1962): 4.

22. Ibid., 3 and 4.

23. Ibid., 5.

24. Ibid.

25. Ibid.

26. Senghor cited in Kenworthy and Ferrari, *Leaders of New Nations*, 105.

27. Senghor, "What Is Negritude?" 5.

28. Ibid.

29. Ibid.

30. Sylvia Washington Ba, *The Concept of Negritude in the Poetry of Leopold Sedar Senghor* (Princeton, NJ: Princeton University Press, 1973), 264.

31. Vaillant, 244.

32. Ibid., 207.

33. Ibid., 223-230.

34. Ibid., 235.

35. Ibid., 240.

36. Senghor, *On African Socialism*, trans., Mercer Cook (New York: Frederick A. Praeger, 1964), 45 and 46.

37. Ibid., 83.

38. Ibid., 87.

39. Senghor, "A Community of Free and Equal Peoples With the Mother Country," in David K. Marvin, ed., *Emerging Africa In World Affairs* (San Francisco, CA: Chandler Publishing Co., 1965), 174-180. For a definition of African socialism, see pages 169-174.

40. Senghor, *On African Socialism*, 144.

41. Irving Leonard Markovitz, *Leopold Sedar Senghor and the Politics of Negritude* (New York: Atheneum, 1969), 119.

42. Ibid., jacket-cover.

43. Madubuike, vii.

44. Ibid., 139.

45. Ibid.

46. Ibid., 144.

47. Ibid., 140.

48. Ibid., 141.

49. Ibid., 145.

50. Ibid., 148.

51. Robert H. Jackson and Carl G. Rosberg, *Personal Rule in Black Africa*, 95.

52. Ibid., 91. See also Gwendolen M. Carter, ed., *African One-Party States* (Ithaca, NY: Cornell University Press, 1962), 87-148.

53. Jackson and Rosberg, 89.

54. Ibid., 93.

55. Sanford J. Ungar, *Africa*, 345.

56. Ayittey, *Africa Betrayed*, 118.

Chapter 11:

1. Nelson Mandela, *Long Walk To Freedom: The Autobiography of Nelson Mandela* (Boston, MA: Little, Brown and Co., 1994), 3. See also Fatima Meer, *Higher Than Hope: The Authorized Biography of Nelson Mandela* (New York: Harper and Row, 1988), 3-22.

2. Mandela, *Long Walk To Freedom*, 5.

3. Ibid., 6.

4. Ibid.

5. Ibid., 7.

6. Ibid., 8.

7. Ibid., 8-9.

8. Ibid., 10.

9. Ibid., 10-12.

10. Ibid., 14.

11. Ibid., 16

12. Ibid., 17.

13. Ibid., 18 and 19.

14. Ibid., 21.

15. Leonard Thompson, *A History of South Africa*, 3rd. ed., (New Haven, CT: Yale University Press, 2001), 1-153.

16. Alan Lester, *From Colonization To Democracy: A New Historical Geography of South Africa* (London: I. B. Tauris Publishers, 1996), 15-36. See also Richard Elphick and Herman Giliomee, eds., *The Shaping of South African Society, 1652-1840.* (Middletown, CT: Wesleyan University Press, 1979); Patti Waldmeir, *Anatomy of A Miracle: The End of Apartheid and the Birth of the New South Africa* (New York: W. W. Norton and Co., 1997); and W. H. Wilkins, ed., *South Africa A Century Ago* (New York: Kraus Reprint Co., 1969). For an excellent chronology of developments in South Africa, see Desmond Tutu, *The Rainbow People of God: The Making of A Peaceful Revolution* (New York: Doubleday, 1994).

17. Mandela, *Long Walk To Freedom*, 26.

18. Ibid.

19. Ibid., 28.

20. Ibid., 32 and 33.

21. Ibid., 36.

22. Ibid.

23. Ibid., 38.

24. Ibid., 40.

25. Ibid., 43 and 45.

26. Ibid., 129.

27. Albert Luthuli, "A Voice Crying in the South African Wilderness," *Negro Digest* (December 1961): 3-7 and *Africa's Freedom* (London: Unwin Books, 1964). Luthuli was the first black South African to receive the Nobel Peace Prize in 1961.

28. Mandela, *Long Walk To Freedom*, 83.

29. One should compare and contrast Afrikanerism with "the ideological creed of the ANC" found in its constitution and in the Freedom Charter adopted in June 1955. See Mandela, *Long Walk To Freedom*, 149-153, 319-320, and Kohn and Sokolsky, *African Nationalism*, 58-72. For treatments of the ideological and theological origins of Afrikaner nationalism, see J. Alton Templin, *Ideology On A Frontier: The Theological Foundation of Afrikaner Nationalism, 1652-1910* (Westport, CT: Greenwood Press, 1984) and Irving Hexham, *The Irony of Apartheid: The Struggle For National Independence of Afrikaner Calvinism Against British Imperialism* (New York: The Edwin Mellen Press, 1981).

30. Mandela, *Long Walk To Freedom*, 125.

31. Jennifer Crwys-Williams, ed., *In the Words of Nelson Mandela* (Secaucus, NJ: Carol Publishing Group, 1998), 21 and 80.

32. Ibid., 41 and 64.

33. Ibid., 42.

34. Mandela, *Long Walk To Freedom*, 322.

35. Ibid., 493. See also pages 485-486 and 491.

36. Crwys-Williams, 36.

37. Ibid., 37.

38. Ibid., 85.

39. Thompson, 260 and Mandela, *Long Walk To Freedom*, 501-502.

40. Tutu, *The Rainbow People*, 209-219.

41. Crwys-Williams, 33, 47 and 49.

42. Tutu, *The Rainbow People*, 193.

43. David Aikman, *Great Souls: Six Who Changed the Century* (Nashville, TN: Word Publishing, 1998), 61-123.

Chapter 12:

1. J. Bryan Hehir, "Human Rights From A Theological and Ethical Perspective," in Kenneth W. Thompson, ed., *The Moral Imperatives of Human Rights: A World Survey* (Lanham, MD: University Press of America, 1980), 10. See also Robert K. Fullinwider and Claudia Mills, eds., *The Moral Foundations of Civil Rights* (Totowa, NJ: Rowman and Littlefield, 1986), Joseph Raz, *The Morality of Freedom* (Oxford: Clarendon Press, 1986) and Murray N. Rothbard, *The Ethics of Liberty* (Atlantic Highlands, NJ: Humanities Press, 1982).

2. See Norman L. Stamps, *Why Democracies Fail: A Critical Evaluation of the Causes For Modern Dictatorship* (Notre Dame, IN: University of Notre Dame Press, 1957) and Daniel Chirot, *Modern Tyrants: The Power and Prevalence of Evil In Our Age* (New York: The Free Press, 1994), 403-421 for his penetrating insights on the eight conditions which breed tyranny.

3. Ptah-hotep cited in Bartlett, *Familiar Quotations*, 3.

4. See *The Holy Bible*, St. John's Gospel, chapter 14:6.

5. Samuel Butler cited in Bartlett, *Familiar Quotations*, 291.

6. Blaise Pascal cited in Bartlett, *Familiar Quotations*, 300.

7. Henry Frederic-Amiel cited in Bartlett, *Familiar Quotations*, 580.

8. William Cullen Bryant cited in Bartlett, *Familiar Quotations*, 471.

9. Franklin Roosevelt cited in Bartlett, *Familiar Quotations*, 779.

10. Mortimer J. Adler, *Six Great Ideas* (New York: Collier Books, 1981), 20-27. See also Barbara Ward, *Five Ideas That Changed the World* (New York: W. W. Norton and Co., 1959).

11. Zachariah Chafee, Jr., *The Blessings of Liberty* (Westport, CT: Greenwood Press, 1973), 102.

12. Ibid., 103.

13. Ibid., 105.

14. Ibid., 110.

15. Benjamin Disraeli cited in Bartlett, *Familiar Quotations*, 502.

16. See *The Holy Bible*, Amos 5:24.

17. Mortimer J. Adler, *Six Great Ideas* (New York: Collier Books, 1981), 135-136.

18. Ibid., 136.

19. Ibid., 137.

20. Ibid., 193.

21. *The Holy Bible*, Proverbs, 14:34.

22. *The Holy Bible*, Proverbs, 16:12.

23. Abraham Edel, "Right and Good," in Philip P. Wiener, ed., *Dictionary of the History of Ideas: Studies of Selected Pivotal Ideas*, vol. 4 (New York: Charles Scribner's Sons, 1973), 173.

24. Ibid., 174.

25. William David Ross, *The Right and the Good* (Oxford: Clarendon Press, 1967), 21-22. This book was first published in 1930. See also Victor Grassian, *Moral Reasoning: Ethical Theory And Some Contemporary Moral Problems* (Englewood Cliffs, NJ: Prentice-Hall, 1981), 109.

26. Ross, 41.

27. Clarence Irving Lewis, *The Ground and Nature of the Right* (New York: Columbia University Press, 1955), 52.

28. Henry David Thoreau cited in Bartlett, *Familiar Quotations*, 557.

29. See my book, *A Walk Through the Wilderness* (New York: Carlton Press, 1990), 15.

30. Shailer Mathews and Gerald Birney Smith, eds., *A Dictionary of Religion and Ethics* (London: Waverley Book Co., 1921), 210.

31. *The Holy Bible*, Hebrews, 11:1.

32. John W. Gardner, *On Leadership* (New York: The Free Press, 1990), 199.

33. John Roger and Peter McWilliams, *Wealth 101: Getting What You Want – Enjoying What You've Got* (Los Angeles, CA: Prelude Press, 1992), 361.

34. Barbara Ward, *Faith and Freedom* (New York: W. W. Norton and Co., 1954), 262.

35. *The Holy Bible*, 2 Cor. 5:7

36. Ward, *Faith and Freedom*, 264-265.

37. Ibid., 265.

38. Ibid., 275.

39. Ibid., 264.

40. Emma S. Etuk, *What's So Good About Christianity? Five Amazing Ways the Gospel Has Influenced and Blessed Our Lives* (Washington, D.C.: Emida International Publishers, 2000), 81- 111.

41. Ward, *Faith and Freedom*, 275.

42. Billy Graham, *Hope For the Troubled Heart* (Dallas, TX: Word Publishing, 1991), ix.

43. Ibid.

44. Robert E. Luccock, *On Becoming the Best We Can Be* (Cleveland, OH: The Pilgrim Press, 1991), 51-61.

45. Jill Haak Adels, *The Wisdom of the Saints: An Anthology* (New York: Oxford University Press, 1987), 48.

46. Ibid., 50.

47. Aly Wassil, *The Wisdom of Christ* (New York: Harper and Row, 1965), 209.

48. Hy Pickering, *Twelve Baskets Full of Original Outlines and Bible Studies* (London: Pickering and Inglis, Ltd., 1905, reprint, 1968), 109.

49. *The Holy Bible*, I Cor. 15:19.

50. Thomas Paine cited in Bartlett, *Familiar Quotations*, 385, italics added for emphasis.

51. Robert Maynard Hutchins cited in Bartlett, *Familiar Quotations*, 845.

52. Italics added for emphasis.

53. Leonard E. Read, *The Love of Liberty* (Irvington-on-Hudson, NY: The Foundation For Economic Education, Inc., 1975), 54.

54. Adler, *Six Great Ideas*, 155-163.

55. Ibid., 156.

56. Ibid., 160.

57. Read, 54.

58. Adler, *Six Great Ideas*, 164.

59. Ibid., 165.

60. Ibid., 166.

61. Ibid., 167.

62. Ibid.

63. Ibid., 172.

64. Ward, *Faith and Freedom*, 283.

65. Emerson cited in Mortimer J. Adler and Charles Van Doren, eds., *Great Treasury of Western Thought: A Compendium of Important Statements On Man and His Institutions By the Great Thinkers in Western History* (New York: R. R. Bowker Co., 1977), 693.

66. Philip Sidney cited in David Powell, *The Wisdom of the Novel: A Dictionary of Quotations* (New York: Garland Publishing, 1985), 340.

67. J. Bruce Long, "Love," in Mircea Eliade, ed., *The Encyclopedia of Religion* (New York: Macmillan Publishing Co., 1987), 9: 31. See also W. R. Boyce Gibson, et.al., "Love," in James Hastings, ed., *Encyclopedia of Religion and Ethics* (New York: Charles Scribner's Sons, 1922), 151-183 and Denis De Rougemont, "Love," in Wiener, *Dictionary of the History of Ideas*, 3: 94-108.

68. Long, 37.

69. Plato cited in Adler and Doren, 724.

70. I am indebted to Professor Sulayman Nyang of Howard University for his advice that I include this chapter.

Chapter 13:

1. Herbert Hoover, *The Challenge To Liberty* (New York: Charles Scribner's Sons, 1934), 193.

2. Ibid., 2.

3. Ibid., 198.

4. Huston Smith, *The World's Religions: Our Great Wisdom Traditions* (New York: HarperCollins Publishers, 1991), 235-236.

5. Ibid., 239. See also Arvind Sharma, ed., *Our Religions* (New York: HarperCollins Publishers, 1993), 425-532.

6. S. G. F. Brandon, "Sin and Salvation," in Philip P. Wiener, ed., *Dictionary of the History of Ideas*, 4:224 and 230.

7. Ibid., 231. The Koranic reference is 2:45.

8. Roosevelt cited in Bartlett, *Familiar Quotations*, 779.

9. Lao-tzu cited in Bartlett, *Familiar Quotations*, 64. See also Rene Dumont, *False Start in Africa*, trans. Phyllis Nauts Ott (New York: Frederick A. Praeger, 1969) and Karl Federn, *The Materialist Conception of History: A Critical Analysis* (Westport, CT: Greenwood Press, 1971).

10. Don Marquis cited in Gerald F. Lieberman, *3,500 Good Quotes For Speakers* (New York: Doubleday, 1983), 30.

11. See Bartlett, *Familiar Quotations*, 760.

12. Toyin Falola, *The History of Nigeria* (Westport, CT: Greenwood Press, 1999), 167 and 173.

13. Thomas Paine cited in Anson Phelps Stokes, *Church and State in the United States: Historical Development and Contemporary Problems of Religious Freedom Under the Constitution*, vol. 1 (New York: Harper and Brothers, 1950), 23. The quote is taken from Paine's book, *The Rights of Man*, page 58.

14. Maurice Cranston, "Toleration," in Paul Edwards, ed., *The Encyclopedia of Philosophy*, vol. 8 (New York: Macmillan Publishing Co., 1967), 143-146.

15. Ibid.

16. Ibid.

17. Plato cited in Lieberman, *3500 Good Quotes For Speakers*, 136 and 252.

18. Franklin H. Littell, "Foundations and Traditions of Religious Liberty." Keynote Address to the Bicentennial Conference On Religious Liberty held at Philadelphia, Pennsylvania, on April 26, 1976, page 4.

19. Stokes, 17.

20. Charles Kimball, *Striving Together: A Way Forward in Christian-Muslim Relations* (Maryknoll, NY: Orbis Books, 1991), Badru D. Kateregga, *Islam and Christianity: A Muslim and A Christian In Dialogue* (Grand Rapids, MI: William B. Eerdmans, 1981) and Kenneth Cragg, *Muhammad and the Christian: A Question of Response* (Maryknoll, NY: Orbis Books, 1984).

21. See John Kenneth Galbraith, *American Capitalism: The Concept of Countervailing Power* (Boston, MA: Houghton Mifflin Co., 1952), 18 and Allen Hollis, *The Bible and Money* (New York: Hawthorn Books, 1976), 111.

22. Ali A. Mazrui, *Political Values and the Educated Class in Africa* (Berkeley: University of California Press, 1978), 203. See also pages 346-354 and Lilyan Kesteloot, *Intellectual Origins of the African Revolution* (Washington, D.C.: Black Orpheus Press, 1972), 25-26.

23. Nzeogwu cited in Leo Dare, "Politics Since Independence," in Richard Olaniyan, ed., *Nigerian History and Culture* (Lagos: Longman Nigeria Ltd., 1985), 194-195 and N. J. Miners, *The Nigerian Army, 1956-1966* (London: Methuen and Co., 1971), 177. For a fuller treatment of Nzeogwu's role in the 1966 Nigerian coup, see Adewale Ademoyega, *Why We Struck: The Story of the First Nigerian Coup* (Ibadan: Evans Brothers, 1981); Olusegun Obasanjo, *Nzeogwu: An Intimate Portrait of Major Chukwuma Kaduna Nzeogwu* (Ibadan: Spectrum Books, 1987); Robin Luckham, *The Nigerian Military: A Sociological Analysis of Authority and Revolt 1960-67* (Cambridge: University Press, 1971), 1-50; and Walter Schwarz, *Nigeria* (New York: Frederick A. Praeger, 1968), 196.

24. Holmes cited in Bartlett, *Familiar Quotations*, 644.

25. Bala J. Takaya and Soni Gwanle Tyoden, eds., *The Kaduna Mafia* (Jos, Nigeria: Jos University Press Ltd., 1987) and *Webster's Ninth New Collegiate Dictionary*, 1985 ed., 715.

26. See "The North Is For June 12," *Tell* (August 15, 1994): 8-16.

27. Takaya and Tyoden, 6 and 11.

28. Simeon Okezuo Nwobi, *Sharia Law In Nigeria: What A Christian Must Know* (Abuja, Nigeria: Totan Publishers Ltd., 2000), 16 and 29, suggests that Ahmadu Bello introduced the Kaduna Mafia into Nigerian politics and religion.

29. Ibid., 90-91.

30. Ibid., 92.

31. Cited in *African News Weekly* (September 16, 1994): 7.

32. H. O. Davies, *Nigeria: The Prospects For Democracy*, 68 and 100-101.

33. Azikiwe, "Tribalism: A Pragmatic Instrument For National Unity," in J. Ayo Langley, *Ideologies of Liberation in Black Africa 1856-1970: Documents On Modern African Political Thought From Colonial Times to the Present* (London: Rex Collings, 1979), 458-459.

Chapter 14:

1. Philip Wylie, *Generation of Vipers* (New York: Rinehart and Co., 1942, 1955), 316.

2. Treadgold, *Freedom: A History*, 415-416.

3. Isaac Umunna, "Forty Years of Freedom," *NewsAfrica* (October 23, 2001): 10-14. See also pages 6-8 and 15-27 for country by country profile of the state of freedom.

4. Baffour Ankomah, "The Greatest Crime Against Humanity!," *New African* (July/August, 2001): 20-21. See also pages 22-25 and 28-34.

5. See "Violent Clashes That Threaten Democracy Under Obasanjo," *Vanguard* (October 16, 2001): 9. See also Nathaniel Ikyur, "Protests In Kano Over U. S. Raids On Taliban," *Sunday Vanguard* (October 14, 2001): 1-2, Yakubu Musa, "Violence Marks Anti-U. S. Demonstration In Kano," *This Day*

(October 14, 2001): 1 and 4, and Dulue Mbachu and Douglas Fabah, "200 May Be Dead In Nigerian Riots," *The Washington Post* (October 15, 2001): A9.

6. Paul Marshall, *Their Blood Cries Out*, 62-65 and Nina Shea, *In the Lion's Den*, 27-55.

7. Nigeria is very likely to explode, if not handled with extreme care, because of the ethno-religious clashes caused by the imposition of the *sharia* upon some northern states. See the editorial opinion, "Nigeria In Turmoil," *West Africa* (October 22-28, 2001): 6, Dokun Oloyede, "Nigeria's Hot Spots: Any Remedy Yet?," *ThisDay* (September 24, 2001): 60-61, and Napoleon Ovie Igbuku-Otu, "Islamic Fundamentalism: Nigerian Connection," *TheNews* (April 30, 2001): 20.

8. See "Special Report: The Dele Giwa Story," *Africa Today* (October 2001): 10-30.

9. Ray Ekpu, "The Gruesome Murder of Dele Giwa," *Newswatch* (October 22, 2001): 52-55.

10. Ademola Adegbamigbe, "The Fall Guy," *TheNews* (April 30, 2001): 19.

11. Myles Monroe, *The Burden of Freedom* (Lake Mary, FL: Creation House, 2000), 239.

12. *The Holy Bible*, John 8:32 and 36.

SELECTED BIBLIOGRAPHY

Abraham, W. E., *The Mind of Africa*. Chicago, IL: The University of Chicago Press, 1962.

Addo, Herb. *Imperialism: The Permanent Stage of Capitalism*. Tokyo: The United Nations University, 1986.

Adels, Jill Haak. *The Wisdom of the Saints: An Anthology*. New York: Oxford University Press, 1987.

Ademoyega, Adewale. *Why We Struck: The Story of the First Nigerian Coup*. Ibadan: Evans Brothers, 1981.

Adler, Mortimer J. *The Idea of Freedom: A Dialectical Examination of the Conceptions of Freedom*. Garden City, NY: Doubleday and Co., 1958.

Adler, *Six Great Ideas*. New York: Collier Books, 1981.

____, *Truth in Religion: The Plurality of Religions and the Unity of Truth: An Essay in the Philosophy of Religion*. New York: Collier Books, 1990.

Adler and Doren, Charles Van, eds. *Great Treasury of Western Thought: A Compendium of Important Statements On Man and His Institutions By the Great Thinkers in Western History*. New York: R. R. Bowker Co., 1977.

Aptheker, Herbert. *Abolitionism: A Revolutionary Movement*. Boston, MA: Twayne Publishers, 1989.

Arendt, Hannah. *The Origins of Totalitarianism*. New York: Harcourt, Brace and World, 1966.

Arlinghaus, Bruce E. *Military Development in Africa: The Political and Economic Risks of Arms Transfers*. Boulder, CO: Westview Press, 1984.

_____ and Baker, Pauline H., eds. *African Armies: Evolution and Capabilities*. Boulder, CO: Westview Press, 1986.

276

Arthur, John. *Freedom For Africa*. Accra, Ghana: Government Printer, 1961.

Assensoh, A. B. *African Political Leadership: Jomo Kenyatta, Kwame Nkrumah, and Julius K. Nyerere*. Malabar, FL: Krieger Publishing Co., 1998.

Awogu, F. Olisa. "The Bill of Rights in the United States and Nigeria: A Comparative Study." M. C. J. Thesis, Howard University, Washington, D.C., 1969.

Awolowo, Obafemi. *Awo: The Autobiography of Chief Obafemi Awolowo*. Cambridge: The University Press, 1960.

_____ *Path to Nigerian Freedom*. London: Faber and Faber Ltd., 1947.

_____ *Voice of Reason: Selected Speeches of Chief Obafemi Awolowo, vol. 1*. Akure, Nigeria: Fagbamigbe Publishers, 1981.

_____ *Freedom and Independence For Nigeria: A Statement of Policy*. Ibadan: PDA, 1958.

_____ *Thoughts On Nigerian Constitution*. Ibadan: Oxford University Press, 1966.

Ayittey, George B. N. *Africa Betrayed*. New York: St. Martin's Press, 1992.

_____ *Africa In Chaos*. New York: St. Martin's Press, 1998.

_____ *Indigenous African Institutions*. Ardsley-on-Hudson, NY: Transnational Publishers, 1991.

Azikiwe, Nnamdi. *My Odyssey: An Autobiography*. New York: Praeger, 1970.

_____ *Democracy With Military Vigilance*. Nsukka: African Book Co., 1974.

_____ *Ideology For Nigeria: Capitalism, Socialism or Welfarism?* Lagos: Macmillan Nigeria Publishers Ltd., 1980.

_____ *Zik: A Selection From the Speeches of Nnamdi Azikiwe*. Cambridge: The University Press, 1961.

Ba, Sylvia Washington. *The Concept of Negritude in the Poetry of Leopold Senghor*. Princeton, NJ: Princeton University Press, 1973.

Babatope, Ebenezer. *Inside Kirikiri (Prison Memoirs of a Politician)*. Enugu: Fourth Dimension Publishing, 1989.

Balaban, Oded and Erev, Anan. *The Bounds of Freedom: About the Eastern and Western Approaches to Freedom*. New York: Peter Lang Publishing, 1995.

Barnes, Harry Elmer. *An Intellectual and Cultural History of the Western World*. 3 vols. New York: Dover Publications, 1965.

Barnett, Randy E. *The Structure of Liberty: Justice and the Rule of Law*. NY: Oxford University Press, 1998.

Bartlett, John. *Familiar Quotations*. Boston, MA: Little, Brown and Co., 1980.

Bay, Christian. *The Structure of Freedom*. Stanford, CA: Stanford University Press, 1970.

Bebler, Anton. *Military Rule in Africa: Dahomey, Ghana, Sierra Leone, and Mali*. New York: Praeger Publishers, 1973.

Bello, Ahmadu. *My Life*. Cambridge: The University Press, 1962.

Bennett, Norman R. *Africa and Europe: From Roman Times to National Independence*. New York: Africana Publishing Co., 1984.

Benson, Mary. *Nelson Mandela: The Man and the Movement*. New York: W. W. Norton and Co., 1986.

Bergmann, Frithjof. *On Being Free*. Notre Dame, IN: University of Notre Dame Press, 1996.

Berkeley, Bill. *The Graves Are Not Yet Full: Race, Tribe and Power in the Heart of Africa*. New York: Basic Books, 2001.

Berlin, Isaiah. *The Power of Ideas*. Princeton, NJ: Princeton University Press, 2000.

_____ *Four Essays On Liberty*. New York: Oxford University Press, 1969.

Betts, Raymond F., ed. *The "Scramble" For Africa: Causes and Dimensions of Empire*. Lexington, MA: D. C. Heath and Co., 1966.

Biale, David. *Power and Powerlessness in Jewish History*. New York: Schoken Books, 1986.

Biddle, Francis. *The Fear of Freedom*. Garden City, NY: Doubleday and Co., 1952.

Bienen, Henry. *Armies and Parties in Africa*. New York: Africana Publishing Co., 1978.

Binder, Leonard. *Islamic Liberalism: A Critique of Development Ideologies*. Chicago, IL: The University of Chicago Press, 1988.

Bjornson, Richard. *The African Quest for Freedom and Identity: Cameroonian Writing and the National Experience*. Bloomington: Indiana University Press, 1991.

Blake, John W. *European Beginnings in West Africa 1454-1578. A Survey of the First Century of White Enterprise in West Africa, With Special Emphasis Upon the Rivalry of the Great Powers*. Westport, CT: Greenwood Press, 1937.

Boahen, A. Adu. *African Perspectives On Colonialism*. Baltimore, MD: The Johns Hopkins University Press, 1987.

Boller, Jr., Paul F. *Freedom and Fate in American Thought From Edwards to Dewey*. Dallas, TX: SMU Press, 1978.

Booth, General William. *In Darkest England and the Way Out*. Atlanta, GA: The Salvation Army, 1984.

Borgin, Karl and Corbett, Kathleen. *The Destruction of a Continent: Africa and International Aid*. San Diego, CA: Harcourt Brace Jovanovich, Publishers, 1982.

Boulares, Habib. *Islam: The Fear and the Hope*. Atlantic Highlands, NJ: Humanities Press, 1990.

Brett, E. A. *Colonialism and Underdevelopment in East Africa: The Politics of Economic Change 1919-1939*. London: Heinemann, 1973.

Brooker, Paul. *Twentieth-Century Dictatorships: The Ideological One-Party States*. Washington Square: New York University Press, 1995.

Brown, J. F. *Surge to Freedom: The End of Communist Rule in Eastern Europe*. Durham, NC: Duke University Press, 1991.

Carlyle, A. J. *Political Liberty: A History of the Conception in the Middle Ages and Modern Times*. Westport, CT: Greenwood Press, 1980.

Carter, Gwendolen M., ed. *African One-Party States*. Ithaca, NY: Cornell University Press, 1962.

Carter, Ian. "The Independent Value of Freedom." *Ethics* 105, 1995.

Cary, Joyce. *The Case For African Freedom*. New York: McGraw-Hill Book Co., 1964.

Chafee, Jr., Zechariah. *The Blessings of Liberty*. Westport, CT: Greenwood Press, 1973.

Christianity and Freedom: A Symposium. London: Hollis and Carter, 1955.

Clark, Andrew F. and Phillips, Lucie Colvin. *Historical Dictionary of Senegal*. Metuchen, NJ: The Scarecrow Press, 1994.

Clark, J. P. *America, Their America*. New York: Africana Publishing Co., 1969.

Cochran, David C. *The Color of Freedom: Race and Contemporary American Liberalism*. New York: State University of New York Press, 1999.

Coleman, James S. *Nigeria: Background to Nationalism*. Berkeley: University of California Press, 1971.

Cooper, John W. *The Theology of Freedom: The Legacy of Jacques Maritain and Reinhold Niebuhr*. Macon, GA: Mercer University Press, 1985.

Cox, Harold. *Economic Liberty*. London: Longmans, Green and Co., 1920.

Cox, Richard. *Kenyatta's Country*. New York: Frederick A. Praeger, Publishers, 1965.

Cragg, Kenneth. *Muhammad and the Christian: A Question of Response*. Maryknoll, NY: Orbis Books, 1984.

Cranston, Maurice. *Freedom: A New Analysis*. London: Longmans, Green and Co., 1953.

Crwys-Williams, Jennifer, ed. *In the Words of Nelson Mandela*. Secaucus, NJ: Carol Publishing Group, 1998.

Curry, Dean C. *A World Without Tyranny: Christian Faith and International Politics*. Westchester, IL: Crossway Books, 1990.

Curtin, Philip D. *The Image of Africa: British Ideas and Action*. 2 vols. Madison: The University of Wisconsin Press, 1973.

_____ ed., *Imperialism*. New York: Harper and Row, Publishers, 1971.

Danford, John W. *Roots of Freedom: A Primer On Modern Liberty.* Wilmington, DE: ISI Books, 2000.

D'Angelo, Edward. *The Problem of Freedom and Determinism.* Columbia: University of Missouri Press, 1968.

Darlington, Charles F. and Darlington, Alice B. *African Betrayal.* New York: David McKay Co., 1968.

Darwall, Stephen, ed. *Equal Freedom: Selected Tanner Lectures On Human Values.* Ann Arbor: The University of Michigan Press, 1995.

Davidson, Basil. *The Blackman's Burden: Africa and the Curse of the Nation-State.* New York: Times Books, 1992.

_____ *Let Freedom Come: Africa in Modern History.* Boston, MA: Little, Brown and Co., 1978.

Davies, A. Powell. *American Destiny: A Faith For America.* Boston, MA: The Beacon Press, 1942.

Davies, H. O. *Nigeria: The Prospects For Democracy.* London: Weidenfeld and Nicolson, 1961.

Decalo, Samuel. *Psychoses of Power: African Personal Dictatorships.* Boulder, CO: Westview Press, 1989.

_____ *Coups and Army Rule in Africa: Motivations and Constraints.* New Haven, CT: Yale University Press, 1990.

Delf, George. *Jomo Kenyatta: Towards Truth About "The Light of Kenya."* New York: Doubleday and Co., 1961.

Devlin, Patrick. *The Enforcement of Morals.* London: Oxford University Press, 1965.

Dewey, John. *Freedom and Culture.* Amherst, NY: Prometheus Books, 1989.

Dike, K. Onwuka. *Trade and Politics in the Niger Delta 1830-1885: An Introduction to the Economic and Political History of Nigeria.* Oxford: Clarendon Press, 1956.

Dilman, Ilnam. *Free Will: An Historical and Philosophical Introduction.* London: Routledge, 1999.

Diop, Cheikh Anta. *The African Origin of Civilization: Myth or Reality*. Westport, CT: Lawrence Hill and Co., 1974.

Downing, F. Gerald. *Jesus and the Threat of Freedom*. London: SCM Press, 1987.

Duggan, William Redman and Civille, John R. *Tanzania and Nyerere: A Study of Ujamaa and Nationhood*. Maryknoll, NY: Orbis Books, 1976.

Dumont, Rene. *False Start in Africa*. New York: Frederick A. Praeger, 1969.

Dunn, John, ed. *Democracy: The Unfinished Journey 508 B.C. to A.D. 1993*. New York: Oxford University Press, 1992.

Ebenstein, William. "Liberty." In *The Encyclopedia Americana*, vol. 17. Danbury, CT: Grolier, 2000.

Edwards, Paul, ed. *The Encyclopedia of Philosophy*, vol. 8. New York: Macmillan Publishing Co., 1967.

Eliade, Mircea, ed. *The Encyclopedia of Religion*. New York: Macmillan Publishing Co., 1987.

Enahoro, Anthony. *Fugitive Offender: The Story of a Political Prisoner*. London: Cassell and Co., 1965.

Enayat, Hamid. *Modern Islamic Political Thought*. Austin: University of Texas Press, 1982.

Ernst, Morris L. *The First Freedom*. New York: The Macmillan Co., 1946.

Esposito, John and Voll, John O. *Islam and Democracy*. New York: Oxford University Press, 1996.

_____ *The Islamic Threat: Myth or Reality?* New York: Oxford University Press, 1992.

Etuk, Emma S. *Destiny Is Not A Matter of Chance: Essays in Reflection and Contemplation on the Destiny of Blacks*. New York: Peter Lang, 1989.

_____ *A Walk Through the Wilderness*. New York: Carlton Press, 1990.

_____ *What's So Good About Christianity? Five Amazing Ways the Gospel Has Influenced and Blessed Our Lives*. Washington, D.C.: Emida International Publishers, 2000.

Evans, M. Stanton. *The Theme Is Freedom: Religion, Politics, and the American Tradition*. Washington, D.C.: Regnery Publishing, Inc., 1994.

Fagan, Brian M. *A Short History of Zambia From the Earliest Times Until A.D. 1900*. Nairobi: Oxford University Press, 1966.

Falola, Toyin. *The History of Nigeria*. Westport, CT: Greenwood Press, 1999.

Faust, Drew Gilpin, ed. *The Ideology of Slavery: Proslavery Thought in the Antebellum South, 1830-1860*. Baton Rouge: Louisiana State University Press, 1981.

Federn, Karl. *The Materialist Conception of History: A Critical Analysis*. Westport, CT: Greenwood Press, 1971.

Fischer, John Martin, ed. *God, Foreknowledge, and Freedom*. Stanford, CA: Stanford University Press, 1989.

Fisher, Humphrey J. *Slavery in the History of Muslim Black Africa*. Washington Square: New York University Press, 2001.

Flatham, Richard E. *The Philosophy and Politics of Freedom*. Chicago, IL: The University of Chicago Press, 1987.

Fleischacker, Samuel. *A Third Concept of Liberty: Judgment and Freedom in Kant and Adam Smith*. Princeton, NJ: Princeton University Press, 1999.

Fluehr-Lobban, Carolyn. *Islamic Society in Practice*. Gainesville: University Press of Florida, 1994.

Foltz, William J. and Bienen, Henry S. *Arms and the African: Military Influences On Africa's International Relations*. New Haven, CT: Yale University Press, 1985.

Forman, Frank. *The Metaphysics of Liberty*. Dordrecht, the Netherlands: Kluwer Academic Publishers, 1989.

Friedrich, Carl J. and Brzezinski, Zbigniew K. *Totalitarian Dictatorship and Autocracy*. Cambridge, MA: Harvard University Press, 1965.

Fromm, Erich. *Escape From Freedom*. New York: Henry Holt and Co., 1994.

Fruchtman, Jack, Jr. *Thomas Paine: Apostle of Freedom*. New York: Four Walls Eight Windows, 1994.

Fullinwider, Robert K. and Mills, Claudia, eds. *The Moral Foundations of Civil Rights.* Totowa, NJ: Rowman and Littlefield, 1986.

Galbraith, John Kenneth. *American Capitalism: The Concept of Countervailing Power.* Boston, MA: Houghton Mifflin Co., 1952.

Gann, L. H. and Duignan, Peter, eds. *Colonialism in Africa.* vol. 2. Cambridge: University Press, 1982.

Gardner, John W. *On Leadership.* New York: The Free Press, 1990.

Garnsey, Peter. *Ideas of Slavery From Aristotle to Augustine.* Cambridge: Cambridge University Press, 1996.

Gellar, Sheldon. *Senegal: An African Nation Between Islam and the West.* Boulder, CO: Westview Press, 1982.

Gibbs, Benjamin. *Freedom and Liberation.* New York: St. Martin's Press, 1976.

Gilbert, Christopher P. *The Impact of Churches on Political Behavior: An Empirical Study.* Westport, CT: Greenwood Press, 1993.

Graham, Billy. *Hope For the Troubled Heart.* Dallas, TX: Word Publishing, 1991.

Grassian, Victor. *Moral Reasoning: Ethical Theory and Some Contemporary Moral Problems.* Englewood Cliffs, NJ: Prentice-Hall, 1981.

Greenawalt, Kent. "Civil Rights and Liberties." in *The Encyclopedia Americana*, vol. 6, Danbury, CT: Grolier Inc., 1993.

Grotpeter, John J. *Historical Dictionary of Zambia.* Metuchen, NJ: The Scarecrow Press, 1979.

Gutierrez, Gustavo. *The Power of the Poor in History*, trans. Robert R. Barr. Maryknoll, NY: Orbis Books, 1984.

Gutteridge, W. F. *Military Regimes in Africa.* London: Methuen and Co., 1975.

Haddad, Yvonne Yazbeck and Haddad, Wadiz, eds. *Christian-Muslim Encounters.* Gainesville: University Press of Florida, 1995.

Hall, Richard. *The High Price of Principles: Kaunda and the White South.* London: Hodder and Stoughton, 1969.

Hallowell, John H. *The Moral Foundation of Democracy*. Chicago, IL: The University of Chicago Press, 1973.

Halperin, Morton H. et al. *The Lawless State: The Crimes of the U. S. Intelligence Agencies*. New York: Penguin Books, 1976.

Handlin, Oscar and Mary. *The Dimensions of Liberty*. Cambridge, MA: Harvard University Press, 1961.

Hanna, William John, ed. *Independent Black Africa: The Politics of Freedom*. Chicago, IL: Rand McNally and Co., 1964.

Harbeson, John W., ed. *The Military in African Politics*. New York: Praeger, 1987.

Harlow, Carol. "What Is Wrong With Rights?" *Public Law and Politics* (1986).

Harris, Joseph E. *Africans and Their History*. New York: New American Library, 1972.

_____ *The African Presence in Asia: Consequences of the East African Slave Trade*. Evanston, IL: Northwestern University Press, 1971.

Harvey, William Burnett. *Freedom, University and the Law: The Legal Status of Academic Freedom in the University of Black Africa*. Lagos: University of Lagos Press, 1978.

Hastings, James, ed. *Encyclopedia of Religion and Ethics*. New York: Charles Scribner's Sons, 1922.

Hatch, John. *Two African Statesmen: Kaunda of Zambia and Nyerere of Tanzania*. Chicago, IL: Henry Regnery Co., 1976.

Hayek, Friedrich A. *The Constitution of Liberty*. Chicago, IL: The University of Chicago Press, 1960.

_____ *The Road to Serfdom*. Chicago, IL: The University of Chicago Press, 1994.

Heinecke, P. *Freedom in the Grave: Nigeria and the Political Economy of Africa*. Okpella, Nigeria: S. Asekome, 1986.

Hexham, Irving. *The Irony of Apartheid: The Struggle For National Independence of Afrikaner Calvinism Against British Imperialism*. New York: The Edwin Mellen Press, 1981.

Hilliard, Constance B., ed. *Intellectual Traditions of Pre-Colonial Africa*. Boston, MA: The McGraw-Hill Co., 1998.

Hodgkin, Thomas. *Nationalism in Colonial Africa*. New York: New York University Press, 1957.

Hollis, Allen. *The Bible and Money*. New York: Hawthorn Books, 1976.

Honderich, Ted., ed. *Essays on Freedom of Action*. London: Routledge and Kegan Paul, 1973.

Hoover, Herbert. *The Challenge to Liberty*. New York: Charles Scribner's Sons, 1934.

Hughes, Langston. *An African Treasury: Articles/Essays/Stories/Poems By Black Africans*. New York: Pyramid Books, 1961.

_____ "Freedom Train: A Poem." *New Republic*, 117, 27, (1947).

Hunold, Albert, ed. *Freedom and Serfdom: An Anthology of Western Thought*. Dordrecht, Holland: D. Reidel Publishing Co., 1961.

[Ibekwe], Chinweizu. *The West and the Rest of Us: White Predators, Black Slavers and the African Elite*. New York: Random House, 1975.

_____ *Decolonising the African Mind*. Lagos: Pero Press, 1987.

Ikeotuonye, Vincent C. *Zik of Africa*. London: P. R. Macmillan Ltd., 1961.

Iliffe, John. *The African Poor: A History*. Cambridge: Cambridge University Press, 1987.

_____ *Africans: The History of A Continent*. Cambridge: Cambridge University Press, 1995.

Inikori, J. E., ed. *Forced Migration: The Impact of the Export Slave Trade on African Societies*. New York: Africana Publishing Co., 1982.

Isichei, Elizabeth. *A History of Nigeria*. London: Longmans, 1983.

Jackson, John G. *Introduction to African Civilizations*. Secaucus, NJ: The Citadel Press, 1970.

Jackson, Robert H., and Rosberg, Carl G. *Personal Rule in Black Africa: Prince, Autocrat, Prophet, Tyrant.* Berkeley: University of California Press, 1982.

Jaffa, Harry V. *Equality and Liberty: Theory and Practice in American Politics.* New York: Oxford University Press, 1965.

Jasper, William F. *Global Tyranny ... Step By Step: The United Nations and the Emerging New World Order.* Appleton, WI: Western Islands Publishers, 1992.

Jones, Amos. *Paul's Message of Freedom.* Valley Forge, PA: Judson Press, 1984.

Jones, Howard Mumford, ed. *Primer of Intellectual Freedom.* Cambridge, MA: Harvard University Press, 1949.

Jouvenel, Bertrand de. *On Power: Its Nature and the History of Its Growth.* New York: The Viking Press, 1949.

July, Robert W. *The Origins of Modern African Thought: Its Development in West Africa During the Nineteenth and Twentieth Centuries.* New York: Frederick A. Praeger, 1967.

Kallen, Horace M. *A Study of Liberty.* Yellow Springs, OH: The Antioch Press, 1959.

Kandeke, Timothy K. *Fundamentals of Zambian Humanism.* Lusaka: NECZAM, 1977.

Kateregga, Badru D. *Islam and Christianity: A Muslim and a Christian in Dialogue.* Grand Rapids, MI: William B. Eerdmans, 1981.

Kaunda, Kenneth D. *Zambia Shall Be Free: An Autobiography.* London: Heinemann, 1979.

_____ *Black Government? A Discussion Between Colin Morris and Kenneth Kaunda.* Lusaka: United Society for Christian Literature, 1960.

_____ *A Humanist in Africa: Letters to Colin Morris.* London: Longmans, 1966.

_____ *Letter to My Children.* London: Longman Group Ltd., 1973.

_____ *The Riddle of Violence.* New York: Harper and Row, 1980.

Kautsky, John H., ed. *Political Change in Underdeveloped Countries: Nationalism and Communism.* New York: John Wiley and Sons, 1962.

Kenworthy, Leonard and Ferrari, Erma. *Leaders of New Nations.* Garden City, NY: Doubleday and Co., 1968.

Kenyatta, Jomo. *Facing Mount Kenya: The Tribal Life of the Gikuyu.* London: Secker and Warburg, 1953.

_____ *Harambee! The Prime Minister of Kenya's Speeches 1963-1964: From the Attainment of Internal Self-Government to the Threshold of the Kenya Republic.* Nairobi: Oxford University Press, 1964.

_____ *Suffering Without Bitterness: The Founding of the Kenya Nation.* Nairobi: East African Publishing House, 1968.

Kesteloot, Lilyan. *Intellectual Origins of the African Revolution.* Washington, D.C.: Black Orpheus Press, 1972.

Kadduri, Majid. *The Islamic Conception of Justice.* Baltimore, MD: The Johns Hopkins University Press, 1984.

_____ *Political Trends in the Arab World: The Role of Ideas and Ideals in Politics.* Westport, CT: Greenwood Press, 1983.

Kimball, Charles. *Striving Together: A Way Forward in Christian-Muslim Relations.* Maryknoll, NY: Orbis Books, 1991.

Klein, Martin A. *Islam and Imperialism in Senegal: Sine-Sabum, 1847-1914.* Stanford, CA: Stanford University Press, 1968.

Klitgaard, Robert. *Tropical Gangsters.* New York: Basic Books, 1990.

Knight, Frank H. *Freedom and Reform: Essays in Economics and Social Philosophy.* New York: Harper and Brothers, 1947.

Kohn, Hans and Sokolsky, Wallace. *African Nationalism in the Twentieth Century.* Princeton: D. Van Nostrand Co., 1965.

Konvitz, Milton R. *Fundamental Liberties of a Free People: Religion, Speech, Press, Assembly.* Ithaca, NY: Cornell University Press, 1957.

Kramer, Martin. *Political Islam.* Beverly Hills, CA: Sage Publications, 1980.

LaHaye, Tim. *The Battle for the Mind.* Old Tappan, NJ: Fleming H. Revell Co., 1980.

Lamont, Corliss. *Freedom of Choice Affirmed*. New York: Horizon Press, 1967.

Lane, Rose Wilder. *The Discovery of Freedom: Man's Struggle Against Authority*. San Francisco, CA: Fox and Wilkes, 1993.

Langley, J. Ayo. *Ideologies of Liberation in Black Africa 1856-1970: Documents On Modern African Political Thought From Colonial Times to the Present*. London: Rex Collings, 1979.

Lapping, Brian. *End of Empire*. New York: St. Martin's Press, 1985.

Lasswell, Harold D. *National Security and Individual Freedom*. New York: McGraw-Hill Book Co., 1950.

Lee, Dorothy. *Freedom and Culture*. Englewood-Cliffs, NJ: Prentice-Hall, 1959.

Lee, J. M. *African Armies and Civil Order*. New York: Frederick A. Praeger, 1969.

Lefever, Ernest W. *Spear and Scepter: Army, Police and Politics in Tropical Africa*. Washington, D.C.: The Brookings Institution, 1970.

Legesse, Asmarom. *Gada: Three Approaches to the Study of African Societies*. New York: The Free Press, 1973.

Legum, Colin, ed. *Zambia: Independence and Beyond. The Speeches of Kenneth Kaunda*. London: Thomas Nelson, 1966.

_____ and Newson, Marion, eds. *African Contemporary Record: Annual Survey and Documents 1987-1988*. New York: Africana Publishing Co., 1989.

Lewis, Bernard. *Race and Slavery in the Middle East: An Historical Enquiry*. New York: Oxford University Press, 1990.

Lewis, Clarence Irving. *The Ground and Nature of the Right*. New York: Columbia University Press, 1955.

Lewis, H. D. *Freedom and History*. London: George Allen and Unwin Ltd., 1962.

Lieberman, Gerald F. *3500 Good Quotes For Speakers*. New York: Doubleday and Co., 1983.

Lipschutz, Mark R. and Rasmussen, R. Kent. *Dictionary of African Historical Biography*. Berkeley: University of California Press, 1986.

Listowel, Judith. *The Making of Tanganyika*. London: Chatto and Windus, 1965.

Lloyd, P. C. *Africa in Social Change: West African Societies in Transition*. New York: Praeger, 1967.

Logan, Rayford. *The Betrayal of the Negro From Rutherford B. Hayes to Woodrow Wilson*. New York: Collier Books, 1965.

Lovejoy, Paul E., ed. *Africans in Bondage: Studies in Slavery and the Slave Trade*. Madison: The University of Wisconsin Press, 1986.

_____ *The Ideology of Slavery in Africa*. Beverly Hills, CA: Sage Publications, 1981.

Lucas, Eric., ed. *What Is Freedom?* London: Oxford University Press, 1963.

Luccock, Robert E. *On Becoming the Best We Can Be*. Cleveland, OH: The Pilgrim Press, 1991.

Luckham, Robin. *The Nigerian Military: A Sociological Analysis of Authority and Revolt 1960-67*. Cambridge: University Press, 1971.

Lugard, Frederick. *The Dual Mandate in British Tropical Africa*. Hamden, CT: Archon Books, 1965.

Macdonald, Duncan B. *Development of Muslim Theology, Jurisprudence and Constitutional Theory*. New York: Charles Scribner's Sons, 1903.

MacDonald, Scott., ed. *Being and Goodness: The Concept of the Good in Metaphysics and Philosophical Theology*. Ithaca, NY: Cornell University Press, 1991.

Madubuike, Ihechukwu. *The Senegalese Novel: A Sociological Study of the Impact of the Politics of Assimilation*. Washington, D.C.: Three Continent Press, 1983.

Magdoff, Harry. *Imperialism: From the Colonial Age to the Present*. New York: Monthly Review Press, 1978.

Maier, Karl. *This House Has Fallen: Midnight in Nigeria*. New York: Public Affairs, 2000.

Majdalany, Fred. *State of Emergency: The Full Story of Mau Mau*. Boston, MA: Houghton Mifflin Co., 1963.

Malinowski, Bronislaw. *Freedom and Civilization*. New York: Roy Publishers, 1944.

Mandela, Nelson. *The Struggle Is My Life*. New York: Pathfinder Press, 1986.

_____ *Long Walk to Freedom: The Autobiography of Nelson Mandela*. Boston, MA: Little, Brown and Co., 1994.

_____, Winnie. *Part of My Soul Went With Him*. New York: W. W. Norton and Co., 1984.

Maneli, Mieczyslaw. *Freedom and Tolerance*. New York: Octagon Books, 1984.

Maritain, Jacques. *Man and the State*. Chicago, IL: The University of Chicago Press, 1951.

Markakis, John and Waller, Michael, eds. *Military Marxist Regimes in Africa*. London: Frank Cass, 1986.

Markovitz, Irving Leonard. *Leopold Sedar Senghor and the Politics of Negritude*. New York: Atheneum, 1969.

Marmon, Shaun E., ed. *Slavery in the Islamic Middle East*. Princeton, NJ: Markus Wiener Publishers, 1999.

Marsha, Tony Toyin. "Liberty in Contemporary Thought." M.A. Thesis, Howard University, Washington, D.C., 1977.

Marvin, David K., ed. *Emerging Africa in World Affairs*. San Francisco, CA: Chandler Publishing Co., 1965.

Masood, Steven. *The Bible and the Qur'an: A Question of Integrity*. Waynesboro, GA: OM Publishing, 2001.

Mathews, Shailer and Smith, Gerald Birney, eds. *A Dictionary of Religion and Ethics*. London: Waverley Book Co., 1921.

Mayer, Ann Elizabeth. *Islam and Human Rights: Tradition and Politics*. Boulder, CO: Westview Press, 1995.

Mazrui, Ali A. *Political Values and the Educated Class in Africa*. Berkeley: University of California Press, 1978.

Mboya, Tom. *Freedom and After*. Boston, MA: Little, Brown and Co., 1963.

McKeon, Richard. *Freedom and History and Other Essays*. Chicago, IL: The University of Chicago Press, 1990.

Meebelo, Henry. *Main Currents of Zambian Humanist Thought.* Lusaka: Oxford University Press, 1973.

Meer, Fatima. *Higher Than Hope: The Authorized Biography of Nelson Mandela.* New York: Harper and Row, 1988.

Melady, Thomas Patrick. *Kenneth Kaunda of Zambia: Selections From His Writings.* New York: Frederick A. Praeger, 1962.

Memmi, Albert. *The Colonizer and the Colonized.* Boston, MA: Beacon Press, 1991.

Meredith, Martin. *Nelson Mandela: A Biography.* New York: St. Martin's Press, 1997.

Mernissi, Fatima. *Islam and Democracy: Fear of the Modern World.* trans. Mary Jo Lakeland. Cambridge, MA: Perseus Books, 1992.

Metrowich, F. R., ed. *African Freedom Annual, 1978.* Sandton: Southern African Freedom Foundation, 1978.

Mezu, S. Okechukwu and Desai, Ram, eds. *Black Leaders of the Centuries.* Buffalo, NY: Black Academy Press, 1970.

Mill, John Stuart. *On Liberty.* New York: Penguin Books, 1985.

Miller, David L. *Modern Science and Human Freedom.* Austin: University of Texas Press, 1959.

Miners, N. J. *The Nigerian Army, 1956-1966.* London: Methuen and Co., 1971.

Mitchell, Joshua. *The Fragility of Freedom: Tocqueville on Religion, Democracy, and the American Future.* Chicago, IL: The University of Chicago Press, 1995.

Mohaddessin, Mohammad. *Islamic Fundamentalism: The New Global Threat.* Washington, D.C.: Seven Locks Press, 1993.

Morel, Edmund D. *The Black Man's Burden: The White Man in Africa From the Fifteenth Century to World War I.* New York: Monthly Review Press, 1969.

Morewedge, Parviz, ed. *Islamic Philosophical Theology.* Albany: State University of New York Press, 1979.

Mulford, David C. *Zambia: The Politics of Independence 1957-1964.* London: Oxford University Press, 1967.

Muller, Herbert J. *Issues of Freedom: Paradoxes and Promises.* New York: Harper and Brothers Publishers, 1960.

_____ *Freedom in the Western World From the Dark Ages to the Rise of Democracy.* New York: Harper and Row, 1964.

Munroe, Miles. *The Burden of Freedom.* Lake Mary, FL: Creation House, 2000.

Murray-Brown, Jeremy. *Kenyatta.* London: George Allen and Unwin, 1972.

Murray, John Courtney. *Freedom and Man.* New York: P. J. Kennedy and Sons, 1965.

Museveni, Yoweri K. *What Is Africa's Problem?* Minneapolis: University of Minnesota Press, 2000.

Nancy, Jean-Luc. *The Experience of Freedom.* Stanford, CA: Stanford University Press, 1993.

Nkrumah, Kwame. *Challenge of the Congo.* New York: International Publishers, 1967.

_____ *Ghana: The Autobiography of Kwame Nkrumah.* New York: International Publishers, 1957.

_____ *I Speak of Freedom: A Statement of African Ideology.* New York: Frederick A. Praeger, Publishers, 1961.

_____ *Towards Colonial Freedom: Africa in the Struggle Against World Imperialism.* London: Heinemann, 1962.

Nwobi, Simeon Okezuo. *Sharia Law in Nigeria: What A Christian Must Know.* Abuja, Nigeria: Totan Publishers Ltd., 2000.

Nyerere, Julius K. *Freedom and Unity/Uhuru na Umoja: A Selection from Writings and Speeches 1952-65.* Dar Es Salaam: Oxford University Press, 1966.

_____ *Freedom and Development/Uhuru na Maendeleo: A Selection From Writings and Speeches 1968-1973.* London: Oxford University Press, 1973.

_____ *Freedom and Socialism/Uhuru na Ujamaa: A Selection From Writings and Speeches 1965-1967.* London: Oxford University Press, 1968.

Oaks, John B. *The Edge of Freedom*. New York: Harper and Brothers, 1961.

Obasanjo, Olusegun. *Nzeogwu: An Intimate Portrait of Major Chukwuma Kaduna Nzeogwu*. Ibadan: Spectrum Books, 1987.

_____ and d'Orville, Hans, eds. *Challenges of Leadership in African Development*. New York: Crane Russak, 1990.

Obi, Amanze. "The Return of Umaru Dikko." *African News Weekly*, 1994.

Odetola, T. O. *Regimes and Development: A Comparative Analysis of African States*. London: George Allen and Unwin, 1982.

Odinga, Ajuma Oginga. *Not Yet Uhuru: The Autobiography of Oginga Odinga*. New York: Hill and Wang, 1967.

Ogot, B. A. and Ochieng, W. R. *Decolonization & Independence in Kenya 1940-93*. London: James Currey, 1995.

Ogunmodede, Francis Ishola. *Chief Obafemi Awolowo's Socio-Political Philosophy: A Critical Interpretation*. Rome: n.p., 1986.

Ojike, Mbonu. *I Have Two Countries*. New York: The John Day Co., 1947.

Olaniyan, Richard, ed. *Nigeria History and Culture*. London: Longman Group Ltd., 1985.

Orizu, Akweke Abyssinia Nwafor. *Without Bitterness: Western Nations in Post-War Africa*. New York: Creative Age Press, 1944.

Paoli, Arturo. *Freedom to Be Free*. Maryknoll, NY: Orbis Books, 1973.

Parenti, Michael. *Democracy For the Few*. 4th ed. New York: St. Martin's Press, 1983.

Parrinder, Geoffrey. *Jesus in the Qur'an*. Oxford: Oneworld Publications, 1995.

Patterson, Orlando. *Freedom*, vol. 1: *Freedom in the Making of Western Culture*. New York: Basic Books, 1991.

Payne, Robert. *The History of Islam*. New York: Dorset Press, 1990.

Peters, Rudolph. *Islam and Colonialism: The Doctrine of Jihad in Modern History*. The Hague: Mouton Press, 1984.

Pickering, Hy. *Twelve Baskets Full of Original Outlines and Bible Studies*. London: Pickering and Inglis Ltd., 1968.

Pipes, Richard. *Property and Freedom*. New York: Vintage Books, 1999.

Platt, Suzy, ed. *Respectfully Quoted: A Dictionary of Quotations*. New York: Barnes and Noble, 1993.

Pohlenz, Max. *Freedom in Greek Life and Thought: The History of An Ideal*. Dordrecht, Holland: D. Reidel Publishing Co., 1966.

Pool, Ithiel de Sola. *Technologies of Freedom*. Cambridge, MA: The Belknap Press, 1983.

Powell, David. *The Wisdom of the Novel: A Dictionary of Quotations*. New York: Garland Publishing, 1985.

Powell, Jim. *The Triumph of Liberty: A 2,000-Year History, Told Through the Lives of Freedom's Greatest Champions*. New York: The Free Press, 2000.

Quarles, Benjamin. *Black Abolitionists*. New York: Oxford University Press, 1969.

Raz, Joseph. *The Morality of Freedom*. Oxford: Clarendon Press, 1986.

Read, Leonard E. *The Love of Liberty*. Irvington-on-Hudson, NY: The Foundation For Economic Education, Inc., 1975.

Reynolds, Charles. *Modes of Imperialism*. New York: St. Martin's Press, 1981.

Rhodes, Robert I., ed. *Imperialism and Underdevelopment: A Reader*. New York: Monthly Review Press, 1970.

Ricoeur, Paul. *Freedom and Nature: The Voluntary and the Involuntary*. n.p: Northwestern University Press, 1966.

Riesman, Paul. *Freedom in Fulani Social Life: An Introspective Ethnography*. Chicago, IL: University of Chicago Press, 1977.

Roberts, Andrew. *A History of Zambia*. New York: Africana Publishing Co., 1976.

Robinson, Ronald and Gallagher, John. *Africa and the Victorians: The Official Mind of Imperialism*. London: Macmillan and Co., 1961.

Rodney, Walter. *How Europe Underdeveloped Africa*. Washington, D.C.: Howard University Press, 1982.

Roger, John and McWilliams, Peter. *Wealth 101: Getting What You Want – Enjoying What You've Got*. Los Angeles, CA: Prelude Press, 1992.

Rosenthal, Franz. *The Muslim Concept of Freedom Prior to the Nineteenth Century*. Leiden: E. J. Brill, 1960.

_____ *A History of Muslim Historiography*. Leiden: E. J. Brill, 1952.

Ross, William David. *The Right and the Good*. Oxford: Clarendon Press, 1967.

Rothbard, Murray N. *The Ethics of Liberty*. Atlantic Highlands, NJ: Humanities Press, 1982.

Rubin, Barry. *Modern Dictators: Third World Coup Makers, Strongmen, and Populist Tyrants*. New York: New American Library, 1987.

Russell, Bertrand. *Power: A New Social Analysis*. New York: Routledge, 1992.

Sampson, Anthony. *Mandela: The Authorized Biography*. New York: Alfred A. Knopf, 1999.

Sanneh, Lamin O. *West African Christianity: The Religious Impact*. Maryknoll, NY: Orbis Books, 1983.

_____ "Christian Experience of Islamic Da'wa: With Particular Reference to Africa." *International Review of Missions*, 1976.

Schillebeeckx, Edward and Iersel, Bas van, eds. *Jesus Christ and Human Freedom*. New York: Herder and Herder, 1974.

Schwarz, Walter. *Nigeria*. New York: Frederick A. Praeger, 1968.

Segal, Ronald. *Islam's Black Slaves: The Other Black Diaspora*. New York: Farrar, Strauss and Giroux, 2001.

Semmel, Bernard. *Imperialism and Social Reform: English Social-Imperial Thought 1895-1914*. Garden City, NY: Anchor Books, 1968.

Sen, Amartya. *Development As Freedom*. New York: Anchor Books, 2000.

Senghor, Leopold Sedar. *On African Socialism*. Mercer Cook, trans. New York: Frederick A. Praeger, 1964.

_____ *Liberte 1: Negritude et humanisme*. Paris: Le Seuil, 1964.

_____ "What Is Negritude?" *Negro Digest*, 1962.

_____ "The Spirit of Civilisation, or the Laws of African Negro Culture" in *The First Conference of Negro Writers and Artists*. Paris: Presence Africaine, 1956.

Sharif, Miyan Muhammad, ed. *A History of Muslim Philosophy*. 2 vols. Wiesbaden: O. Harrassowitz, 1963.

Sharma, Arvind, ed. *Our Religions*. New York: HarperCollins, 1993.

Shils, Edward. "The Intellectuals in the Political Development of the New States." in John H. Kausky, ed. *Political Change in Underdeveloped Countries: Nationalism and Communism*. New York: Wiley and Sons, 1962.

Sklar, Richard L. *Nigerian Political Parties: Power in An Emergent African Nation*. Princeton, NJ: Princeton University Press, 1963.

Smith, Huston. *The World's Religions: Our Great Wisdom Traditions*. New York: HarperCollins Publishers, 1991.

Smith, William Edgett. *We Must Run While They Walk: A Portrait of Africa's Julius Nyerere*. New York: Random House, 1971.

Soroush, Abdolkarim. *Reason, Freedom and Democracy in Islam: Essential Writings of Abdolkarim Soroush.*, eds. Mahmoud Sadri and Ahmad Sadri. New York: Oxford University Press, 2000.

Stamps, Norman L. *Why Democracies Fail: A Critical Evaluation of the Causes For Modern Dictatorship*. Notre Dame, IN: University of Notre Dame Press, 1957.

Steger, E. Ecker. *The Many Dimensions of the Human Person*. New York: Peter Lang Publishing, 1994.

Stokes, Anson Phelps. *Church and State in the United States: Historical Development and Contemporary Problems of Religious Freedom Under the Constitution*, vol. 1. New York: Harper and Brothers, 1950.

Takaya, Bala J. and Tyoden, Soni Gwanle, eds. *The Kaduna Mafia*. Jos, Nigeria: Jos University Press Ltd., 1987.

Templin, J. Alton. *Ideology On a Frontier: The Theological Foundation of Afrikaner Nationalism, 1652-1910*. Westport, CT: Greenwood Press, 1984.

The Encyclopedia Americana, vol. 16. Danbury, CT: Grolier, 1999.

"The Return of Dikko: An Acute Case of People's Amnesia?" *African News Weekly*, 1994.

Thomas, Clive Y. *The Rise of the Authoritarian State in Peripheral Societies*. New York: Monthly Review Press, 1984.

Thomas, Tony. *The Freedom Struggle in South Africa*. New York: Pathfinder Press, 1976.

Thompson, Kenneth W., ed. *The Moral Imperatives of Human Rights: A World Survey*. Lanham, MD: University Press of America, 1980.

Thompson, Leonard. *A History of South Africa*, 3rd ed. New Haven, CT: Yale University Press, 2001.

Thornton, A. P. *Imperialism in the Twentieth Century*. Minneapolis: University of Minnesota Press, 1977.

Toland, John. *Adolf Hitler*. 2 vols. Garden City, NY: Doubleday and Co., 1976.

Treadgold, Donald W. *Freedom: A History*. New York: New York University Press, 1990.

Trimingham, John S. *The Influence of Islam Upon Africa*. New York: Frederick A. Praeger, 1968.

_____ *A History of Islam in West Africa*. London: Oxford University Press, 1959.

Trueblood, Elton. *Declaration of Freedom*. New York: Harper and Brothers, 1955.

Ungar, Sanford J. *Africa: The People and Politics of An Emerging Continent*. New York: Simon and Schuster, 1986.

Uwechue, Ralph. *Makers of Modern Africa: Profiles in History*. London: Africa Books Ltd., 1991.

_____ "The Military in Nigerian Politics." *Tell* (Nigeria), 1994.

Uzoigwe, G. N. *Britain and the Conquest of Africa: The Age of Salisbury*. Ann Arbor: The University of Michigan Press, 1974.

Vaillant, Janet G. *Black, French, and African: A Life of Leopold Sedar Senghor*. Cambridge, MA: Harvard University Press, 1990.

Ward, Barbara. *Faith and Freedom*. New York: W. W. Norton and Co., 1954.

_____ *Five Ideas That Changed the World*. New York: W. W. Norton and Co., 1959.

Warraq, Ibn. *Why I Am Not A Muslim*. Amherst, NY: Prometheus Books, 1995.

Warren, Bill. *Imperialism: Pioneer of Capitalism*. London: NLB and Verso Editions, 1980.

Wassil, Aly. *The Wisdom of Christ*. New York: Harper and Row, 1965.

Watt, William Montgomery. *Christian-Muslim Encounter: Perceptions and Misperceptions*. London: Routledge and Kegan Paul, 1991.

_____ *Islamic Political Thought*. New York: Columbia University Press, 1980.

Welch, Jr., Claude E. and Meltzer, Ronald, I, eds. *Human Rights and Development in Africa*. Albany: State University of New York Press, 1984.

Whitaker, Jennifer Seymour. *How Can Africa Survive?* New York: Harper and Row, Publishers, 1988.

Wiener, Philip P., ed. *Dictionary of the History of Ideas: Studies of Selected Pivotal Ideas*, vol. 4. New York: Charles Scribner's Sons, 1973.

Williams, Chancellor. *The Destruction of Black Civilization: Great Issues of a Race From 4500 B.C. to 2000 A.D.* Chicago, IL: Third World Press, 1987.

Williams, Geoffrey J. *Independent Zambia: A Bibliography of the Social Sciences, 1964-1979*. Boston, MA: G. K. Hall and Co., 1984.

Willis, John Ralph, ed. *Slaves and Slavery in Muslim Africa*, vol. 1 *Islam and the Ideology of Enslavement*. London: Frank Cass, 1985.

Woetzel, Robert K. *The Philosophy of Freedom*. Dobbs-Ferry, NY: Oceana Publications, Inc., 1966.

Woody, J. Melvin. *Freedom's Embrace*. University Park: The Pennsylvania State University Press, 1998.

Wright, Robin. "Islam, Democracy and the West." *Foreign Affairs*, 72, 13, (1992).

_____ *Sacred Rage: The Wrath of Militant Islam.* New York: Simon and Schuster, 1985.

Yee, Shirley J. *Black Women Abolitionists: A Study in Activism, 1828-1860.* Knoxville: University of Tennessee Press, 1992.

Ye'or, Bat. *The Dhimmi: Jews and Christians Under Islam.* Rutherford, NJ: Fairleigh Dickinson University Press, 1985.

Zulu, J. B. *Zambian Humanism: Some Major Spiritual and Economic Challenge.* Lusaka: NECZAM, 1970.

INDEX

A

Abacha, Sani, 24, 140, 228
Abubakar, Abdulsalami, 158
Achebe, Chinua, 165
Adels, Jill Haak, 199
Adler, Mortimer J., 59, 183, 202
African National Congress, 170
Aggrey, James Emman Kwegyir, 41, 132
Aikman, David, 179
Akintola, S. L., 127
Albright, Madeline, K., 102
Amin, Idi, 18, 23, 47, 86, 100, 153, 228
Ani-Okokon, Edem, 129
apartheid, 105, 109, 118, 146, 159, 173, 177, 212
Aquinas, Thomas, 59
Arabs, 2, 3, 4, 5, 11, 27, 28, 29, 31
Ashantis, 67
assimiliation, 142, 144, 146, 148, 154
Athie, Mohammed N., 32
Awolowo, Obafemi, 69, 119, 121
Ayoola, Theo, 19
Ayittey, George, 101
Azikiwe, Nnamdi, 20, 42, 63, 66, 69, 119, 121, 128, 235

B

Ba, Sylvia Washington, 149
Babangida, Ibrahim, 24, 125, 140, 221, 242

Bashir, Omar, 29
Banning, Emile, 9
Barnett, Randy E., 58
Basil the Great, 199
Begin, Menachem, 53, 55, 239
Bello, Ahmadu, 137, 232
Benjamin, James Mayan, 30
Bentham, Jeremy, 190
Berger, Gaston, 154
Berlin Conference, 9, 12
Berlin, Isaiah, 58, 61
Biko, Steve, 226
Bisalla, I. D., 233
Bloc Democratique Senegalais, 152
Blyden, Edward, 131
Botsio, Kojo, 76
Boulton, Matthew, 226
Brandon, S. G. F., 214
Brassey, Thomas, 226
Bryant, William Cullen, 183
Buhari, Muhammed, 221, 233
Buthelezi, Mangosuthu, 177
Butler, Samuel, 182

C

Calder, Ritchie, 11
Cervantes, Miguel de, 192
Cesaire, Aime, 150
Chafee, Jr., Zechariah, 183
chieftaincy, 164
Cochran, David C., 58
coercion, 56, 57, 58, 59, 181, 222, 223, 229

Coleman, James S., 20
colonial, 1, 13, 15
colonialism, 5, 7, 9, 14, 15, 17,
    18, 21, 22, 29, 63, 66, 78, 81,
    85, 91, 93, 96, 122, 140, 147,
    150, 153, 167, 169, 187, 203,
    225, 230
colonizers, 6, 7, 8, 9
Convention Peoples' Party, 72
coups, 227
Cranston, Maurice, 221
Crowther, Samuel Ajayi, 41
Curran, John Philpot, 35

D
Danquah, Joseph B., 71, 77
Davies, H. O., 129, 234
de Gaulle, Charles, 145
de Klerk, F. W., 176, 177
de Wet, Quartus, 175
despotism, 140, 153, 187, 201,
    215, 221, 228
Dia, Mamadou, 151, 157
Diop, Cheikh Anta, 132, 157
Diouf, Abdou, 158
Disraeli, Benjamin, 186
Dostert, Pierre Etienne, 11
Douglass, Frederick, 5, 131
Doyle, Arthur Conan, 11
Drake, Francis, 5
Dubois, Leon, 143
DuBois, W. E. B., 131, 146

E
Edison, Thomas Alva, 227
Ekpo, Margaret Udo, 69
Ekpu, Ray, 243
emancipation, 2
Enahoro, Anthony, 131
equality, 201-205
ethnicity, 234

exploitation, 236
Ezeanya, Austin, 233

F
Fabianism, 135
faith, 194-198
Fanti Constitution, 74
First, Ruth, 69
Fodio, Usman Dan, 232
Frederic-Amiel, Henry, 182

G
Gandhi, Mahatma, 106, 116
Gardner, John W., 194
Garfield, James A., 132
Garrison, William Lloyd, 5
Garvey, Marcus, 132
Giwa, Dele, 242
Gold Coast, 12, 13, 71, 75
gradualism, 71
Graham, Billy, 199
Grassian, Victor, 191
greed, 216
Gueye, Lamine, 151, 157

H
Hansberry, William Leo, 131
hamartiology, 213
Hawkins, Jim, 5
Hayek, Friedrich A., 53, 57
Hehir, J. Bryan, 181
Helvetius, Claude-Adrien, 56
Henry, Patrick, 54
Herskovits, Melville, 132
Hobbes, Thomas, 56
Holmes, Jr., Oliver Wendell, 228
honesty, 192-194
Hoover, Herbert, 212
hope, 199-201
Hume, David, 56
Hutchins, Robert Maynard, 201

I

Ibibio, 67
Igbos, 65, 66
Igbuku-Otu, Napoleon
  Ovie, 243
Ikoli, Ernest, 129
imperialism, 13, 16, 42, 73, 81,
  83, 85, 132, 140, 230
International Igbo
  Conference, 233
intolerance, 221
Ironsi, Aguiyi, 139
Isichei, Elizabeth, 133
Islam, 2, 3, 6, 26, 27, 31,
  125, 214

J

Jabavu, D.D.T., 169
Jefferson, Thomas, 54, 153, 201
Johnson, James, 112
July, Robert W., 142
justice, 186-188

K

Kant, Immanuel, 190
Kapwepwe, Simon, 107
Kaunda, Kenneth, 69, 103, 147
Kawawa, Rashidi, M., 97
Kenya African Democratic
  Union, 86
Kenya African National
  Union, 83
Kenya Peoples' Union, 85
Kenyatta, Jomo, 15, 22, 61, 69,
  80, 81
Kerr, Alexander, 170
King Leopold II, 9, 10, 11, 12
King, Jr., Martin Luther, 176
Kipling, Rudyard, 79

L

Lao-tzu, 216
Leakey, L. S. B., 132
Lenin, Vladimir, 153
liberalism, 212
liberty, 54, 55, 56, 57, 58, 145,
  174, 179, 204, 222
Lincoln, Abraham, 56, 106, 170
Littell, Franklin, H., 223
Livingston, David, 103
Locke, Alain, 132
Long, J. Bruce, 207
love, 205-209
Luccock, Robert E., 199
Lugard, Frederick, 8
Lumumba, Patrice, 12
Luthuli, Albert, 171, 174

M

Macaulay, Herbert, 19, 20, 129
MacLeod, Iain, 116
Madubuike, Ihechukwu, 154
mafiaism, 231
Maji Maji Resistance, 88
Malinowski, B., 82
Mandela, Nelson, 69, 159
Mangope, Lucas, 177
Marchall, Paul, 242
Marquis, Donald Robert
  Perry, 217
Marx, Karl, 153
Matthews, Z.K., 169
Mau Mau Rebellion, 15, 83
Maxeke, Charlotte, 69
Mazrui, Ali A., 226
Mbeki, Thabo, 178
Mboya, Tom, 69, 78
McKay, Claude, 132
Mengistu, Haile Mariam, 24
Messaoud, Boubacar, 32
Mill, John Stuart, 56, 59, 190

Milton, John, 55
Mohammed, Murtala, 47
Munroe, Myles, 244
Morel, Edmund Denille, 11
Moslems, 6, 26, 30, 125
Muslim, 151, 224, 233, 241, 242

N
National Independence
    Party, 138
nationalism, 70, 71, 78, 127,
    128, 138, 154, 209
Ndaw, Ibrahima Seydou, 151
negritude, 144, 148, 150
Nehru, Jawaharlal, 174
Ngala, Ronald, 86
Ngengi, Kamau Wa, 15
Nguema, Francisco, 18, 23
Nkomo, Joshua, 80
Nkrumah, Kwame, 11, 42, 69, 70
Nkumbula, Harry, 109
Nyerere, Julius K., 65, 69, 87, 88
Nyssa, Gregory, 199
Nzeogwu, Chukwuma
    Kaduna, 228

O
Obasanjo, Olusegun, 24,
    158, 209
Obote, Milton, 23
Odinga, Oginga, 85
Ogunmodede, Francis
    Ishola, 122
Ojike, Mazi Mbonu, 21
Okello, Tito, 23
Okpara, M. I., 138
Orizu, A. A. Nwafor, 45, 46

P
Paine, Thomas, 201, 221
Pascal, Blaise, 182

Paton, Alan, 173
Patterson, Orlando, 60
Peters, Carl, 87
Pickering, Hy, 200
Plato, 209
plutocracy, 219
political ambition, 217

R
Radebe, Gaur, 172
Read, Leonard E., 202, 204
regimentalism, 228
Rhodes, Cecil, 103
Riebeeck, Jan Van, 165
righteousness, 188-192
Roberts, Andrew, 103
Rodrigues, Deodolinda, 69
Roosevelt, Franklin D., 19,
    183, 216
Ross, William David, 190
Rousseau, Jean Jacques, 55

S
Seko, Mobutu Seso, 12, 23, 47
Senghor, Leopold, 69, 141, 142
Shagari, Shehu, 47, 218
Sharp, Granville, 5
Shea, Nina, 242
Sidney, Sir Philip, 206
Sisulu, Walter, 171
slave trade, 3, 4, 11, 13, 17, 18,
    27, 28, 31, 196
slavery, 3, 4, 5, 13, 18, 21, 22,
    27, 29, 32, 55, 56, 90, 132,
    196, 203, 211, 225, 241, 244
Smith, Ian, 118
Smuts, Jan, 170
Sobukwe, Robert, 171
Sokoni, John, 107
Sonquishe, Daniel, 105
Spencer, Herbert, 55

Stalin, Josef, 153
statism, 230
Stephenson, George, 226
Stokes, Anson Phelps, 223

T
Tambo, Oliver, 170
Tanganyika African
    Association, 89
Thoreau, Henry David, 192
toleration, 221
Treadgold, Donald W., 61, 240
tribalism, 234
trust, 219
truth, 182-186
Turnbull, Richard, 93
Tutu, Desmond, 24, 178
Twain, Mark, 11

U
Umar, Abubakar Dangiwa, 231
Umunna, Isaac, 240
Ungar, Sanford, J., 101, 117
utilitarianism, 189, 190
Uzoigwe, G. N., 12

V
Vatsa, Mamman, 233
Verwoerd, Hendrik F., 177

W
Wangila, Rhoi, 67
Ward, Barbara, 195
Washington, Booker T., 132
Watt, James, 226
Wesley, John, 5
Whitney, Eli, 227
Wilberforce, William, 5
Williams, Chancellor, 189
Wilson, Woodrow, 19
Wolofs, 143
Wright, Richard, 132
Wylie, Philip, 239

Y
Yutar, Percy, 177

Z
Zambian African National
    Congress, 113, 115

ABOUT THE AUTHOR

Award-winning author, speaker and professional historian, Emma Samuel Etuk is the Founder and Director of Nigeria For Christ Ministries. A graduate of Howard University in Washington, D.C., he obtained a Ph.D. in United States History, with minors in African History and International Relations.

Formerly a civil servant, Etuk attended the Polytechnic, Calabar, in Nigeria, where he received a Higher National Diploma in Estate Management. He also received a B.A. degree in Business Administration from Malone College, Canton, Ohio, a M.A. in Church History from Ashland Theological Seminary; and did graduate work at the Institute of Church and State at Baylor University in Waco, Texas. At seminary, Etuk studied under Drs. David A. Rausch, Douglas Chismar and Jerry R. Flora.

Etuk is a motivational speaker who has taught history at Howard, Dillard and Morgan State Universities, as well as at Bethune-Cookman College. He has lectured in Nigeria and in the United States, and has written six books, several articles and essays which have been widely read. He has been heard on more than 200 radio talk-show and television programs covering USA, Canada, the Caribbean and Europe. He was recently a guest on the Voice of America.

In 1999, Etuk and his family were honored at the U.S. Congress as "Parents of the Year" for the State of Maryland "for their outstanding example of creating a God-centered home, demonstrating sacrificial love towards others and ministering to parents and families in their community." The same year, two of Etuk's books won the Writer's Digest 1999 National Self-Published Book Awards.

Etuk is currently a member of the National Speakers Association and the National Speakers Association-D.C. He is also a member of the Small Publishers Association of North America (SPAN). He conducts workshops and lectures on leadership, Christian evangelism, soul-winning techniques and on the topics related to his books. "LISTEN AFRICANS: Freedom Is Under Fire!" is his seventh book. He can be reached by e-mail: *emida1@yahoo.com*.